Cyber Reconnaissance, Surveillance and Defense

Cyber Reconnaissance, Surveillance and Defense

Robert Shimonski

John Zenir, Esq, Contributing Editor

Allison Bishop, Technical Editor

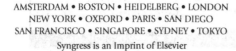

AMSTERDAM • BOSTON • HEIDELBERG • LONDON
NEW YORK • OXFORD • PARIS • SAN DIEGO
SAN FRANCISCO • SINGAPORE • SYDNEY • TOKYO
Syngress is an Imprint of Elsevier

Acquiring Editor: *Chris Katsaropoulos*
Editorial Project Manager: *Benjamin Rearick*
Project Manager: *Punithavathy Govindaradjane*
Designer: *Mark Rogers*

Syngress is an imprint of Elsevier
225 Wyman Street, Waltham, MA 02451, USA

Notices
Knowledge and best practice in this field are constantly changing. As new research and experience broaden our understanding, changes in research methods, professional practices, or medical treatment may become necessary.

Practitioners and researchers must always rely on their own experience and knowledge in evaluating and using any information, methods, compounds, or experiments described herein. In using such information or methods they should be mindful of their own safety and the safety of others, including parties for whom they have a professional responsibility.

To the fullest extent of the law, neither the Publisher nor the authors, contributors, or editors, assume any liability for any injury and/or damage to persons or property as a matter of products liability, negligence or otherwise, or from any use or operation of any methods, products, instructions, or ideas contained in the material herein.

Library of Congress Cataloging-in-Publication Data
Shimonski, Robert.
  Cyber reconnaissance, surveillance, and defense / Robert Shimonski ; Allison Bishop, technical editor.
    pages cm
  ISBN 978-0-12-801308-3 (paperback)
  1. Electronic intelligence. 2. Internet in espionage. 3. Cyber intelligence (Computer security)
4. Internet–Security measures. 5. Computer crimes. I. Title.
  TK7882.E2S56 2014
  327.12–dc23
                                            2014031815

British Library Cataloguing in Publication Data
A catalogue record for this book is available from the British Library

ISBN: 978-0-12-801308-3

For information on all Syngress publications
visit our website at http://store.elsevier.com/Syngress

Working together
to grow libraries in
developing countries

www.elsevier.com • www.bookaid.org

Dedication

I dedicate this book to my children Dylan and Vienna – my greatest love, my biggest joy.

May your dreams stay big and your worries stay small.

Contents

About the Authors

Rob Shimonski, Author

Rob Shimonski (www.shimonski.com) is an experienced entrepreneur and an active participant in the business community. Rob is a best-selling author and editor with over 15 years of experience developing, producing, and distributing print media in the form of books, magazines, and periodicals. To date, Rob has successfully created over 100 books that are currently in circulation. Rob has worked for countless companies to include CompTIA, Microsoft, Cisco, the National Security Agency, and Elsevier. As an Author, Rob has helped produce well over 50 security-centric books covering topics such as cybercrime, cyberwarfare, hacking, penetration testing, and security engineering. Rob started to train others while in the US Marine Corps. Since then Rob has held a NY State teaching certificate as well as multiple trainer roles in colleges and trade schools across the world and continues his goal of always trying to help others learn difficult topics.

John M. Zenir ESQ., Contributing Editor

John M. Zenir ESQ. (www.jmzesq.com) is an experienced law attorney. He has been practicing law in the state of New York since 1992. John is a frequent lecturer and has been honored by both the Nassau and the Suffolk County Bar Associations. He is also a member of the New York State Bar Association, for which he serves on the Committee for Children and the Law. From 2004 to 2005, he was a member of the Board of Directors of the Legal Aid Society of Nassau County. John has been a member of the 18-B Family Court Panel for Nassau County for both trials and appeals since 1994 and is currently a member of the Law Guardian Panel for Nassau County. John has shown a strong commitment to the community through his participation in *pro bono* activities for the Volunteer Lawyers Project for Nassau County since he began practicing law.

Allison Bishop, Technical Editor

Allison Bishop is a highly experience criminal reviewer with 10 years of experience reviewing cases, criminal research, and criminal activity. Allison also works as a paralegal performing tasks such as briefing cases and reviewing case law and working within the legal process. As an editor, Allison enjoys reviewing and editing works based on criminal justice, legal studies, security topics, and cybercrime. When Allison is not entrenched in studies, she loves to exercise, cook, and travel.

Acknowledgments

Writing a book is normally an enormous task, one that takes months to complete with many revisions, and many "back and forth" sessions between editors and all those who help. The team that helped assemble this book operated with 100% professionalism and I could not have been more grateful.

Chris, as usual, thank you for all work up front, putting the ideas together, and getting this book on the schedule. You are always available when needed and helpful.

Ben, I am grateful for all of your assistance while putting this book together. Having worked with you on a few books now, I appreciate all of the work you do behind the scenes.

Allison, without your attention to detail, diligence, and hard work, this book would not be the best it could be. Thank you for all of the hard work you put into reviewing all of chapters and contributing as much as you did.

John, you are a great lawyer and your work in reviewing the legal and ethical aspects of this book is greatly appreciated.

I would also like to extend a thank you to Muzz Hafeez for assisting with providing much needed legal research when needed.

Last, I would like to extend a thank you to the readers and the security community in general. As security practitioners, we have big shoes to fill – keeping ourselves, our peers, friends and family, and the world at large safe from a bigger evil. It is amazing how connected our world has become, it's nice to see a connected community, who works together so closely to ensure safety and privacy, and ethics that are considered and enforced.

Introduction

Cybercrime. Cyberwarfare. What has the world become?

Where were we 20 years ago when the world really started to get "interconnected?"

Children played outside in the street and came home when the sun started to set. The only way to communicate with them was to literally go out and hunt them down.

Folks went on vacation and for a week were off the grid. You learned about how their vacation was when they got home and shared the details. It may have even taken a week or so to get the pictures developed to "see" what transpired.

Your personal details were personal, private, and shared between close friends and family members, and even if a secret got out, it didn't go "viral" overnight to millions of interconnected eyes and ears.

Today, we live in a much different world. With the introduction of the personal computer, we have evolved into carrying a mobile tracking device with us everywhere we go and worse, we "share" everything we do. Although this book may not touch on a brand new topic, I have designed it to help alert those who may need the wake-up call to today's dangers – no more privacy! Now we must know where our children are at all times and track them. We must post all information about everything we will do, think of doing, or have done for the world to see. We must share all of our personal information. What is the cost?

In this book, I attempt to alert you of the dangers of using technology, how it's been used to commit crimes, and how to protect yourself against the common and not so common attacks that now impact our lives in ways that could be so damaging, it may take a lifetime to reverse.

This book was not put together to provide shock and awe to your already busy lives, but to assist you with limiting the footprint you leave everywhere you go. In some ways, you will learn that you cannot escape the eyes upon you; however, knowing that they are there may give you something to think about when you think your privacy is evaded. This book may help you decide what you want your elected officials to do while they are in office – vote on pork or vote on the removal of systems that read through your personal information and store it.

Originally, I wanted to write a book on "how to spy" and it was deemed to be too dangerous to put into the hands of the public; so as a team, we formed the book into *Digital Surveillance, Reconnaissance, and Defense* that revolves more around the security practitioner and not the thousands of hackers and script kiddies that lay waiting for a "how to" guide. Many of the remnants of the original manuscript are still here, but because of the content and topics covered, we decided to bring a lawyer into the writing process to assist in making it 100% clear that there are serious consequences to those who break cyberlaw.

There are many cases of spying, information gathering, and personal exploitation taking place today. Current events will tell you that social media accounts are being duplicated to steal identities, web cameras are being exploited to show your families activities while in the home, pictures posted online are being hacked to discover the location of where the picture was taken, phones are being tapped to track and trace geographical location, and even the National Security Agency is filtering through your e-mails. Edward Snowden while being considered a whisteblower, traitor, or whatever you would like to think has done nothing but alert us to what is going on without our knowledge. It is Edward, this book, and other information you can gather on your own that will fully make you a believer that every day that passes, your rights are being taken away.

Throughout the book, we will also learn in depth about how the government is conducting surveillance worldwide. Not just the US government, but any government. When you think about spying, think about one of my favorite quotes from Kevin Mitnick listed here …

> The Patriot Act is ludicrous. Terrorists have proved that they are interested in total genocide, not subtle little hacks of the U.S. infrastructure, yet the government wants a blank search warrant to spy and snoop on everyone's communications.
>
> **Kevin Mitnick**

Regardless, we have a job to do and that job is to be aware, make others aware, and do what security practitioners do – provide security where possible. We have also taken on the role of educators, teaching those around us and making them aware of the dangers that lurk in the digital world and outside of it as well. We ask ourselves, why must we carry around tracking devices everywhere we go? Why must we post everything we do? Are we even aware of these dangers?

In this book, we start with Chapter 1 and it covers the basics of digital surveillance, reconnaissance, and defense. You will learn about the history and practice of digital surveillance, reconnaissance, and defense and how it has grown into our digital world. In Chapters 2–7, you will learn about all of the specific ways in which digital surveillance, reconnaissance, and defense can take place – mobile devices, video cameras, tracking devices, and many more. In each chapter, we cover a legal case where these activities were brought before a court of law and why. In Chapter 8, we summarize the book and provide a master list of how to protect yourself from these threats.

Before you read this book, consider watching the news or read through your local newspaper and think about all of the reports on privacy invasion, digital threats, government espionage, legal issues, and hacking issues if you do not already. This book was based on providing a framework of knowledge behind the constant flow of these issues being reported, a framework to help explain why it's a growing issue but, more importantly, what WE can do about it moving forward.

Rob Shimonski
www.spynewswire.com

CHAPTER 1

Digital Reconnaissance and Surveillance

DIGITAL RECONNAISSANCE AND SURVEILLANCE

Today, the world operates on a digital landscape. Wearable technology is the latest buzz word and everyone seems to be connected via their phones, pads, and laptops. Virtually everyone everywhere is becoming more and more interconnected and sharing data and socializing. Using this medium has become the norm. While the world continues to grow digitally, so does the risk of exposure. As the landscape grows exponentially, so does the threat of those who would, and will abuse this medium for their own gain.

Modern societies cannot hold back growth and innovation because of fear; those same societies must learn to overcome challenges of a growing interconnected world as seen in Figure 1.1.

Because technological advancements grow exponentially, the security innovations must encapsulate and work within them. Security is not a new consideration; it is an age old practice applied to new situations such as a growing digital landscape.

Reconnaissance and surveillance have been practiced for centuries, primarily as a way for militaries to conduct observation of enemy activities and monitor targets to gain strategic advantage. Reconnaissance and surveillance teams would go out to gather information about enemy activities in hopes to find out location information, size, and strength of their targets and/or to place targeting information for incoming strikes.

Digital reconnaissance (or digital recon for short) is the "digital" form of what these teams or individuals do, except primarily in a computer-based world. These experts perform many of these same basic functions of their military counterparts and the target could be strategic advantage, financial gain, leverage, or to place targeting information for more attacks in a corporate or private landscape. The landscape is not the traditional battlefield, but the cyberworld where computers and mobile technology can be manipulated, video cameras

1

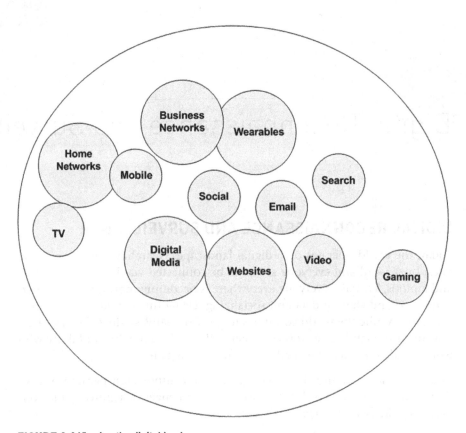

FIGURE 1.1 Viewing the digital landscape.

can be hacked into, and databases of personal information can be stolen to gain strategic advantage.

Not all who perform reconnaissance and surveillance activities have bad intentions; some perform these activities in order to protect. In recent news, the National Security Agency (NSA) has been filtering data of the Americans and others in the name of national security. Because it wasn't disclosed and seemed to overreach, it was immediately brought into questions by the American public when it was brought into light by Edward Snowden, an employee who worked with the NSA and leaked how the NSA was capturing inappropriate data. The threat of government's spying on individuals is not new; however, it seems to have grown more post 9/11 because of the threat of terrorist attack, the assembling of the Department of Homeland Security (DHS) in the United States, and the ability for many to use technology as a way to gather information quickly about anyone or anything.

In this chapter, we will detail the fundamentals of digital reconnaissance and surveillance, provide some history on the topic, and set the tone for the remaining chapters where we will go into detail on how these activities take place, how vulnerable we are, and how to fortify our defenses and mitigate risk on a more personal level.

Art and History of Spying

As we have just discussed, reconnaissance and surveillance is not new; it's been practiced for centuries. The term "spying" may come to mind when you read about or watch movies where a "spy" is used to capture information about a target. In this book, we will use this term interchangeably, so when the term spy is referenced, we use it to explain the person or activity of collecting and reporting information on a specific target.

What is surveillance? The word surveillance comes from the French word "watching over." Surveillance involves monitoring persons or locations to identify behaviors, activities, and other changing information. This will be the primary topic and focus throughout the book, covering the current landscape and attack vectors. Learning how to mitigate and defend against digital surveillance is tricky; today almost everything you do is captured on camera or tracked. We will cover more on this topic as we progress through the book; however, understanding the passive and the aggressive form of surveillance is important.

There are different forms of surveillance to include adversarial surveillance that is to gather information in preparation for an aggressive action and likely criminal in nature. Examples of adversarial surveillance are terrorism (domestic and international), destruction of property (logical or physical), and other crimes against individuals of entities to include theft, stalking, and espionage. Espionage (which is used interchangeably with spying) is defined as the practice of spying on or spying by governmental and military entities to gain information.

Surveillance has also advanced to the point where unmanned aircraft (typically called Drones), as seen in Figure 1.2, is responsible for conducting "spy"

FIGURE 1.2 Security drone.

missions to gather data and information on targets. This has brought about a large amount of controversy about how privacy is impacted and what legal issues arise from such activity.

One of the most historical legal concepts of spying is the Espionage act of 1917. This highly outdated and misused law does not fully protect those who are charged with spying. Cybercrime is not covered, security clearances are not covered, and it is consistently becoming more and more important in the realm of prosecuting criminals at the highest levels of government. It also brings to light what are the legal implications of spying on your neighbor, such as using their wireless connection, and infiltrating their home. What about the Electronic Communications Privacy Act of 1986 that prohibited the storing of certain data on others. As we will learn for decade's, protection has been put into place to draw specific boundaries to keep privacy of citizens in check; however, this has brought about many legal challenges along the way. In this chapter and throughout the book, we will cover these legal aspects alongside the technical how to and defense tactics you need to put into place for safety and security. You will see in this book, as we progress through the chapters, and looking at how digital spying is conducted, you will find that many of the old tactics used outside of the digital realm still apply. As an example, stalking digitally can also lead to traditional stalking and vice versa. Understanding the concerns and risks of both are relevant to understanding the threat as a whole.

This does not mean that any person or team that conducts surveillance is a threat. Investigative, forensic, and security teams today conduct investigations legally and may require a warrant or some form of legal backing to conduct any type of information gathering; however, not all need to operate within these boundaries. Therefore, it's important to understand some legal concepts when either you are the victim of these activities or, if perpetrating an attack, what you may or may not be held liable for.

THREAT OF DIGITAL RECONNAISSANCE AND SURVEILLANCE

What is at stake? Currently, much is at stake. Your privacy is at stake. Your safety could be at stake. Your identity can be stolen. You can be impacted financially. As the digital landscape grows, so does the threat exponentially. We will cover each of these in depth; however, it's safe to say that the threat is very real and the need to understand it and protect yourself should be considered and practiced.

The threat of digital spying is also growing at a rapid rate, generationally, and more and more are creating an online footprint. As more people get mobile devices and attach to the public Internet, there are more opportunities for attackers to conduct surveillance on selected targets.

Your identity can be stolen. You finances can be impacted. Your safety can be threatened.

To understand this concept in more detail, we need to consider the size, depth, and breadth of the threat landscape.

Threat Landscape

As mentioned before, threats grow exponentially. The math is simple. As more people connected to the public Internet via a growing number of devices to include mobile phones, laptops, wearable technology, and pads, the number of possible victims also grows. The attack vector also extends.

The Internet fueled by search engines, social media, and the ability to retain all that it collects is a digital spy's goldmine when doing reconnaissance work. Considerably, one of the biggest threats today on the Internet is in the form of search engines and social media. You can virtually learn a person's history, what they like, their location, and who their friends and family are. You can learn where they work. You can even track their movement day by day. This is a reminder that George Orwell's book "1984" may indeed have come to 2014 and Big Brother is watching. In fact, this book may turn you into a Winston Smith, looking for ways to evade Big Brother's roving eye! Today's roving eye looks more in line with the millions of cameras that can be found in stores, businesses, and home across the world as seen in Figure 1.3.

Search engines are so far one of the first (and easiest) tools to use to start reconnaissance on a target. You may even attempt to safeguard your personal

FIGURE 1.3 Digital surveillance camera.

information or the websites you use may attempt to safeguard it; however, let's take a look at how easy it is to gather information on a target.

In this example, we will look at the growing world of online dating. One would think that by going online and filling out a profile on a website that is marketed as safe, one could simply find and meet their perfect "match." Before the online dating craze took hold, traditionally a person may get a "reference check" from a friend of family member about a person who may be right for them. They may meet somewhere and get to know each other, perhaps at a school, work, or a venue. They may talk on the phone and get to know each other. Today, you simply need to create an online profile and sit back and wait.

You may think it's safe; you are not identifying yourself by last name, you may not be putting up a picture, or you may lie about who you are. But what if you were honest? What if you put a few key pieces of information up like your first name, last initial, your occupation, and the town where you reside? This is all that is needed to give a spy (or worse, a stalker) enough information to begin to track you in a search engine. For example, Rhonda K., a Horticulturist who resides in Kissimmee, Florida, may be enough to find your LinkedIn profile. Now, there is enough to begin to track more information about you. As we progress through the book, we will learn how to dig deeper and find more information; however, this is enough for now. To show you the "threat landscape" and how deep and wide it goes. Rhonda may have just been divorced and looking for a safe way to date that fit into her busy lifestyle; however, by attempting to remain anonymous while she tested the online dating waters may have exposed herself to stalking.

Social media is also another treasure trove of information. By simply infiltrating someone's social sites, you may be able to launch attacks directly against a victim in the form of bullying, stalking, and worse, criminal behavior. With sites such as Twitter, Facebook, and Linkedin, one could conduct surveillance and reconnaissance of a target and gain information such as identity, occupation, location, movement patterns, and more.

Mobile technology has widened the threat landscape by giving each and every user of a mobile device a way to track their every movement. A stolen, hacked, or bugged phone can provide information on a user's identity, location, movement patterns, and communication history. Digital pads from Microsoft, Google and Apple are also commonplace today and they store just as much information. What makes these devices all the more enticing to someone who is tracking you is, they are not left at home! If a phone is bugged, normally it never leaves the owner's side providing data on everywhere they go, everything they do.

Stationary devices are just as much of a threat now as they had ever been. Computers are used at work and at home and if exposed locally or remotely,

FIGURE 1.4 Traffic cameras.

can also provide a great deal of information to those collecting it. Other stationary devices such as video cameras are now found everywhere. While driving, cameras track your movements and report location to a centralized collection system. While walking into stores, schools, work, or now in personal homes, cameras track your movement in the name of safety and security. What if those cameras were used for reasons other than good?

A good example of use can be seen in Figure 1.4. Here, we see traffic camera's providing services such as allowing citizens to see what a major roadway may look like to pick a better route to work, one that may be less congested or accident free. It provides a way for law enforcement to maintain safe driving patterns by ticketing those who break laws such as running red lights. It allows law enforcement agencies to track a child abductor by tracking a license plate through such cameras. However, these systems can be quickly misused.

We also need to consider the digital threats that only add on to the already existing threats that existed prior to the existence of the public Internet, mobile phones, and computers. The reason why it's pertinent is that you understand the threat landscape is because it is growing. It's everywhere you go, everything you use, everything you touch, and everything you send digitally. Nothing is safe, nothing is untraceable. In this chapter, we learn how to safeguard as much as possible to ensure that you do not easily become a victim to surveillance and reconnaissance.

WHY SPY?

Now that we have discussed the foundations of digital reconnaissance and surveillance, let's look at some of the current newsworthy high profile stories of how digital spying is affecting the world. It is difficult to turn on the news today and not hear about the NSA and Edward Snowden, to date, one of the biggest news stories around covering the topics of digital spying by the American government on its own citizens. Other news stories will be covered; however, this is one of the biggest stories to break the new media about spying in the past few years.

We also need to understand why spying takes place. What is to gain? What is to lose? Spying is done on purpose … there are reasons someone spies on another person, organization, or entity. Those reasons will be discussed in depth in this chapter. It's important to understand the motivations behind those who spy, by doing so you may be able to proactively know when you are at risk.

We will also cover the details on who the bad guys are and who the good guys are and how the lines blur. Not all spying is done by a stalker, an ex-boy or girlfriend, or by a husband or wife. Not all spying is done by organizations looking to achieve competitive advantage over other entities.

Some surveillance is done simply to protect interests. For example, military organizations perform surveillance and reconnaissance missions to gather information about an entity. Some governments perform these functions as a way to protect its citizens. As mentioned above, however, those lines are easily blurred.

In this section of this chapter, we will also cover the fundamentals of digital forensics. Since we will be covering investigations (both criminal and noncriminal), it only makes sense to discuss the science of digital forensics.

NSA and Edward Snowden

In terms of spying, surveillance and reconnaissance, and intelligence collection, the NSA is an intelligence agency that operates under the Department of Defense (DoD) for the US Government. The NSA is tasked with collecting intelligence to keep the country safe.

The NSA is allowed to operate in a manner that may seem inappropriate in hopes to safeguard the United States and its interests abroad. How the agency does this is through mass surveillance of communications, phone records, Internet transactions, and e-mail. It collects this data, filters it, and software mines it for key words and other triggers.

So why so much news media about the NSA lately if this is what they were tasked to do?

Edward Joseph Snowden, an American computer analyst working as a contractor, was accused of allegedly leaking top secret information about the NSA who he accused of spying on the American citizens by collecting data on them as seen in Figure 1.5. He claimed that all data being collected seemed to fall outside of the boundaries of targeting individuals who may be deemed a threat. Instead, the NSA was collecting and filtering data on everyone who communicated within the United States, as well as outside of it.

FIGURE 1.5 Edward Snowden.

Although some of the biggest news during the printing of this book is revolving around Edward Snowden and the NSA, this is not a new topic. It should not be shocking, although it is. As mentioned earlier, for centuries, governments and military organizations have been performing intelligence and counter-intelligence operations. This is also not the first government scandal to take place (America or otherwise). The secret Five Eyes organization made up of five ally countries (made up of countries such as the United States, the United Kingdom, and Australia) routinely share information among each other. Edward Snowden released that the United States had been sending Israel unfiltered data to a foreign country that contained private information about the US citizens. Had it not been for the current leak of information, this practice that has been going on for decades would not be of personal public interest because it would not have been a top story in the news.

Another interesting story to consider would be how the US public is surveilling its own government. When the story of Wikileaks broke in the news, not only was it very popular but also it became the subject of a newly released movie. Wikileaks released data of US military missions online for all to see as seen in Figure 1.6. This was a very controversial move by the citizens to show that spying can also be dangerous to the government if they do not protect their secrets, and secrets that are made public can cause a government major problems such as put agents at risk or destroy trust.

So what is breeding paranoia and fueling fear that tests public trust? The same question may come up as to why I decided to write this book and perhaps why you have decided to read it. The answer may be simple … it may be that there is a lack of public trust these days, now more than ever. Perhaps, it is because there are too many stories on the news about how easy it is to hack into social

Roger. Currently engaging approximately eight individuals, uh KIA, uh RPGs, and AK–47s.

FIGURE 1.6 Military surveillance.

media accounts and conduct cyber-bullying. Perhaps, it is because identity theft has become a common crime. Perhaps, it's because everywhere you turn there is a video camera recording your every move, or because everyone carries a mobile device that can capture the moment and post it online for the world to see within seconds. It may be an answer that is more radical it may just be that fear and paranoia make a great news story and ratings have never been higher. No matter what the reason, the threat is real, and in this book, we will cover how to defend yourself, mitigate risk, protect your identity, and close attack vectors whenever possible.

Public Trust

Honestly, everyone likes a great spy novel. Famous movies are abundant and 007 James Bond is a household name. We get excited about these movies and we read spy novels, but what if you were actually spied on? How does it feel to be excited about seeing a spy in a movie use their cool gadgets developed for espionage? Then to find out someone was stalking you online and following you around without your knowledge after tracing your movement patterns? It is interesting that a culture excited about the prospect of excitement in the world of spying would be polling so low when it comes to the fact that they have become the stars of the latest spy thriller.

These questions come down to public trust. Public trust is low these days and while writing this book, it can be considered to be at an all time low. In recent Gallup polling, it is no wonder folks do not trust their governments – they are polling and showing results that public trust is a cause and effect based on how negatively the news is portraying governments involved in what they have been doing for a long time.

FIGURE 1.7 Newspaper headlines denoting spy activity.

The news media is a large distributor of propaganda to sell products and gain views from those who are willing to view their products as seen in Figure 1.7. The term "spy" is used often to generate fear, probe those who distrust or are unsure, and question their privacy in a way to build paranoia to sell products. This doesn't make what they are saying is untrue; however, it needs to be viewed in a way that is educating and not in a way that causes citizens to worry about their privacy, or in a way that causes them to fear everything and everyone around them.

That being said, let's move away from the world of international spies and military covert operations and move into the day-to-day operations most of us live today – our personal lives. Public trust in each other and our neighbors, the people we work with, and our families and friends should not be rocked by government scandals and daily news stories on how your privacy is not safe. The truth is, your privacy may not be safe and it's up to you to safeguard it. We will teach you how to do so in this book.

So why disclose this information to you in this chapter? To show you that spying is nothing new, nothing uncommon and seemingly done often without concern for the law. It's mentioned to explain to you, the citizen, how you can protect yourself from spying at any level, how you can be spied on, and how you can better protect yourself from these actions.

Is paranoia breeding the growth of more surveillance? Today, people are setting up digital surveillance systems in their own homes, businesses, and elsewhere for safety and security. As we will learn in this chapter, there are those who can access those systems to spy on you.

Consider the following. You are worried about your own safety so you get a digital surveillance system to protect your home, business, or other property. The first

FIGURE 1.8 Companies performing surveillance.

question to consider is, will you be monitoring this system yourself or will you hire a company to do it for you. There are many companies today who offer this service and Internet service providers (ISPs) are starting to offer it as a part of their Internet connectivity and digital TV packages.

An example of an entity monitoring your privacy for security reasons is seen in Figure 1.8.

Let's say you do not personally own it; however, you get it as a service through your ISP. You need to understand that other people are maintaining it, monitoring it. How can you trust them? How can you ensure that your private life is not being watched by someone you do not trust? What happens to that trust when the entities monitoring your cameras have a security breach? These questions are hypothetical to build critical thinking among you and your family to consider, for each benefit there could be a consequence.

Cybercrime

So now that we covered government and military, what about the local and the state laws against criminal behavior. Can you be stalked online and charged with a crime? Obviously, it's hard to charge an entire government that has been given carte blanche to "spy" in order to keep the public safe, what about the public itself?

Cybercrime is crimes committed using a computer and/or a computer on a network. It's a simple definition; however, there are many considerations such as does it take place on workplace computers? Over the Internet? Does it take place using e-mail, mobile phones, or within chat-rooms owned by a service provider?

This becomes important because if someone is caught spying and it's over the Internet from another country, how is the crime prosecuted? It can be conducted over the public Internet that then makes it cross-border crimes since it

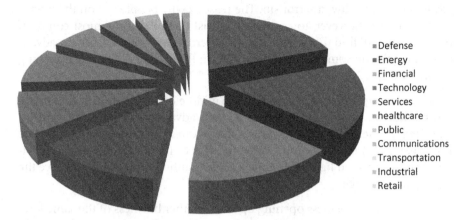

- Defense
- Energy
- Financial
- Technology
- Services
- healthcare
- Public
- Communications
- Transportation
- Industrial
- Retail

FIGURE 1.9 Cybercrime activity.

touches the global landscape. For an example of the size and scope of cyber-crime activities, please refer to the chart as seen in Figure 1.9.

What is important to consider is that these are in fact crimes and because of that, there is a process involved. Criminal activity if caught must follow specific protocols operating within the realm of law. After these crimes have been committed, normally digital forensics are used to substantiate the evidence brought to trial, as industry experts comb over the computers, phones, and networks to preserve evidence and bring it within the court of law.

As we mentioned earlier, espionage can also be considered a major cybercrime. This ties into the motivations those have to conduct cybercrimes … a major one would be financial theft, another identity theft. So why would someone do these things? What are their motivations?

Why Spy? Motivation

At a bigger level, we mentioned why organizations, governments, and militaries spy. Although we do not cover the details of all computer-related crimes, we do cover some of them here so you can understand that stalking someone online is no different than stalking someone at a public location. We do cover spying in general so that we can teach you how to protect yourself overall; the best way to understand how to protect against someone wishing and willing to do you harm is to understand why they want to do such a thing.

At a macrolevel, reconnaissance and surveillance are performed by the government agencies and the military for security and safety reasons, to gain tactical advantage and to thwart terrorism. The reasons why people spy on the micro-level are many; however, to create a small list of some of the most common reasons, you will find that whether at the macro or microlevel, leverage, advantage, and gain are some of the most common threads that bind any reasoning to any who spy.

Consider a couple divorcing and is in the middle of a legal custody and financial battle. You have heard it before, to gain advantage in the court (tactical advantage), one of the injured parties may request the assistance of a private investigator (PI) to "spy" on the other to learn of their activities. Those activities if shown to shed light in an unfavorable manner in the court may give the other party leverage.

Consider a small business opening up near another business of the same kind and the two entrepreneurs visiting each other's establishment in order to gain competitive advantage. Of course, they do so without each other knowing who they are. Taking this into the digital realm, these same entrepreneurs visit each other's web properties to perform the same tasks. Consider that one of these parties chooses to deface, discredit, or defraud the other in hopes of injuring their reputation.

Consider someone who realizes that their spouse is looking through their phone when they are not around to see what they are up to, who they are talking to, what sites they have been to, and what their e-mail content is.

Consider an author publishing a new book that directly competes with a title of similar content and launches a smear campaign using the comments section of the site in which it's sold to discredit the title.

Consider a high school student who is consistently picked on (bullied) and only way to get back at those who are conducting these actions launches a cybercrime against the perpetrators, for example, hacks into and defaces their public Twitter page.

What if an ex-boyfriend wanted to stalk an ex-girlfriend and posed as someone else on Facebook to track, monitor, and interact with her? Facebook and other social media site as seen in Figure 1.10 are a large source of controversy today in regard to privacy. These sites are easily used to provide portals into private lives and give those who use them for the wrong reason to track you, find out where you live, when you take a vacation, and where you work.

At a more microlevel, an individual can spy to learn more about another person. For example, if someone you worked with wanted to get to know more about you … instead of just asking you or trying to get to know you, they search for you online in a search engine.

FIGURE 1.10 Social media concerns.

The motivations are endless, they are many. Legal reasons, divorce, leverage, financial, theft, revenge … the list goes on and on. This is why people may decide to conduct their own investigations on others, why they would consider spying on others. Make no mistake; however, most of these activities are spying and many of them may be considered a cybercrime.

What Is to Gain? Reward

When someone spies it's always to achieve a specific goal. Whether the goal is to learn information, take photos, or document activities, this is where spying and actual crime can become a challenge to define. It is easy to understand if you split the two into two separate activities. Surveillance is conducted to gather information about individuals, organizations, businesses, and infrastructure. It may be gathered in order to commit an act of terrorism or other crime. At both the macro and microlevel, there is much to gain. There are massive rewards.

In the United States, the banking and finance sector accounts for more than 8% of the annual gross domestic product and can be considered one of the major arteries of the entire world economy. Spying on these targets at any level to produce information to sell or to produce intelligence for a digital attack can be extremely rewarding.

At the microlevel, gains can be just as rewarding to those who wish to do wrong. For example, you want to find out if your neighbor's wireless is open for use so you do not have to pay for yours. You do some reconnaissance work and scan the area to find a signal. You attach to the wireless Service Set Identifier and bypass the password configured. Later, you find that you are able to attach to the main network and connect to their in-home video surveillance security system. Some would think that being able to watch their neighbors unsuspected would be a reward.

In another example, pictures were scoured off the Internet from young girls taking "selfies" that provided their location (possibly home address) within the metadata of the picture. This enabled those who wish to do wrong the ability to track and possibly stalk these girls.

As you can see, there is much to gain especially by those with ill-conceived notions. That's where the possible crimes take place and afterward, the investigations into those crimes possibly as part of a case in the court of law.

Digital Forensics

Digital forensics is considered the investigation work done after a crime is committed on digital devices and networks. Although we have only described a small handful of possible crimes that can take place in the cyberworld, it's important to understand for the purpose of this chapter that as you commit cybercrimes, they can be detected, thwarted, and brought into the court of law. For example, if you wanted to use an application to track someone using their phone, if that phone winds up in the hands of a digital forensic analyst, it's likely that they will be able to produce that software and show the cyberattack in detail in the court of law.

Digital forensics can be used for surveillance as well. As we will learn, some of the data gathered from your devices memory, logs, and storage devices can be very revealing. These items can disclose where you have been online, sometimes where you have been physically, what you have done, what you have said, and what you have stored, and give those who are performing surveillance a bird's eye view into your digital behaviors. An example of the amount of storage devices that data can be gleaned from is seen in Figure 1.11.

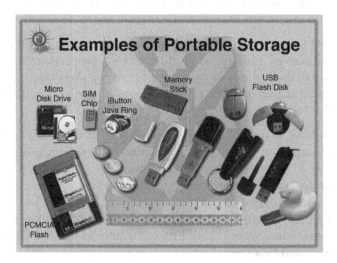

FIGURE 1.11 Portable storage devices.

These same digital devices can be brought inconspicuously into your home or business and data from your devices can be transferred onto them without your knowledge.

One thing to note is that digital forensics can recover for the investigative purposes almost anything on a computer or network system as long as it has not been tampered with. For example, information kept in memory may be lost if the device is turned off. Although a major discussion on forensic science falls outside the scope of this book, we will in fact cover forensic specifics throughout the book when discussing relevant topics.

WHO SPIES?

We covered the nuts and bolts of why reconnaissance and surveillance takes place. We discussed the legal aspects of it; however, before we end this chapter and move into the details of how it is conducted, we should take a close look at those who spy and specifically, if they are doing it for the right or wrong reasons.

Who spies? It's easy to just say "everyone" at some level because of human nature and how people can be curious; however, we will break down key categories so that you can understand not only who, but why. A good saying is "Curiosity killed the cat". Its human nature to take interest in things they want to know or learn about; however, ethically there are boundaries.

The government spies in the name of national security. The military will spy to conduct covert operations.

Organizations spy to gain competitive advantage. The public spies for many reasons to include harmless curiosity all the way to conducting major crimes.

One topic we did not cover is the list of diverse professionals who work within the digital realm to conduct investigations, surveillance, and reconnaissance work on a daily basis. We just recently covered the legal aspects of conducting surveillance work and touched on the role of PI; however, there are many other roles that conduct surveillance work, investigation work, and not all of them are "bad guys." Some of them are and we will cover the distinctions throughout the book when we delve into the actual "how" it's done; however, to start, lets take some time to review the professionals today who conduct digital surveillance and reconnaissance work and the reasons they do.

Professional Roles

Digital surveillance and reconnaissance is conducted by many. As we have discussed earlier, the military, the government, your neighbor, and your co-worker may for some reason or another, wish to gather data or intelligence on another or another entity for specific or even no-specific reasons.

There are those, however, who work professionally in the field. These professionals are also experts in working in the digital realm or technology. Digital forensics, cybercrime investigators, penetration testers, and law enforcement specialists are only but a few of the diverse offerings within the field of digital security.

What we will not cover here that we have already discussed in this chapter are military and government agents who conduct reconnaissance and surveillance work for gathering intelligence.

Hackers (White, Gray, and Black)

One of the biggest threats today in the digital world is the "Hacker," who traditionally manipulated your computer, mobile, and video systems so that they could tamper with them, gain access, or acquire information from them. These same folks were able to create malware (malicious software) to perform these same functions; however, some of these programs were able to track your activities, impersonate you, and or steal your identity. What a hacker does is broad; however, it needs to be understood that the malicious form of the term hacker has been rebranded.

Black hat hacker's are those who wish to do harm, are malicious or operate in an unethical manner. White hats are considered to be hackers who are non-malicious. White hats are generally computer system experts who work in the security field to find problems with systems that their malicious counterparts would look to expose for financial reasons, leverage, or simply for fun. Gray hats are said to cross both black and white boundaries and generally will not be overly malicious.

There is a reason you need to understand why these types of experts spy; they spy to gain something and unfortunately since they may happen upon your computer system with your personal information stored, they may collect it for their own personal use or to sell for a profit. They may attach to your systems without your knowledge and conduct their operations in a clandestine manner in which you may not detect.

Digital Forensics Examiner

As we discussed earlier when covering the world of digital forensics, there is much to be gleaned from digital devices and most, if not all, activity can be found and brought into a court of law to bolster a case as evidence. Unfortunately, if you are the malicious party, it's likely that you will have all of your activity presented unless you masterfully know how to cover your tracks and/or dispose of evidence correctly.

These experts are often brought in to testify as experts in their field and present evidence in the form of data, logs, and provable activity. Digital forensic examiners use special tools and software (Encase is one of the most commonly used) to scour a computer system or device in order to find data and, as long as the crime scene or evidence is untampered with, can be used to show all activity of those using such systems and devices.

Cyber Intelligence Analyst

Intelligence agents (or analysts) are those who work in the Intelligence field and typically are employed by military and government agencies. When Intelligence is gathered on a target, these individuals or teams review and assist with the activities revolving around building cases, fighting crime, stopping malicious activities from taking place, and more.

These experts work on cybercrime cases and assist with the analysis of the data collected. For example, if a Virus was used to steal government data, these intelligence experts may work with developers, companies, other software teams, and so on to assist with reviewing the findings and assisting them with the stopping of the criminal behavior taking place.

Cyber Security Engineer

Security engineers (or analysts, in general) work within the field of information technology security and typically assist with the design and assembly of digital computer security systems. For example, they may be firewall, intrusion detection/prevention system experts who understand access control, authentication, and accounting in depth.

In regard to surveillance and spying of and on systems and people using systems, these experts are those who are in charge with building and engineering systems that offer security to prevent unauthorized access to private networks, computers, and systems.

Penetration Tester

Penetration testers (or pen tester for short) are charged with testing access of systems that have already been engineered. These experts verify that access cannot be gained, and if it is, they provide reports on what needs to be fixed. It would be extremely difficult to spy on a home through their video cameras if this weakness was considered, tested, and then locked down post test.

They use software such as Backtrack, Nessus, and others to verify that access cannot be gained unless permitted and exposure is limited. They mitigate the possibility of problems taking place by exposing that they are problems to begin with and give such findings to those charged with locking open holes down. They are also highly employed by those looking to ensure that systems and networks that are to be and remain compliant are in fact configured correctly to be compliant to policy.

Private Investigator

Private investigation is a form of surveillance work. We discuss it here in this section of this chapter coincidentally; it's a common form of work performed to gather information on a target. Private investigation is a trade where trained professionals conduct surveillance work for clients as per request.

A PI is a professional who performs investigations. Although we have touched on this topic throughout the chapter, PI's are responsible for conducting private investigation for those who request their services. They often conduct surveillance activities for those who hire them and can be considered a private detective conducting investigations for criminal cases, civil cases, and for collection of evidence. Sometimes referred to as a private eye, these professionals commonly work for attorneys who need to collect evidences to support legal cases.

They can (and often are) hired to spy on individuals to bolster cases with documented evidence commonly produced by video and camera footage (Figure 1.12). Today, professionals undergoing these work activities are generally licensed to do so and operate within ethical standards.

Law Enforcement

Law enforcement professionals (such as police, agents, and detectives) are commonly used to conduct and/or stop surveillance activities. If a crime is suspected, for example, detectives may be called in to open a case and start to collect and review evidence. To do so, these experts must at times do reconnaissance and surveillance work in order to build cases and report on them, and/or use such evidence in the court of law.

FIGURE 1.12 Private investigation.

LEGAL AND ETHICAL PRINCIPLES

Until now, we have talked about a lot of scary stuff and how it relates to the court of law; however, there are many factors to consider when it comes to digital spying when brought in front of a judge. We know what experts are counted on to bolster cases and we know the types of malicious characters who may be committing crimes. We now know that there is a blurry line separating government and public activities and some of the legislature created to create clearer lines to follow.

To close this chapter, we should discuss legal and ethical principles revolving around surveillance activities. In the remaining of this book, we will cover surveillance at a more personal level; however, it's important to understand that for those committing spying and stalking crimes (for example), there could be a punishment. As easily as it may be to use the digital landscape to conduct your crime, it's as easy to gather the evidence of it happening.

Ethics

Ethically you should not use any of the information learned in this book to conduct a crime. It is here for one purpose, awareness. The goal of this book is to help security professionals in the field and/or the typical citizen remain aware of digital surveillance issues taking place today and to assist those parties with providing a way to be aware of them, mitigate them, and protect against it. It is by no means a book that shows someone with a vengeful heart a way to conduct such unlawful activities.

Ethically, you should always consider that there are those with ill intentions out in the world and you should learn how to protect yourself against them, not become one of them. You should also consider that since you are protected by laws, so if you do suspect you are a victim, you should not retaliate or counterattack. This behavior is not only counterproductive and inflammatory but also could be illegal and used against you.

The Law

With the growing digital landscape, cybercrime has grown just as quickly as the networks, systems, and applications have. Because of this, legally, lines have been blurred as cyberlaw has attempted to keep up. Cyberlaw is the cyber-based legal dealings of any legal issues and actions that take place in the digital world. The reason why this is critically so important to consider is that if you become a victim of cybercrime, what is your recourse? Also, if you are thinking of committing a cybercrime, think again – the police, FBI, and other federal intelligence groups are keeping an eye open and are armed with evidence collection methods, laws, and safeguards to protect and serve the innocent.

Some of the most common issues that raise questions in the court of law is, how does the Internet fall into jurisdiction issues? What about privacy rights? In our attempts to answer these questions, we will review a cybercrime case to show how cyberlaw works and how those who fall victim can be protected and those who perpetrate crimes can be held accountable. In some cases, such as that of Alexis Pilkington (New York) who committed suicide allegedly from cyberbullying, the crimes perpetrated could lead to death.

Surveillance and Cybercrime Sample Law

In the next section, we will review a case where the United States and Erik Bowker had their day in court. On September 25, 2001, Bowker was charged with one count of interstate stalking, in violation of 18 U.S.C. § 2261A(1); one count of cyberstalking, in violation of 18U.S.C. § 2261A(2); one count of theft of mail, in violation of 18 U.S.C. § 1708; and one count of telephone harassment, in violation of 47 U.S.C. § 223(a)(1)(C). On June 6, 2002, a jury returned guilty verdicts on all charges. The government moved for an upward departure from the sentencing guidelines based on the victim's extreme psychological harm. On September 10, 2002, the district court sentenced Bowker to 96 months incarceration, 3 years supervised release, and a $400 special assessment. In assessing the term of incarceration, the district court granted the government's motion for an upward departure.

Count1 (interstate stalking)[1], Count 2 (cyberstalking)[2], and Count 4 (telephone harassment)[3] track the language of the relevant statutes. Count 1 alleges that between July 10 and July 30, 2001, Bowker knowingly and intentionally traveled across the Ohio state line with the intent to injure, harass, and intimidate Tina Knight, and as a result of such travel placed Knight in reasonable fear of death or serious bodily injury, in violation of 18 U.S.C. § 2261A(1). Count 2 alleges that between December 25, 2000 and August 18, 2001 Bowker, located in Ohio, knowingly and repeatedly used the Internet to engage in a course of conduct that intentionally placed Knight, then located in West Virginia, in reasonable fear of death or serious bodily injury, in violation of 18 U.S.C. § 2261A(2). Count 4 alleges that between June 12, 2001 and August 27, 2001, Bowker, located in Ohio, knowingly made telephone calls, whether or not conversation or communication ensued, without disclosing his identity and with the intent to annoy, abuse, threaten, and harass Knight, in violation of 47 U.S.C. § 223(a)(1)(C). Because the indictment stated all of the statutory elements of the offenses, and because the relevant statutes state the elements unambiguously, the district court properly denied Bowker's motion to dismiss Counts 1, 2, and 4 of the indictment. The indictment's reference to the specific dates and locations of the offenses, as well as the means used to carry them out (travel, Internet, telephone), provided Bowker fair notice of the conduct with which he was being charged.

We hold that the above-described facts amply justified the district court's upward departure determination. Cf. United States v. Otto, 64 F.3d 367, 371 (8th Cir.1995) (affirming upward departure where stalking victim lived in constant fear for herself and for her children and was always on the lookout for the defendant; could not eat or sleep; lost weight; required counseling; and feared the defendant's ultimate release); United States v. Miller, 993 F.2d 16, 21 (2d Cir.1993) (affirming upward departure after the defendant had engaged in a 3-year campaign of harassment; noting that the victim had been afraid to answer the telephone or open her mail for 3 years; was afraid to remain in the New York area; and believed that the years of harassment had hastened her husband's demise).

---

372 F.3d 365 (2004)

UNITED STATES of America, Plaintiff-Appellee,

v. Erik BOWKER, Defendant-Appellant.

No. 02-4086.

United States Court of Appeals, Sixth Circuit.

Submitted: March 10, 2004.

Decided and Filed: June 11, 2004.

366*366 367*367 368*368 369*369 370*370 Edward F. Feran (briefed), Assistant United States Attorney, Cleveland, OH, for Appellee.

Jay Milano (briefed), Milano & Co., Rocky River, OH, for Appellant.

Before MARTIN and CLAY, Circuit Judges; MILLS, District Judge.[*]

Opinion
CLAY, Circuit Judge.

Defendant-Appellant Erik S. Bowker appeals his convictions and sentence for one count of interstate stalking, in violation of 18 U.S.C. § 2261A(1); one count of cyberstalking, in violation of 18 U.S.C. § 2261A(2); one count of theft of mail, in violation of 18 U.S.C. § 1708; and one count of telephone harassment, in violation of 47 U.S.C. § 223(a)(1)(C). Bowker also appeals the district court's failure to rule on his motion to return seized property and the district court's enhancement of his sentence based on extreme psychological harm to the victim. For the reasons that follow, we AFFIRM Bowker's convictions and sentence, but REMAND to the district court for a ruling on Bowker's motion to return seized property.

I Facts
A. Procedural History
On August 28, 2001, United States Magistrate Judge George J. Limbert signed a criminal complaint charging Erik. S. Bowker ("Bowker") with one count of telephone harassment in violation of 47 U.S.C. § 223(a)(1)(C). Bowker was arrested on August 29, 2001. On September 7, 2001, the magistrate judge held a preliminary examination and detention hearing for Bowker. The magistrate judge determined that probable cause for Bowker's arrest had been established, and he ordered Bowker detained.

On September 25, 2001, a federal grand jury returned a four-count indictment against Bowker. Bowker was charged with one count of interstate stalking, in violation of 18 U.S.C. § 2261A(1); one count of cyberstalking, in violation of 18U.S.C. § 2261A(2); one count of theft of mail, in violation of 18 U.S.C. § 1708; and one count of telephone harassment, in violation of 47 U.S.C. § 223(a)(1)(C).

371*371 Bowker filed several pretrial motions which are the subject of this appeal – a *pro se* motion to represent himself, a motion to dismiss Counts 1, 2, and 4 of the indictment, a motion to sever Count 3 from the indictment, a motion to suppress evidence, and a *pro se* motion for return of seized property and items, pursuant to Rule 41 of the Federal Rules of Criminal Procedure. The district court denied all of the foregoing motions, except for the motion to return seized property, on which the district court never ruled. On March 26, 2002, after the denial of Bowker's *pro se* motion to represent himself, Bowker's counsel moved to withdraw from the case, and Bowker signed a separate statement asking the court to grant the motion and assign him new counsel. The district court granted the motion and assigned Bowker new counsel.

Bowker's jury trial commenced on June 3, 2002. On June 6, 2002, the jury returned verdicts of guilty against Bowker on all counts. On September 5, 2002, the government moved for an upward departure from the sentencing guidelines based on the victim's extreme psychological harm. On September 10, 2002, the district court sentenced Bowker to 96 months' incarceration, three years of supervised release, and a $400 special assessment. In assessing the term of incarceration, the district court granted the government's motion for an upward departure.

B. Substantive Facts

In March, 2000, Tina Knight began working as a part-time general assignment reporter at WKBN Television in Youngstown, Ohio. WKBN has a general email account for most employees, and in June, 2000, WKBN received a number of emails relating to Knight. The emails were sent from several different email addresses and purported to be from an individual variously identified as "User x," Eric Neubauer, Karen Walters, and "BB." Several of the emails attached photographs with verbal captions. One caption referred to Knight being shot with a pellet gun, and another email said, "Thanks for my daily Tina Knight fix. Thanks for helping me get my nuts off," and another said "More Tina Knight, that is what I want and need." After receiving approximately nine of these types of email, WKBN's news director took them to the station's general manager. They then contacted Special Agent Deane Hassman of the FBI. Soon thereafter, Knight was shown the emails, and she was stunned and frightened.

FBI Agent Hassman began investigating the Tina Knight emails in July, 2000. Hassman was concerned about Knight's personal safety based on the content of the emails. One of the emails that concerned Hassman stated, "I'm not the type of obsessed viewer that hides in the bushes near your home to watch you come home from work, but we shall see. That may actually be fun." Another disturbing email stated, in part, "Dear Ms. Knight. Now I'm really pissed that you were looking even cuter than normally. You fucked up a little bit and here I am watching on this black and white thrift store TV. Cute, cute, cute. I bet you were a Ho at Ohio University in Athens, doing chicks and everything. Wow."

On July 25, 2000, Hassman sent emails to the various email addresses on the correspondence pertaining to Knight. Hassman asked the sender of the emails to contact him so that he could determine the sender's intent. Within 24 to 48 hours, Hassman received a telephone call from an individual who identified himself as Erik Bowker. Hassman wanted to set up a meeting with Bowker so Hassman could positively identify the sender of the emails and also ask him to cease and desist from 372*372 contacting Knight. They arranged to meet at the public library in Youngstown, but Bowker never showed.

A few weeks later, Knight began receiving hand-written notes at WKBN, the majority of which were signed by "Doug Wagner." By September, the letters were arriving at the station almost every couple of days. One of the letters included the phrase, "All this week I will be playing the role of Doug Wagner." A letter dated August 9, 2000 was signed "Chad Felton"; stated, "I think you are a super babe"; and included a necklace. The return addresses on the letters were one of two P.O. Boxes registered to Erik Bowker or his mother.

Knight left her employment at WKBN in November, 2000 to take a position at WOWK CBS13 in Charleston, West Virginia. WKBN did not inform the general public of Knight's new location.

In late December, 2000, Knight's parents, who reside in Medina, Ohio, received a card and a hand-written note at their home. The card purported to be from "Kathryn Harris." The letter read, "Dear Tina Knight: I am Kathryn Harris today. I didn't want your parents asking you a lot of questions, nor did I want to attract a lot of attention to you. My letters to you are all online at yahoo.com in a standard mail account. It is all explained there so please check in and read what I have written.... The E-mail address is *tinahatesme@yahoo.com*." Agent Hassman visited the email address to check if any letters had been sent to the email address mentioned in the letter. Hassman discovered that an email had been sent December 25, 2000. At the end of the email, the name "Doug Wagner" was typed. The email read, in part, "I told you I would not contact you by mail anymore but I am sorry, I am in agony. I'm thinking about you all the time. You really are my dream girl.... I am blinded with affection for you. I did not ask for this. Nope, it's all your fault.... Please don't cat dance on my emotions by failing to respond to me at all."

In February, 2001, Bowker filed a lawsuit against Knight in the Mahoning County Common Pleas Court. Knight's social security number was stated in the complaint, which was served at Knight's home address in West Virginia. Bowker's lawsuit accused Knight of stalking him. Agent Hassman attended a status conference for the lawsuit on March 16, 2001, so that he could make face-to-face contact with Bowker. After meeting Bowker at the hearing and confirming that Bowker had been sending the unsolicited correspondence to Knight, Hassman told Bowker that the correspondence was unwelcome and might be a violation of federal law. Hassman advised Bowker that if the conduct continued, it might result in his arrest. Bowker responded that he had a First Amendment right to engage in that type of conduct. Nevertheless, during the meeting, Bowker wrote and signed a note stating, "I understand that Tina M. Knight wishes all further contact with her or any family member to stop and I agree to do so, pursuant to conversation with Deane Hassman, special agent, Federal Bureau of Investigation...." Bowker also agreed to voluntarily dismiss his lawsuit against Knight.

Despite Bowker's March, 16, 2001 agreement to cease and desist from any further contact with Knight, on that very same day, Bowker mailed a letter to Knight. Bowker also continued to attempt telephone contact with Knight. Between January 26 and August 29, 2001, Bowker made 146 telephone calls from his cell phone to WOWK CBS 13, where Knight worked. Bowker also made 16 calls to Knight's personal residential telephone in 373*373 West Virginia between August 11 and 28, 2001. Knight's number was unlisted and unpublished. According to telephone records, each of the 16 calls placed to Knight's home were preceded by *67, which enables a caller to block identification of his telephone number on the recipient's caller identification display. Bowker also called Knight's co-worker and a neighbor.

As the telephone calls to Knight's television station persisted through the summer of 2001, Agent Hassman believed it was important to capture Bowker's voice on tape, so Hassman provided Knight with a recording device at the television station. On June 12, 2001, Knight recorded a 45 minute telephone call from Bowker who, at one point, identified himself as "Mike." During the conversation, Bowker referred to Knight's neighbors, her family members and her social security number. He also indicated he might be watching Knight with his binoculars. Knight provided the tape to the FBI and never spoke to Bowker again on the telephone.

On July 16, 2001, Knight received a letter at the television station. In the letter, Bowker referred to Knight's parents and stated several times, "You do not hang up on me." The letter also crassly referred to Knight's car, threatened to file a mechanic's lien on her car and her co-worker's car, accused Knight and her colleague of being "fuck-ups, assholes and seriously emotional and mentally unbalanced," and contained numerous sexual references. The letter stated that Bowker would be contacting Knight's neighbors, pointed out that Knight had not registered her car in West Virginia, and concluded with the words, "So bye-by, fuck you, you are an asshole and a sociopath and an embarrassment to mothers everywhere sir.... Adios, Eric.... Smooch, Smooch."

On August 10, 2001, Knight received a certified letter mailed to her residence in West Virginia. Accompanying the letter were numerous photographs of Bowker at various locations in West Virginia, Knight's home state. The letter stated, in part, "Send me an E-Mail address. It keeps me long distance, you know what I mean." Knight forwarded the letter and the photographs to the FBI. Bowker's credit card statement later revealed purchases from a Kmart and a Kroger near Knight's place of employment and residence in West Virginia between June 12 and July 30, 2001.

In August 2001, Bowker left a series of messages on Knight's answering machine asking that Knight or Knight's friend call him back, which did not occur. Among other things, Bowker stated:

I don't even know why I'm nice to you ever at all, you and your fucked-up friend should not even be working in the media. You know you gotta mother-fucking realize there's like 50 percent men in this country and you better mother-fucking learn that you're going to have to deal with us sometime....

Well, it looks like nobody is going to answer me if Tina Knight is okay, so I'm gonna take the 1:00 a.m. bus out of Columbus, Ohio and come down there and see for myself. Okay, I'll be there about 6:00 a.m. Bye.

Knight testified that these messages made her afraid to leave the house everyday, and she feared that Bowker might try to rape her. She gave the answering machine recordings to the FBI.

Bowker was arrested on August 29, 2001 at a self-storage facility in Youngstown where he kept some of his possessions. Among other things recovered from the storage facility, Bowker's car and other locations, were a police scanner set to the frequency of the Youngstown Police Department, 374*374 a paper with scanner frequencies from the Dunbar, West Virginia Police Department, letters bearing the name "Chad Felton," a credit report for Tina Knight, Knight's birth certificate, a map of Dunbar, West Virginia, Greyhound bus schedules with West Virginia routes, and photos taken by Bowker during a West Virignia trip on July 11, 2001, which included pictures of Knight's place of work, her car and CBS news trucks. The FBI also discovered that Bowker had in his possession a Discover Card credit card bill addressed to Tina Knight in West Virginia. Knight never received that statement in the mail.

II Probable Cause for Bowker's Arrest

Bowker argues that the magistrate judge erroneously found that there was probable cause to issue a warrant for his arrest premised on an alleged violation of 47 U.S.C. § 223(a)(1)(C), which prohibits telephone harassment. He further argues that trial court committed the same error when it denied Bowker's motion to suppress evidence obtained through the arrest warrant. We reject Bowker's arguments for the reasons stated below.

A. Standard of Review

The Court considers the evidence that the warrant-issuing magistrate judge had before him only to ensure that the magistrate had a substantial basis for concluding that probable cause existed. *See United States v. Jones,* 159 F.3d 969, 973 (6th Cir.1998) (citing *Illinois v. Gates,* 462 U.S. 213, 238-39, 103 S.Ct. 2317, 76 L.Ed.2d 527 (1983)). The Court defers to findings of probable cause made by a magistrate, and will not set aside such findings unless they were arbitrarily made. *United States v. Brown,* 147 F.3d 477, 484 (6th Cir.1998). When reviewing a district court's denial of a motion to suppress, the Court reviews the district court's findings of fact for clear error and its conclusions of law *de novo. Id.*

B. Analysis

At the preliminary hearing, the government brought a one-count criminal complaint against Bowker for the crime of telephone harassment, in violation of 47 U.S.C. § 223(a)(1)(C). That section provides for a fine, imprisonment, or both for anyone, who in interstate or foreign communications:

makes a telephone call or utilizes a telecommunications device, whether or not conversation or communication ensues, without disclosing his identity and with intent to annoy, abuse, threaten, or harass any person at the called number or who receives the communications.

47 U.S.C.A. § 223. Incorporated into the criminal complaint was the affidavit of FBI Agent Deane Hassman, who alleged that Bowker had made numerous telephone calls to Tina Knight in which Bowker did not identify himself, including a conversation with Knight on June 12, 2001, and messages left on Knight's answering machine on August 17-19 and 25-26, 2001. Agent Hassman's affidavit also provided extensive background details on Bowker's campaign of harassment against Knight via emails, letters and telephone calls.

Bowker concedes that the magistrate judge could have found probable cause on the elements of using the telephone with the intent to annoy, abuse, threaten or harass. He argues, however, that the magistrate had no basis to find the element of failing to disclose identity during the telephone calls because Knight, the recipient of those calls, allegedly recognized his voice, making it unnecessary for him to state his name. *See* J.A. 581 (testimony 375*375 of Agent Hassman: "There came a point in time where Tina [Knight] began to recognize a certain voice on the phone, which she believed to be Eric [sic] Bowker."). Bowker points to the fact that during the June 12, 2001 telephone conversation with Knight, she referred to Bowker as "Eric" [sic].

Bowker's argument is flawed in several respects. His argument does not address the numerous occasions when Bowker called Knight and no conversation ensued and no messages were left or her answering machine. The evidence before the magistrate showed that Bowker used a caller identification blocking feature (*67) to place these calls, thereby concealing his identity. Since the telephone harassment law prohibits calls made with the intent to harass or annoy "whether or not conversation or communication ensues," there was probable cause to find that Bowker had concealed his identity in those instances. Knight's alleged ability to identify Bowker's voice was irrelevant.

Bowker responds that his use of the *67 feature should be legally irrelevant, since it penalizes him for placing telephone calls to numbers with a caller identification service. He contends that criminal liability should not hinge on what telephone features a person pays for each month to the local phone company. Bowker, however, is not being penalized based on the telephone features to which his victim subscribed, but for using the *67 feature in conjunction with his intent to annoy or harass Knight. Had he lacked that intent, no criminal liability would have attached.

Even assuming that Knight was able to identify Bowker's voice, the magistrate judge properly found probable cause to believe that Bowker had not disclosed his identity during the June 12, 2001 conversation in which he mis-identified himself as "Mike" and in August, 2001, when he left messages on Knight's answering machine without providing any name at all. On its face, the telephone harassment statute makes it illegal to place a call, with the intent to annoy, abuse threaten or harass, whenever the caller fails to identify himself. Since Bowker concedes that the magistrate judge could have found probable cause that he had the requisite intent, it was Bowker's provision of a false name and/or his failure to identify himself – not an erroneous judicial determination about the victim's recognition of his voice – that led to the issuance of his arrest warrant.

Bowker similarly argues that the district court, which supervised the trial proceedings, erred in denying his motion to suppress evidence derived from his arrest for telephone harassment. In addition to his argument that the evidence did not support a finding of probable cause to believe that Bowker had failed to disclose his identity (discussed above), Bowker argues that the district court erred in ruling that FBI agent Hassman did not intentionally mislead or omit crucial material facts in his affidavit supporting probable cause. Bowker argues that he showed, by a preponderance of the evidence, materially false representations and omissions by Agent Hassman, and that absent those misrepresentations, probable cause would not have been found.

To prevail on a motion to suppress based on allegations of intentional misrepresentation by a law enforcement officer in the course of obtaining an arrest warrant, Bowker must establish (1) the allegation of perjury or reckless disregard "by the defendant by a preponderance of the evidence" and (2) "with the affidavit's false material set to one side, the affidavit's remaining content is insufficient to establish probable cause, [such that] the search warrant must be voided and the fruits of the search' suppressed." *United* 376*376 *States v. Graham*, 275 F.3d 490, 505 (6th Cir.2001) (quoting *Franks v. Delaware*, 438 U.S. 154, 155-56, 98 S.Ct. 2674, 57 L.Ed.2d 667 (1978)). Bowker has not established that Agent Hassman perjured himself in his affidavit in support of the criminal complaint or at the suppression hearing. At most, he quibbles with Hassman's characterization of Bowker's letters and emails as sexual and threatening. Hassman's characterization, however, largely is a matter of opinion, and the content of Bowker's communications speak for themselves. Thus, there is no indication that the magistrate judge was misled in reaching its probable cause finding. Accordingly, the district court did not err in denying Bowker's motion to suppress evidence.

III Motion to Dismiss Counts 1, 2 and 4 of the Indictment

Bowker argues that the district court erred in failing to dismiss Counts 1 (interstate stalking), 2 (cyberstalking) and 4 (telephone harassment) of the indictment on the ground that the indictment inadequately alleged the elements of the offenses charged, and on the ground that the statutes that the indictment alleged he violated are unconstitutionally vague and overbroad. We review the denial of a motion to dismiss *de novo. United States v. Maney,* 226 F.3d 660, 663 (6th Cir.2000). For the reasons that follow, we affirm the decision of the district court.

A. Sufficiency of the Indictment

Under the Notice Clause of the Sixth Amendment, a criminal defendant has the right "to be informed of the nature and cause of the accusation" against him. U.S. Const. amend. VI. In addition, the Indictment Clause of the Fifth Amendment requires that a defendant be charged with only those charges brought before the grand jury. U.S. Const. amend. V. An indictment satisfies these constitutional requirements "if it, first, contains the elements of the offense charged and fairly informs a defendant of the charge against which he must defend, and, second, enables him to plead an acquittal or conviction in bar of future prosecutions for the same offense." *Maney,* 226 F.3d at 663 (citing *Hamling v. United States,* 418 U.S. 87, 117, 94 S.Ct. 2887, 41 L.Ed.2d 590

(1974); *Russell v. United States*, 369 U.S. 749, 763-64, 82 S.Ct. 1038, 8 L.Ed.2d 240 (1962); *United States v. Sturman*, 951 F.2d 1466, 1478-79 (6th Cir.1991)). "To be legally sufficient, the indictment must assert facts which in law constitute an offense; and which, if proved, would establish prima facie the defendant's commission of that crime." *Id.* (quoting *United States v. Superior Growers Supply, Inc.*, 982 F.2d 173, 177 (6th Cir.1992)).

"An indictment is usually sufficient if it states the offense using the words of the statute itself, as long as the statute fully and unambiguously states all the elements of the offense." *United States v. Landham*, 251 F.3d 1072, 1079 (6th Cir.2001) (citing *Hamling*, 418 U.S. at 117, 94 S.Ct. 2887; *United States v. Monus*, 128 F.3d 376, 388 (1997)). The Supreme Court has cautioned, however, that while "the language of the statute may be used in the general description of the offense, ...it must be accompanied with such a statement of the facts and circumstances as will inform the accused of the specific offense, coming under the general description, with which he is charged." *Hamling*, 418 U.S. at 117-18, 94 S.Ct. 2887 (internal quotation marks and citation omitted)." 'Courts utilize a common sense construction in determining whether an indictment sufficiently informs a defendant of an offense.' *Maney*, 226 F.3d at 377*377 663 (quoting *Allen v. United States*, 867 F.2d 969, 971 (6th Cir.1989)).

Count1 (interstate stalking)[1], Count 2 (cyberstalking)[2] and Count 4 (telephone harassment)[3] track the language of the relevant statutes. Count 1 alleges that, between July 10 and July 30, 2001, Bowker knowingly and intentionally traveled across the Ohio state line with the intent to injure, harass, and intimidate Tina Knight, and as a result of such travel placed Knight in reasonable fear of death or serious bodily injury, in violation of 18 U.S.C. § 2261A(1). Count 2 alleges that between December 25, 2000 and August 18, 2001 Bowker, located in Ohio, knowingly and repeatedly used the internet to engage in a course of conduct that intentionally placed Knight, then located in West Virginia, in reasonable fear of death or serious bodily injury, in violation of 18 U.S.C. § 2261A(2). Count 4 alleges that between June 12, 2001, and August 27, 2001, Bowker, located in Ohio, knowingly made telephone calls, whether or not conversation or communication ensued, without disclosing his identity and with the intent to annoy, abuse, threaten and harass Knight, in violation of 47 U.S.C. § 223(a)(1)(C). Because the indictment stated all of the statutory elements of the offenses, and because the relevant statutes state the elements unambiguously, the district court properly denied Bowker's motion to dismiss Counts 1, 2 and 4 of the indictment. The indictment's reference to the specific dates and locations of the offenses, as well as the means used to carry them out (travel, internet, telephone), provided Bowker fair notice of the conduct with which he was being charged.

Relying on the *Landham* case, *supra,* Bowker argues that the indictment was defective because it does not charge him with making direct threats against Knight and therefore should have contained a statement of facts and circumstances surrounding 378*378 the alleged indirect threats he made against her, such as an explanation of the parties' relationship. *See Landham,* 251 F.3d at 1080 (holding "because the alleged threatening statement must be viewed from the objective perspective of the recipient, which frequently involves the context of the parties' relationship...., it is incumbent on the Government to make that context clear in such an indictment, unless the alleged threat is direct").

Landham is distinguishable, however. There, the Court held that the indictment failed to sufficiently allege a kidnaping threat because the indictment was missing several elements of the offense, specifically, a communication containing a threat and a threat to kidnap. *Id.* at 1082. The indictment failed to acknowledge that the defendant had been in a custody battle with his ex-wife over their daughter and, therefore, the defendant's obscure statements like "I'm going to get her" were either unreasonably perceived to be kidnaping threats and, even if the alleged threat had been carried out, it would not have constituted a crime as a matter of substantive law. *Id.* at 1081-83. The Court further held that the indictment failed to sufficiently allege a threat of bodily harm, because the statement charged in the indictment referred to past conduct of the defendant, not present or future conduct, and, in any event, did not mention a threat to inflict bodily harm. *Id.* at 1082-83. Bowker's indictment, by contrast, did not contain similar deficiencies. All of the statutory elements of the prohibited conduct were properly alleged, including the intent to cause a reasonable fear of death or serious bodily harm. And unlike the parties involved in *Landham,* whose custody battle was highly relevant to the charged conduct, Bowker's relationship with Knight had no relevant bearing on the alleged illegality of his conduct. We therefore reject Bowker's challenge to the sufficiency of the indictment.

B. Overbreadth Challenge

According to the Supreme Court, imprecise laws can be attacked on their face under two different doctrines – overbreadth and vagueness. *City of Chicago v. Morales,* 527 U.S. 41, 119 S.Ct. 1849, 144 L.Ed.2d 67 (1999). The "overbreadth doctrine is a limited exception to the traditional standing rule that a person to whom a statute may constitutionally be applied may not challenge that statute on the basis that it may conceivably be applied in an unconstitutional manner to others not before the court." *Staley v. Jones,* 239 F.3d 769, 784 (6th Cir.2001) (citations omitted). However, "overbreadth scrutiny diminishes as the behavior regulated by the statute moves from pure speech toward harmful, unprotected conduct." *Id.* at 785. "'[P]articularly where conduct and not merely speech is involved, we believe that the overbreadth of a statute must not only be real, but substantial as well, judged in relation to the statute's plainly legitimate sweep.' *Id.* (quoting *Broadrick v. Oklahoma,* 413 U.S. 601, 615-16, 93 S.Ct. 2908, 37 L.Ed.2d 830 (1973)).

Bowker has provided absolutely no argument as to how 18 U.S.C. § 2261A, which prohibits interstate stalking and cyberstalking, is facially overbroad, merely asserting that the statute "reaches large amounts of protected speech and conduct" and "potentially targets political or religious speech." We fail to see how a law that prohibits interstate travel with the intent to kill, injure, harass or intimidate has a substantial sweep of constitutionally protected conduct. 18 U.S.C. § 2261A(1). The same is true with respect to the prohibition of intentionally using the internet in a course of conduct that places a person in reasonable fear of death or seriously bodily 379*379 injury. 18 U.S.C. § 2261A(2). It is difficult to imagine what constitutionally-protected political or religious speech would fall under these statutory prohibitions. Most, if not all, of these laws' legal applications are to conduct that is not protected by the First Amendment. Thus, Bowker has failed to demonstrate how 18 U.S.C. § 2261A is substantially overbroad.

We also reject Bowker's argument as to the purported overbreadth of the telephone harassment statute, 47 U.S.C. § 223(a)(1)(C). Bowker relies on the Supreme Court's decision in *Coates v. City of Cincinnati,* 402 U.S. 611, 91 S.Ct. 1686, 29 L.Ed.2d 214 (1971), which involved a city ordinance that made it a criminal offense for three or more persons to assemble on a sidewalk and to be "annoying" to passersby. *Id.* at 611, 91 S.Ct. 1686. The Court struck down the ordinance, reasoning that it was "unconstitutionally broad because it authorizes the punishment of constitutionally protected conduct." *Id.* at 614, 91 S.Ct. 1686.

Coates is distinguishable. First, the focus of the telephone harassment statute is not simply annoying telephonic communications. It also prohibits abusive, threatening or harassing communications. Thus, the thrust of the statute is to prohibit communications intended to instill fear in the victim, not to provoke a discussion about political issues of the day. *See United States v. Lampley,* 573 F.2d 783, 787 (3d Cir.1978) (holding that in enacting the telephone harassment statute, "Congress had a compelling interest in the protection of innocent individuals from fear, abuse or annoyance at the hands of persons who employ the telephone, not to communicate, but for other unjustifiable motives") (citations omitted). Second, the telephone harassment statute operates in a distinctly different realm of communication than the ordinance in *Coates,* which governed the manner in which individuals could assemble and communicate in the open on public property. Persons who find sidewalk speech annoying usually are not being singled out by the speaker and, in any event, have the option of ignoring that speech by walking away or taking a different route. Because the sidewalk speaker is operating in the open, annoyed listeners have little reason to fear for their safety and can readily identify and confront the speaker if they so choose. Not so with individuals receiving unwelcome, anonymous telephone calls. Call recipients have to deal with much more inconvenience to avoid the speech (e.g., changing telephone numbers or using a call-screening service); these calls usually are targeted toward a particular victim and are received outside of a public forum (e.g., the home or the workplace); and, because the caller does not identify himself, the speech is more likely to instill fear in the listener and, at a minimum, makes it more difficult for the listener to confront the caller. Accordingly, the domain of prohibited speech is far more circumscribed, and the government's interest in protecting recipients of the speech is far more compelling, under the telephone harassment statute compared to the city ordinance at issue in *Coates.*

We acknowledge that the telephone harassment statute, if interpreted to its semantic limits, may have unconstitutional applications. For example, if Bowker had been charged with placing anonymous telephone calls to a public official with the intent to annoy him or her about a political issue, the telephone harassment statute might have been unconstitutional as applied to him. *See United States v. Popa,* 187 F.3d 672, 677-78 (D.C.Cir.1999) (holding that telephone harassment statute was unconstitutional as applied to defendant who had placed seven calls to a U.S. Attorney 380*380 to complain about his treatment by the police and the prosecutor's conduct of a case against him). But Bowker was not so charged. His calls were predominately, if not exclusively, for the purpose of invading his victim's privacy and communicating express and implied threats of bodily harm. This type of speech is not constitutionally protected. *Landham,* 251 F.3d at 1080. But the fact that application of the telephone harassment statute may be unconstitutional in certain instances does not warrant facial invalidation. *See Parker v. Levy,* 417 U.S. 733, 760, 94 S.Ct. 2547, 41 L. Ed.2d 439 (1974) (facial invalidation not appropriate when the remainder of the statute "covers a whole range of easily identifiable and constitutionally proscribable conduct"); *Staley,* 239 F.3d at 786-87 (holding that "several examples of speech or expressive conduct that could conceivably be restricted under the statute" did not render anti-stalking statute unconstitutional). Whatever overbreadth exists in the statute "can be cured on a case-by-case basis." *Staley,* 239 F.3d at 787 (citing *Broadrick,* 413 U.S. at 615-16, 93 S.Ct. 2908). No cure is necessary in this case.

C. Vagueness Challenge

"[E]ven if an enactment does not reach a substantial amount of constitutionally protected conduct, it may be impermissibly vague because it fails to establish standards for the police and public that are sufficient to guard against the arbitrary deprivation of liberty interests." *Morales,* 527 U.S. at 52, 119 S.Ct. 1849 (citing *Kolender v. Lawson,* 461 U.S. 352, 358, 103 S.Ct. 1855, 75 L. Ed.2d 903 (1983)). Vagueness may invalidate a criminal statute if it either (1)fails "to provide the kind of notice that will enable ordinary people to understand what conduct it prohibits" or (2) authorizes or encourages "arbitrary and discriminatory enforcement." *Id.* at 56, 119 S.Ct. 1849 (citing *Kolender,* 461 U.S. at 357, 103 S.Ct. 1855). "It is established that a law fails to meet the requirements of the Due Process Clause if it is so vague and standardless that it leaves the public uncertain as to the conduct it prohibits...." *Giaccio v. Pennsylvania,* 382 U.S. 399, 402-03, 86 S.Ct. 518, 15 L.Ed.2d 447 (1966).

The stalking and telephone harassment statutes charged in Bowker's indictment provide sufficient notice of their respective prohibitions because citizens need not guess what terms such as "harass" and "intimidate" mean. This Court's decision in *Staley v. Jones, supra,* is instructive. That case involved a habeas corpus review of a conviction for stalking under a Michigan law that defines stalking as "a willful course of conduct involving repeated or continuing harassment of another individual that would cause a reasonable person to feel terrorized, frightened, intimidated, threatened, harassed, or molested and that actually causes the victim to feel terrorized, frightened, intimidated, threatened, harassed, or molested." Mich. Comp. Laws Ann. § 750.411i(e). Michigan law defines "harassment" as "conduct directed toward a victim that includes, but is not limited to, repeated or continuing unconsented contact that would cause a reasonable individual to suffer emotional distress and that actually causes the victim to suffer emotional distress." *Id.* § 750.411i(d). Expressly excluded from the definition of "harassment" is "constitutionally protected activity or conduct that serves a legitimate purpose." *Id.* This Court rejected the petitioner's vagueness challenge to the Michigan statute, reasoning as follows:

A person of reasonable intelligence would not need to guess at the meaning of the stalking statutes, nor would his interpretation of the statutory language differ with regard to the statutes' application, 381*381 in part because the definitions of crucial words and phrases that are provided in the statutes are clear and would be understandable to a reasonable person reading the statute…. Also, the meaning of the words used to describe the conduct can be ascertained fairly by reference to judicial decisions, common law, dictionaries, and the words themselves because they possess a common and generally accepted meaning. We therefore conclude that the statutes are not void for vagueness on the basis of inadequate notice.

Staley, 239 F.3d at 791-92.

The Michigan prohibition against willful harassment that causes a reasonable person to feel fear is almost indistinguishable from the federal anti-stalking statute, 18U.S.C. § 2261A(1), which prohibits intentional harassment that causes a reasonable fear of death or serious bodily injury. In fact, the federal statute arguably is less vague because it circumscribes the type of fear a victim must feel, namely a fear of death or serious bodily injury, whereas the Michigan law does not.

Bowker attempts to distinguish the Michigan statute by pointing to the fact that Michigan law defines the word "harassment," whereas federal law does not. The harassment definition under Michigan law, however, contains nothing not already reflected in the federal statute's general prohibition. The Michigan definition of harassment requires conduct directed toward a victim, but this requirement is implicitly reflected in the federal statute's requirement that a perpetrator intend to harass a victim. Michigan's harassment definition also requires that the conduct cause a reasonable individual to suffer emotional distress, but the federal statute requires conduct that causes a fear of death or serious bodily injury. There simply is no principled basis to distinguish the language of the federal statute from the Michigan statute which this Court upheld in *Staley.*

We also reject Bowker's argument that the stalking and telephone harassment statutes' failure to define words like "harass" and "intimidate" render them void for vagueness. As noted by the Court in *Staley,* the meaning of these words "can be ascertained fairly by reference to judicial decisions, common law, dictionaries, and the words themselves because they possess a common and generally accepted meaning." *Staley,* 239 F.3d at 791-92. Indeed, the Michigan anti-stalking statute, which the *Staley* Court upheld, does not appear to define the word "intimidate," a word that Bowker claims is too vague in the federal law. For this reason as well, we reject Bowker's vagueness challenge to the federal law.

Bowker's reliance on *Church of the Am. Knights of the Ku Klux Klan v. City of Erie,* 99 F.Supp.2d 583 (W.D.Pa.2000), also is misplaced. There, the court held that a city ordinance that restricted the wearing of a mask "with the intent to intimidate, threaten, abuse or harass any other person" was unconstitutionally vague. *Id.* at 591 (quotation marks and statutory citation omitted). The court found that each of these terms, given their ordinary meaning, could encompass forms of expression that are constitutionally protected. *Id.* Not only might it prohibit certain types of advocacy, such as advocating the return to segregation, but it also might prohibit the simple act of wearing a mask. *Id.* The court also found that the ordinance did not provide the public with adequate notice of what type of conduct was prohibited. The ordinance, however, is not comparable to the federal anti-stalking statute. The federal anti-stalking statute, which prohibits harassment or intimidation that causes a reasonable fear of death or serious bodily 382*382 harm, imposes a far more concrete harm requirement than the ordinance at issue in *Ku Klux Klan,* which did not require that the harassment or intimidation result in any particular type of reaction in the audience. *See id.* at 592 (holding that ordinance was unconstitutionally vague: "To some extent, the speaker's liability is potentially defined by the reaction or sensibilities of the listener; what is 'intimidating or threatening' to one person may not be to another. And, although the provision has a scienter requirement, it is reasonable to expect that the requisite intent could be inferred from circumstantial factors, which may include the effect that particular speech has on the speaker's audience.").

We further reject Bowker's argument that the federal stalking and telephone harassment statutes authorize or encourage arbitrary or discriminatory enforcement. Although the statutes provide no guidelines on terms like harass and intimidate, the meanings of these terms "can be ascertained fairly by reference to judicial decisions, common law, dictionaries, and the words themselves because they possess a common and generally accepted meaning." *Staley,* 239 F.3d at 791-92. Thus, Bowker has not demonstrated that these statutes fail to provide "sufficiently specific limits on the enforcement discretion of the police to meet constitutional standards for definiteness and clarity." *Morales,* 527 U.S. at 64, 119 S.Ct. 1849 (internal quotation marks and citation omitted).

Only Bowker's vagueness challenge to part of the telephone harassment statute, 47 U.S.C. § 223(a)(1)(C), merits further discussion. As noted above, that statute prohibits using a telephone, without disclosing identity, with the intent to annoy, abuse, threaten, or harass any person at the number called. Bowker argues that the term "annoy" is unconstitutionally vague, relying on the Supreme Court's decision in *Coates, supra.* In rejecting the city ordinance which made it a criminal offense for three or more persons to assemble on a sidewalk and to be "annoying" to passersby, the Court reasoned:

In our opinion this ordinance is unconstitutionally vague because it subjects the exercise of the right of assembly to an unascertainable standard, and unconstitutionally broad because it authorizes the punishment of constitutionally protected conduct. Conduct that annoys some people does not annoy others. Thus, the ordinance is vague, not in the sense that it requires a person to conform his conduct to an imprecise but comprehensible normative standard, but rather in the sense that no standard of conduct is specified at all.

Id. at 614, 91 S.Ct. 1686. The Court further held that the ordinance violated the First Amendment right to freedom of assembly because the "First and Fourteenth Amendments do not permit a State to make criminal the exercise of the right of assembly simply because its exercise may be 'annoying' to some people." *Id.* at 615, 91 S.Ct. 1686.

We agree that the word "annoy," standing alone and devoid of context and definition, may pose vagueness concerns. But that is not the case with the telephone harassment statute. The statute reads "annoy, abuse, threaten, or harass." 47 U.S.C. § 223(a)(1)(C). The Supreme Court has observed that "[c]anons of construction ordinarily suggest that terms connected by a disjunctive be given separate meanings, *unless the context dictates otherwise.*" *Reiter v. Sonotone Corp.,* 442 U.S. 330, 339, 99 S.Ct. 2326, 60 L.Ed.2d 931 (1979) (emphasis added). Here, the statutory language must be read in the context of Congressional intent to protect 383*383 innocent individuals from fear, abuse or annoyance at the hands of persons who employ the telephone, not to communicate, but for other unjustifiable motives. *Lampley,* 573 F.2d at 787. This context suggests that the words annoy, abuse, threaten or harass should be read together to be given similar meanings. Any vagueness associated with the word "annoy" is mitigated by the fact that the meanings of "threaten" and "harass" can easily be ascertained and have generally accepted meanings. *Staley,* 239 F.3d at 791-92,

Even assuming, *arguendo,* that Bowker's vagueness argument theoretically has merit, he cannot rely on it to invalidate the indictment or his conviction for telephone harassment, because the statute clearly applies to the conduct he allegedly committed. The Supreme Court held in *Parker v. Levy supra,* 417 U.S. at 756, 94 S.Ct. 2547:

... [O]ne who has received fair warning of the criminality of his own conduct from the statute in question is [not] entitled to attack it because the language would not give similar fair warning with respect to other conduct which might be within its broad and literal ambit. One to whose conduct a statute clearly applies may not successfully challenge it for vagueness.

Here, Bowker engaged in an anonymous campaign of threatening and harassing conduct directed toward Knight through use of the telephone (as well as the mails and the computer) that clearly fell within the statute's prohibition. This type of conduct lies at the core of what the telephone harassment statute was designed to prohibit. *Lampley,* 573 F.2d at 787. FBI Agent Hassman specifically warned Bowker that he might be arrested if he persisted in his course of telephone harassment, but Bowker ignored that warning. Moreover, the fact that Bowker engaged in this campaign with an intent to threaten or harass mitigates any concern that he may have been punished for merely having a communication over the telephone. As the Third Circuit held in rejecting a vagueness challenge to the very same statutory language:

The section's specific intent requirement renders unconvincing appellant's second claim that [the predecessor to § 223(a)(1)(C) is] unconstitutionally vague. It has long been true that (t)he Court, indeed, has recognized that the requirement of a specific intent to do a prohibited act may avoid those consequences to the accused which may otherwise render a vague or indefinite statute invalid.... (W)here the punishment imposed is only for an act knowingly done with the purpose of doing that which the statute prohibits, the accused cannot be said to suffer from lack of warning or knowledge that the act which he does is a violation of law. *Screws v. United States,* 325 U.S. 91, 101-02, 65 S.Ct. 1031, 1035, 89 L.Ed. 1495 (1945). The appellant cannot claim confusion about the conduct proscribed where, as here, the statute precisely specifies that the actor must intend to perform acts of harassment in order to be culpable.

Lampley, 573 F.2d at 787. Thus, Bowker vagueness challenge fails. The district court did not err in denying his motion to dismiss Counts 1, 2 and 4 of the indictment.

IV Motion to Sever Count 3 from the Indictment

The district court denied Bowker's motion to sever Count3 of the indictment (mail theft) from Counts 1 (interstate stalking), 2 (cyberstalking), and 4 (telephone harassment). Bowker had argued that joinder of these counts would prejudice his rights under the Fifth Amendment 384*384 and Rules 8 and 14 of the Federal Rules of Criminal Procedure. Specifically, he argued that the mail theft count should not be admissible to support the other three counts for stalking and telephone harassment on the ground that the crimes did not possess the same or similar characteristics and that there was no nexus between the mail theft count and the other alleged crimes. He further argued that he wished to testify concerning the stalking and telephone harassment counts, which require the government to prove intent, but not the mail theft count, and that joinder precluded him from exercising his Fifth Amendment right to testify only as to the stalking and telephone harassment counts. Last, he argued that the jury's exposure to evidence pertaining to the stalking and telephone harassment counts would prejudice them in deciding the mail theft count. Bowker renews these arguments on appeal.

A motion for relief from the prejudicial joinder of counts must be renewed at the close of the evidence. *United States v. Hudson,* 53 F.3d 744, 747 (6th Cir.1995). When the defendant fails to renew the motion, this Court can reverse a conviction only upon a showing of plain error. *United States v. Anderson,* 89 F.3d 1306, 1312 (6th Cir.1996). Bowker failed to renew his motion to sever Count 3 of the indictment from Counts 1, 2 and 4 at the close of the evidence. Accordingly, he must demonstrate plain error by the district court.

Federal Rule of Criminal Procedure 8 provides, in relevant part:

(a) Joinder of Offenses. The indictment or information may charge a defendant in separate counts with 2 or more offenses if the offenses charged – whether felonies or misdemeanors or both – are of the same or similar character, or are based on the same act or transaction, or are connected with or constitute parts of a common scheme or plan.

Fed.R.Crim.P. 8(a). Rule 14 provides, in relevant part:

(a) Relief. If the joinder of offenses or defendants in an indictment, an information, or a consolidation for trial appears to prejudice a defendant or the government, the court may order separate trials of counts, sever the defendants' trials, or provide any other relief that justice requires.

Fed.R.Crim.P. 14(a). The record clearly shows that all of the counts in Bowker's indictment were of the same or similar character and that the allegations thereunder were an integral part of Bowker's common scheme to harass and threaten Knight. This scheme involved a 14-month campaign of sending emails and regular mail and placing telephone calls to her workplace in Youngstown; sending mail to her parent's home; placing telephone calls to Knight's unpublished home number in West Virginia; placing telephone calls to Knight's West Virginia workplace; sending mail to Knight's West Virginia home; and stealing Knight's mail from her West Virginia home. Thus, all of the counts properly were joined pursuant to Rule 8, and the district court did not plainly err under Rule 14 by refusing to sever the mail theft count.

Bowker also has not demonstrated that the district court committed plain error when it rejected his argument that severance was required in order to permit him to testify as to the mail theft count, but to avoid testimony as to the stalking and telephone harassment counts. The Tenth Circuit confronted a similar argument in *United States v. Martin,* 18 F.3d 1515, 1518-19 (10th Cir.1994), stating:

Martin contends that the denial of his severance motion "forced [him] to testify 385*385 at trial and convict himself as to the drug count in an attempt to win an acquittal of the gun count."…. Martin further contends that inasmuch as he "had both important testimony to give concerning one count and a strong need to refrain from testifying on the other," …. the district court's refusal to sever the counts deprived him of a fair trial….[N]o need for a severance exists until the defendant makes a convincing showing that he has both important testimony to give concerning one count and a strong need to refrain from testifying on the other. Applying these standards to our case, we hold that Martin failed to demonstrate a convincing need for a severance.

Several other circuits have applied the same or similar standards. *E.g., United States. v. Alosa,* 14 F.3d 693, 695 (1st Cir.1994) (holding that defendant did not deserve severance because he failed to make a convincing showing that he had both important testimony to give concerning one count and a strong need to refrain from testifying on the other); *United States v. Gorecki,* 813 F.2d 40, 43 (3d Cir.1987) (holding that defendant's bare allegation that the joinder of counts prevented his testimony on one count, without a specific showing as to what that testimony may have been, failed to meet the stringent requirements for severance under Rule 14); *United States v. Ballis,* 28 F.3d 1399, 1408 (5th Cir.1994) (affirming denial of severance because defendant did not point out this alleged dilemma in testifying about some counts but not others with sufficient specificity for the trial court to have abused its discretion in denying the motion); *United States v. Alexander,* 135 F.3d 470, 477 (7th Cir.1998) (noting that there may be cases in which a defendant can convincingly show that he has important testimony to give on one count but a strong need to remain silent on another, and in that circumstance, severance may be required; affirming denial of severance because defendant failed to provide specific examples of the exculpatory testimony that he would testify about).

It is clear that Bowker failed to make a "convincing showing" that he had important testimony concerning the interstate stalking and telephone harassment counts, as well as a "strong need" to refrain from testifying on the mail theft count. Indeed, his motion to sever provided absolutely no indication as to what his testimony would be on the stalking and harassment counts, stating only that his testimony was "anticipated to be crucial" because these crimes have a specific intent requirement. In addition, Bowker showed absolutely no need to avoid testifying on the mail theft count, merely arguing that his testimony on this count was "not needed" because mail theft lacks a specific intent requirement. Such non-specific assertions of prejudice are insufficient to warrant severance under Rule 14. For these reasons, the district court did not commit plain error in refusing to sever the counts of the indictment.

V Right to Self-Representation

Bowker argues that he is entitled to a new trial because the district court denied his constitutional right to represent himself. We review such a denial for an abuse of discretion. *Robards v. Rees,* 789 F.2d 379, 384 (6th Cir.1986).

On January 22, 2002, Bowker, then represented by counsel, filed on his own initiative a handwritten motion "for release of appointed attorney." In that motion, Bowker stated, "Now Comes Defendant, being first advised of his rights to an attorney, and does now knowingly, willingly, and intelligently waive his rights, to 386*386 court-appointed counsel." The district court purported to deny that motion via a hand-written minute order on January 28, 2002, stating that "Defendant's pro se motion for new counsel is denied." The court did not refer to the fact that Bowker's motion did not seek new counsel, but to waive his right to counsel. Bowker, however, soon had a change of heart about representing himself because on March 26, 2002, Bowker's attorney moved to withdraw as counsel due to "the fractured lawyer-client relationship." In an attached statement signed by Bowker, Bowker requested that his appointed lawyer withdraw from the case "and that a new lawyer be appointed to represent" him. The court granted the motion on April 10, 2002 and appointed a new federal public defender for Bowker on April 22, 2002.

The sixth and fourteenth amendments guarantee state criminal defendants the right of self-representation at trial. *See Faretta v. California,* 422 U.S. 806, 95 S.Ct. 2525, 45 L.Ed.2d 562 (1975). Since it is more likely than not that a defendant would fare better with the assistance of counsel, *id.* at 835, 95 S.Ct. 2525, he will be permitted to represent himself only when he "knowingly and intelligently" relinquishes his right to counsel. *Id.* Such a knowing waiver must be made by a "clear and unequivocal" assertion of the right to self-representation. *Id.* "Once there is a clear assertion of that right, the court must conduct a hearing to ensure that the defendant is fully aware of the dangers and disadvantages of proceeding without counsel." *Raulerson v. Wainwright*, 732 F.2d 803, 808 (11th Cir.1984) (citation omitted).

We hold that the district court erred in denying Bowker's January 22, 2002 motion to represent himself which was accompanied by a clear and unequivocal assertion of the right to self-representation. At a minimum, the court should have conducted some inquiry into the bases for Bowker's motion. It is not apparent from the record that the district court did anything other than misconstrue the motion as a motion for appointment of new counsel and then deny the motion. Nevertheless, the district court's error was rendered harmless by Bowker's change of heart about self-representation over two months prior to trial. As noted above, after being denied the right to represent himself, Bowker explicitly joined his then-attorney's motion to withdraw from the case and to have new counsel appointed for him. Thus, Bowker's last indication to the district court on the matter was that he did not wish to represent himself. *Cf. id.* at 809 ("Even if Raulerson's letter of July 18, 1980 constituted a clear and unequivocal demand to represent himself, his agreement to proceed with the assistance of an attorney waived that original request...."). Accordingly, the district court's erroneous disposition of the January 22, 2002 motion for self-representation was rendered harmless error by Bowker's subsequent waiver of his right to self-representation. Bowker, therefore, is not entitled to a new trial.

VI Motion to Return Seized Property

On February 5, 2002, Bowker filed a *pro se* motion for return of seized property and items, pursuant to Rule 41 of the Federal Rules of Criminal Procedure. He sought an order from the court directing the government to return all items and tangible objects which were not going to be used as evidence in his case. As of May 29, 2002, the district court had not yet ruled on the motion, so Bowker filed a "request for ruling on motion for return of property." On June 4, 2002, the district court denied Bowker's request for a ruling 387*387 on the motion for return of property. No reasons were provided by the court for the denial, and the district court never held a hearing on, nor has it ever ruled on, the underlying motion for return of property.

Rule 41 provides, in relevant part:

(g) Motion to Return Property. A person aggrieved by an unlawful search and seizure of property or by the deprivation of property may move for the property's return. The motion must be filed in the district where the property was seized. The court must receive evidence on any factual issue necessary to decide the motion. If it grants the motion, the court must return the property to the movant, but may impose reasonable conditions to protect access to the property and its use in later proceedings.

Fed.R.Crim.P. 41(g). In *United States v. Hess*, 982 F.2d 181 (6th Cir.1992), this Court observed that "'[a] district court has both the jurisdiction and the duty to return the contested property once the government's need for it has ended.' *Id.* at 187 (internal quotation marks omitted); quoting *United States v. Martinson*, 809 F.2d 1364, 1370 (9th Cir.1987) (citing *United States v. Wilson*, 540 F.2d 1100, 1103-04 (D.C.Cir.1976)). There, the district court had failed to address the legal or factual issues raised in a party's motion for return of seized records. The Court found it significant that no hearing was held regarding who was entitled to possession of the documents, and the district court had failed to consider the merits of the moving party's arguments. The Court also was troubled because there were no findings of fact or conclusions of law regarding which party was entitled to retain the records. Accordingly, the Court held that the district court did not discharge its duty under Rule 41(g) to hear and decide the issues, reasoning that Rule 41(g) "clearly contemplates a hearing 'on any issue of fact necessary to the decision of the motion.' *Id.* at 186.

Hess is directly on point. The district court below simply ignored Bowker's motion to return records, and when Bowker filed a motion to have the court rule on that motion, the court denied the motion, without ever reaching the merits of the underlying motion. The court held no hearing, took no evidence, and gave no indication that it ever has considered the merits of Bowker's motion. Accordingly, on remand, the district court shall hold a hearing on Bowker's motion for return of records, take evidence on any factual issues necessary to resolve that motion, and promptly rule on that motion.

VII Motion for a Judgment of Acquittal as to Counts 1, 2 and 4

Bowker challenges the district court's failure to grant his motion for a judgment of acquittal on Counts 1, 2 and 4 of the indictment, pursuant to Rule 29 of the Federal Rules of Criminal Procedure. For the reasons that follow, we affirm the judgment of the district court.

A. Standard of Review

"In reviewing a district court's denial of a motion for judgment of acquittal on a claim of insufficient evidence, 'the relevant question is whether after viewing the evidence in the light most favorable to the prosecution, *any* rational trier of fact could have found the essential elements of the crime beyond a reasonable doubt.' *United States v. Lloyd,* 10 F.3d 1197, 1210 (6th Cir.1993) (quoting *Jackson v. Virginia,* 443 U.S. 307, 319, 99 S.Ct. 2781, 61 L.Ed.2d 560 (1979)). "If the evidence, however, is such that a rational fact finder must conclude that a reasonable doubt is raised, this court is obligated to reverse a 388*388 denial of an acquittal motion." *Id.* (quoting *United States v. Collon,* 426 F.2d 939, 942 (6th Cir.1970)). The district court's findings of fact are reviewed for clear error, and circumstantial evidence alone is sufficient to sustain a conviction. *Nationwide Mut. Ins. Co. v. Home Ins. Co.,* 278 F.3d 621, 625 (6th Cir.2002); *United States v. Peters,* 15 F.3d 540, 544 (6th Cir.1994).

B. Interstate Stalking Count

Count 1 of the indictment charges Bowker with interstate stalking, in violation of 18 U.S.C. § 2261A(1). The government was required to prove:

(1)   that the defendant traveled in interstate or foreign commerce;

(2)   with the intent to kill, injure, harass, or intimidate another person; and

(3)   in the course of, or as a result of, such travel places that person in reasonable fear of the death of, or serious bodily injury to, that person, a member of the immediate family of that person, or the spouse or intimate partner of that person.

Bowker argues that the government did not prove, pursuant to the interstate stalking count, that the "result of" Bowker's travel from Ohio to West Virginia in July, 2001, was to put Knight in reasonable fear of her life or bodily injury, because Knight did not learn of Bowker's travels until August 2001, after he had completed his travel. This argument is specious. Knight learned of Bowker's travel to West Virginia because he sent her numerous photographs informing her that he had been in the state the preceding month. Accompanying the photographs was the statement, "Take the photos out to read the backs of them. Send me an E-mail address. It keeps me long distance, you know what I mean." The clear implication of this statement was that Bowker would continue to communicate with Knight, unless she provided him with her email address. The jury was entitled to infer that this statement, combined with the photographs of Bowker at various locations in West Virginia, was intended to intimidate Knight by showing her that Bowker had traveled to her state and would do so in the future. The statute did not require the government to show that Bowker actually intended to harass or intimidate Knight during his travels, only that the result of the travel was a reasonable apprehension of fear in the victim. Since Knight testified that she was afraid that Bowker might rape her, and her fear seemed reasonable, the government proved all of the elements of the interstate stalking count.

C. Cyberstalking Count

Count 2 of the indictment charges Bowker with cyberstalking, in violation of 18 U.S.C. § 2261A(2). The government was required to prove:

(1) Bowker intentionally used the mail or any facility of interstate or foreign commerce;

(2) Bowker engaged in a course of conduct with the intent to place Knight in reasonable fear of death of, or serious bodily injury to, herself, her spouse or intimate partner, or a member of her immediate family; and

(3) Bowker's course of conduct actually placed Knight in reasonable fear of death of, or serious bodily injury to, herself.

The evidence shows that Bowker's intended to instill in Knight a fear of death or serious bodily harm through use of the mails and other facilities of interstate commerce, required elements of the cyberstalking count. During a June 12, 2001 telephone conversation with Knight, Bowker told her:

389*389 You don't know where I'm at. I might be in your house in Dunbar[, West Virginia]; you don't know that…. I know all of your neighbors..... And I have access to all that information, just like anybody else does who knows where to find it. I have an enormous amount of things about you that I'm not going to disclose unless I have to. I'm not going to tell anybody about it except if you lie to me. I might not say anything to you at the time, but that might come back, you know..... I know the names of all your relatives and where they live..... I know your brothers' wives['] names, their ages, their Social Security numbers and their birth dates …. and their property values..... Maybe I live on 20th street in Dunbar..... Maybe I watch you with binoculars all the time and maybe I don't.

(J.A. 985-88, 1000.) A July 16, 2001 letter that Bowker sent to Knight at the television station had both sexual and threatening connotations. It read, in part:

No. 1. You do not hang up on me.

No. 2. You do not hang up on me, ever.

No. 3. If and when I call CBS 13 asking about a news story that you reported on, you do not hang up on me. You must at least do the bare minimum and answer my news related questions.

I know what you value most in life, your bullshit fake ass 1997 Pontiac Grand Am, which is about top on your list as well as two other things. As far as the Grand Am is concerned, say good-bye to it. I am going to file a mechanics lien on it immediately and later seek civil forfeiture.

All that you … would have to do is be polite, be nice, and answer my news-related questions, just like the rest of the reporters, except your buddy April Kaull. I'm going to file a lien on her vehicle too. You are both fuck-ups, assholes and seriously emotionally and mentally unbalanced.....

Also, WOWK will hire just about anyone. Or at least a pretty girl reporter, as long as she does her hair and makeup well.....

That vehicle is exemplary of you, pretty on the outside and very worthless inside. You have female genitals and that is about it. You are a very slander to the word woman. Oh, yeah, you dress like one but so do transvestites. I think I would rather spend the evening with a pretty transvestite than with you.....

Anyhow, I also think that it is time for your neighbors to get to know you better and I will be making attempts to inform them about how the prima donna from Ohio things [sic] she can eat from the top and throw her garbage on the sidewalk of West Virginia and Dunbar.....

I also noticed that you already had the job and residence in West Virginia when you had your Ohio License plates renewed, for one year anyhow.....

So bye-bye, fuck you, you are an asshole and a sociopath and an embarrassment to mothers everywhere, sir. In parenthesis: (I wasn't bringing up the mental case thing again since it is genetic.)

Yes, sir. Adios, Eric [sic]. Smooch. Smooch.

(J.A. 1011-15.) In August 2001, Bowker left a series of messages on Knight's answering machine asking that Knight or Knight's friend call him back, which did not occur. These messages contained statements that Knight reasonably could perceive to be threats to her personal safety. Excerpts include the following statements:

390*390 I don't even know why I'm nice to you ever at all, you and your fucked-up friend should not even be working in the media. You know you gotta mother-fucking realize there's like 50 percent men in this country and you better mother-fucking learn that you're going to have to deal with us sometime.....

Well, it looks like nobody is going to answer me if Tina Knight is okay, so I'm gonna take the 1:00 a.m. bus out of Columbus, Ohio and come down there and see for myself. Okay, I'll be there about 6:00 a.m. Bye.

(J.A. 1226-27.) Since Knight testified that these intentionally intimidating, threatening and harassing interstate communications made her afraid to leave the house everyday and that Bowker might try to rape her, the government proved all of the elements of the cyberstalking count.

D. Telephone Harassment Count
Count 4 of the indictment charged Bowker with telephone harassment, in violation of 47 U.S.C. § 223(a)(1)(C). The government had to prove that:

(1)   Bowker made interstate telephone calls to Knight;
(2)   Bowker did not disclose his identity in the telephone calls; and
(3)   in the telephone calls, whether or not conversation or communication ensued, Bowker intended to annoy, abuse, threaten, or harass Knight or any person at the called number.

Bowker's primary argument against his conviction for telephone harassment is that Knight allegedly was aware of Bowker's identity when she received his calls. The statute, however, does not preclude criminal responsibility merely because the recipient may suspect, or have a very good idea of, the caller's identity. Rather, assuming that Bowker called Knight with the requisite intent to annoy, abuse, threaten, or harass, the only issue is whether Bowker disclosed his identity in those calls. It is clear that in all of the at-issue telephone calls, Bowker never affirmatively identified himself as Erik Bowker. In fact, he denied being Bowker during a conversation with Knight on June 12, 2001, and instead stated that his name was Mike. Thus, a straightforward application of the telephone harassment statute shows that the jury reasonably found the non-disclosure element to be satisfied.

VIII Motion for a New Trial on Counts 1, 2 and 4
The denial of a defendant's motion for a new trial under Federal Rule of Criminal Procedure 33 is reviewed for abuse of discretion. *United States v. Ashworth*, 836 F.2d 260, 266 (6th Cir.1988). The Court is "limited to examining the evidence produced at trial to determine whether the district court's determination that the evidence does not 'preponderate heavily against the verdict' is

a clear and manifest abuse of discretion." *Id.* (citation omitted). As discussed in the preceding section, there was ample evidence to support Bowker's convictions on Counts 1, 2 and 4 of the indictment. Thus, it was not an abuse of discretion to find that the evidence did not preponderate heavily against the verdict.

IX Upward Departure for Extreme Psychological Harm to the Victim

After Bowker's convictions, he was sentenced pursuant to the 2000 edition of the United States Sentencing Commission Guidelines Manual ("Guidelines"). Based upon a final offense level of 19, and a criminal history corresponding to Category 391*391 V, Bowker's Guidelines' range was between 57 and 71 months. The government moved for a three level upward departure in his sentence based on extreme psychological injury to the victim, Tina Knight. The basis for the motion was, in part, Guidelines § 5K2.3. The district court granted the motion for upward departure. Because Bowker argues that the sentence imposed by the district court was outside the applicable guideline range and was based on a factor that is not justified by the facts of the case, this Court reviews the district court's determination under a *de novo* standard. 18 U.S.C. § 3742(e).

Section 5K2.3 of the Guidelines provides:

§ 5K2.3. EXTREME PSYCHOLOGICAL INJURY (POLICY STATEMENT)

If a victim or victims suffered psychological injury much more serious than that normally resulting from commission of the offense, the court may increase the sentence above the authorized guideline range. The extent of the increase ordinarily should depend on the severity of the psychological injury and the extent to which the injury was intended or knowingly risked.

Normally, psychological injury would be sufficiently severe to warrant application of this adjustment only when there is a substantial impairment of the intellectual, psychological, emotional, or behavioral functioning of a victim, when the impairment is likely to be of an extended or continuous duration, and when the impairment manifests itself by physical or psychological symptoms or by changes in behavior patterns. The court should consider the extent to which such harm was likely, given the nature of the defendant's conduct.

Guidelines § 5K2.3 (Nov. 1, 2000). With regard to the crime of stalking, Guidelines § 2A6.2 instructs that "an upward departure may be warranted if the defendant stalked the victim on many occasions over a prolonged period of time." Guidelines § 2A6.2, Application Note 5.

The record shows that Bowker stalked Knight on many occasions and over a prolonged period of time. See Guidelines § 2A6.2, Application Note 5. FBI Special Agent James McNamara, an expert on stalking crimes, testified at the sentencing hearing as to the extreme nature of Bowker's conduct. McNamara pointed to the facts that the harassment occurred over a period of years and in two different states; involved numerous, multi-media contacts (letters, telephone calls, email and interstate travel); and involved contacts with Knight's friends and family members. Further, Bowker's campaign of harassment substantially impaired Knight's "behavioral functioning" as manifested by "changes in [her] behavior patterns." Guidelines § 5K2.3. Knight was so distressed that she was left with profound feelings of paranoia and felt compelled to change banks and unlist her phone number, and have her bills sent to a different address. She also purchased a gun, routinely uses a security escort, and, most unfortunately, decided to forgo her on-air news career.

Knight's Victim Impact Statement movingly captures the extreme psychological distress that Bowker's stalking activities inflicted on her:

The two years that I was stalked changed my family and me. First of all since the stalking began because of my job as a television news reporter it has turned me off to a future in that career.....I don't want to be anyone's favorite newscaster because I fear it will turn into another situation like the one I had.....I am also concerned about major purchases in the future, like a home, 392*392 and how he may be able to track me down.....Even writing this I am careful not to mention anything about my personal life for fear he will read this and it will give him another means by which to contact me.....I am concerned about the rest of my life.....I am not confident this will stop. That is my biggest fear. When he gets out of jail this could start all over again so I truly can never relax. It's just putting off my ultimate fear that someday, no matter what I do, he will show up at my front door with intent to harm me. By now I've given him reason to really hate me in his mind. I testified against him in court and helped put him in jail. I hope he isn't out for revenge.[4]

We hold that the above-described facts amply justified the district court's upward departure determination. *Cf. United States v. Otto,* 64 F.3d 367, 371 (8th Cir.1995) (affirming upward departure where stalking victim lived in constant fear for herself and for her children and was always on the lookout for the defendant; could not eat or sleep; lost weight; required counseling; and feared the defendant's ultimate release); *United States v. Miller,* 993 F.2d 16, 21 (2d Cir.1993) (affirming upward departure after the defendant had engaged in a three year campaign of harassment; noting that the victim had been afraid to answer the telephone or open her mail for three years; was afraid to remain in the New York area; and believed that the years of harassment had hastened her husband's demise).

X Expert Testimony on Stalking

As noted in the preceding section, the government called an expert on stalking crimes, FBI Special Agent James McNamara, to testify at Bowker's sentencing hearing. Bowker argues that the district court's decision to hear the testimony of Agent McNamara was erroneous and that the court's decision should be reviewed for an abuse of discretion under Federal Rule of Evidence 702. The Federal Rules of Evidence, however, are by their own terms expressly inapplicable to sentencing hearings. Fed.R.Evid. 1101(d)(3). According to the federal statute that governs the use of information in sentencing, "[n]o limitation shall be placed on the information concerning the background, character, and conduct of a person convicted of an offense which a court of the United States may receive and consider for the purpose of imposing an appropriate sentence." 18 U.S.C. § 3661. The Supreme Court has explained that this statute "codifies the longstanding principle that sentencing courts have broad discretion to consider various kinds of information." *United States v. Watts,* 519 U.S. 148, 151, 117 S.Ct. 633, 136 L.Ed.2d 554 (1997). Accordingly, this Court reviews the district court's admission of Agent McNamara's testimony for an abuse of discretion in determining that the testimony had "sufficient indicia of reliability to support its probable accuracy." Guidelines § 6A1.3(a).

Agent McNamara has been with the FBI for 15 years and is assigned to the FBI as a behavioral analyst. His duties include looking at the behavior of criminals, conducting research with convicted offenders and disseminating the results of that research, and working on active criminal cases as a law enforcement consultant. 393*393 McNamara has been trained in a variety of disciplines, including criminal justice, psychology, forensic science, anthropology and psychology. Based on his review of transcripts and other materials pertaining to Bowker's case, McNamara testified that Bowker had engaged in multimedia attempts to contact Knight, including letters, email, telephonic contacts, and the sending of gifts. McNamara opined that the sending of gifts in a stalking case is "significantly important in the areas of increased dangerousness." He further testified that Bowker escalated his activity, from contacts through the mail, to telephonic and electronic mail contact, to traveling interstate to pursue Knight. McNamara also indicated that

Bowker's past history of violence, including domestic abuse, was a predictor of future dangerousness or violence. As a consequence of these findings, McNamara concluded that Bowker was a more dangerous type of stalker.

We hold that the district court did not abuse its discretion in admitting Agent McNamara's testimony at the sentencing hearing. His testimony was relevant to the court's application of Guidelines § 2A6.2, which determines how the base offense level is to be calculated for the crime of stalking. Guideline § 2A6.2 provides for a two-level increase in the base offense level for a pattern of activity involving stalking, threatening, harassing, or assaulting the same victim. McNamara's testimony directly addressed this issue. Agent McNamara's testimony also was relevant to determining whether an upward departure was warranted for extreme psychological injury to the victim. *See* Guidelines § 2A6.2, Application Note 5 (instructing that the severity of the stalking may warrant an upward departure). Therefore, the district court did not err in entertaining Agent McNamara's expert testimony at sentencing.

XI Bowker's Right of Allocution

Federal Rule of Criminal Procedure 32(i)(4)(A)(ii) provides that, before imposing a sentence, the court must "address the defendant personally in order to permit the defendant to speak or present any information to mitigate the sentence." Bowker argues that the district court denied him this right of allocution. We apply a *de novo* standard of review. *United States v. Wolfe,* 71 F.3d 611, 614 (6th Cir.1995).

After Bowker's attorney cross-examined Agent McNamara, the FBI expert on stalking, the district court asked Bowker directly, "Is there anything that you have to say to this Court before it imposes sentence?" Bowker responded that he would like to read a lengthy statement, and the court told Bowker to proceed. Bowker began by challenging his prior criminal history. The court then went through each crime that formed the foundation for the assignment of a Criminal History Category V. Bowker then asked to address some things that occurred during his trial, and the court told him to proceed. Bowker gave a lengthy justification for his conduct underlying his convictions, complained about not being able to testify as to his intent, and pointed out that he has severe physical disabilities and mental problems. Bowker next complained about the performance of his attorney. Bowker then asked the court to have his mother testify, which the court permitted. The only request the district court appeared to deny Bowker was his desire to read a 15-page statement into the record. Based on the totality of the circumstances, we see no merit to Bowker's argument that he was denied the right of allocution. *Cf. United States v. Kellogg,* 955 F.2d 1244, 1250 (9th Cir.1992) ("Although the defendant has a 394*394 right of allocution at sentencing, that right is not unlimited.").

XII Conclusion

For all the foregoing reasons, we AFFIRM Defendant Bowker's convictions and sentence. This case shall be REMANDED for the district court to conduct a hearing and to rule on Bowker's motion to return seized property.Retrieved from:

http://scholar.google.com/scholar_case?case=12391284590311589187&hl=en&as_sdt=2&as_vis=1&oi=scholarr

As we have learned in our example, it's important to understand the ethics that revolve around conducting spying and committing cybercrime within the digital domain. Tracking others and stalking them as we have learned can cause harm, loss, and even death. You should also learn how you can be a victim and that is what we will learn in Chapter 2.

SUMMARY

In this chapter, we have discussed the fundamentals of digital surveillance, what reconnaissance is, and what digital spying is. While discussing the history of digital spying, we looked at how government entities, militaries, and others have been practicing for decades to gain tactical advantage and gather intelligence. While discussing these topics, we covered major legislature put in place to provide privacy to those under the fourth amendment as an example.

We flashed forward to today's current events to discuss how the US-based NSA is under scrutiny for crossing boundaries it may or may not have been entitled to do and the whistleblower (Edward Snowden) who brought the issues to public eyes. We also examined why trust is so important when it comes to common surveillance activities that are supposed to keep you safe and secure such as traffic camera's, home monitoring systems, and the government's goal of stopping terrorism by collecting all incoming and outgoing data transmissions into and out of the country.

Those who spy and why they spy were also covered. We discussed experts in the field who help build legal cases, those who are in charge of our security, those who subvert it, and those who collect information for many reasons both good and bad.

Legal and ethical concerns were covered as well as sample case law to show the effects of digital surveillance from a legal perspective to just how important it is to not only protect ourselves but also be aware of the many dangers lurking in the digital darkness.

CHAPTER 2

Information Gathering

INFORMATION GATHERING

When conducting digital surveillance and reconnaissance, one of the priorities of these tasks is to gather information on a target or a group of targets. No simple task, however, within the digital world, it makes it much easier to do and it can be done from afar. If you know how to cover your tracks, it can also be done privately without concern of being discovered. Prior to using technology, to gather information you would need to physically be on location and hope to not be seen or get caught. As technology became more available, it could then be tapped to reveal information about targets. For example, a phone could be "bugged" with a device to listen to a conversation and recorded. This technique was used to leverage the weaknesses in the old publically switched telephone network that operated with analog technology. Now, with the progress made in the digital realm, you can be at a computer terminal or on your mobile device anywhere in the world, connect to the public Internet, and gather a large amount of information on a variety of targets within minutes all while remaining undetected. This chapter covers many of the methods in which this can be done.

Why is this so important? For one, to be able to attack, you need to find vectors in which you can breech your target. The old analog phone example is a good one to understand the increasing attack vector. Now with digital technology, your telephone conversation can be stored digital within a private branch exchange device, locally to the phone or captured in transmission. Applications can be placed on the receiver device to capture or listen to the conversation. There are more points in the transmission to capture data and more locations in which it is stored.

Now that you are aware of the fact that information can be gathered and it can be quickly and easily acquired, we should consider all of the points in which it can be collected. As well, is all information gathering malicious? Once you understand the attack vector, you can consider if your information is truly private and you can learn to protect yourself and mitigate attack.

Am I Being Spied On?

The first question to ask is, "am I being spied on?" This is a question that just invites paranoia into the minds of many. However, it is a good question to ask because by doing so, it makes you think about protecting yourself, your data, and your interests. It also gets you to consider your digital footprint, that is, where you leave your mark in the digital world. For example, sending a simple e-mail from work to another recipient. Consider that the recipient is also at work. If you are concerned about your information being private, you do not need to look any further than your organizations security policy and specifically on e-mail usage and retention. The fact is, if your policy states that the data you send and receive is by default owned by the organization when using their systems, then the answer is no. Your communications are not private. Now, let's consider that you are under investigation by Human Resources for a workplace matter. If an issue, complaint, or security violation is suspected, your e-mail can be reviewed by appropriate parties. Something as harmless as showing interest in co-workers and asking them out for a drink could easily turn into a sexual harassment case.

Now let's consider if you send a private communication from your personal e-mail account to another recipient. Is your communication truly private? The answer is no. Quite simply, if you're under investigation, your data can be subpoenaed by the judge for forensic review within the court. The Internet Service Provider (ISP) who holds your e-mail account would need to comply.

Another consideration is what if I wasn't at work and I wasn't involved in a legal case? Is my transmission private? It could be, however, according to data released on the National Security Agency, data transmissions are captured and filtered. This simple example of an e-mail transmission continues on if you consider that your device could be stolen. You could be hacked or it's possible someone or something has tampered with your system and collecting your data.

The answer to the question, "Am I being spied on?" is not easily provided. The answer could be your data is never truly private and could be collected at any time for just about any reason, legally or maliciously. If maliciously, you may or may not know your privacy is being violated. Attackers wish to remain anonymous, so they usually conduct surveillance activities with the intentions of remaining anonymous and/or going undetected. Also, governments collecting information on their citizens generally do not want to advertise such activity.

How Private Is Your Life?

As we learned in Chapter 1, everything you do within the digital domain can potentially be stored to include video footage of you going to a local store, when you use your mobile phone and it connects to a cell tower, when you access your favorite social media site, or if you log in to your bank to pay a bill.

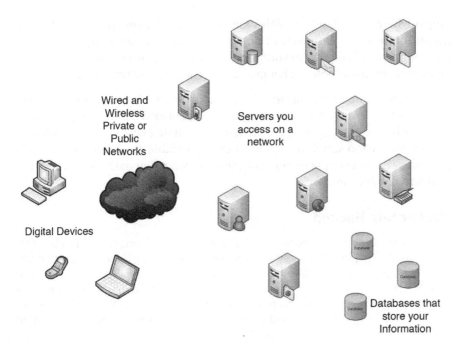

FIGURE 2.1 Information gathering points.

In Figure 2.1, we provide an extremely high-level view of the digital landscape and all of the points within it that data is or can be stored. Every one of these points can also be used for information gathering.

In this example, we see digital devices such as a laptop or a phone accessing a network to use a resource. These resources can include going to a website to purchase goods, to send an e-mail, to upload a file, or to text with a friend. Every transmission from source to destination leaves residual evidence of the transaction in logs if configured. Data and transmissions are time stamped and a digital forensics expert can uncover a complete map of activity.

As seen in the figure, you can use any device to connect through any network to any resource and your activity can be captured. Marketing firms work very hard to conduct tracking activities to know how to track your buying habits in an effort to show you only the items you may be interested in or have an impulse to buy. This does not necessarily mean that someone or an entity is spying on you in a way that seems to imply that you are in danger; however, it does open your mind to the fact that your habits are tracked and if this data was to get into the wrong hands, could be used against you. For example, within social media sites such as Facebook, by simply "liking" a post, it is added to Facebook internal databases and if what you like is something that may be deemed offensive to some, could impact your privacy since it can be freely searched by others.

This is where surveillance activities can also tie in. If someone was looking to gather information about you in hopes to conduct an attack such as identity theft or password cracking of your protected data, understanding what you like gives attackers a foothold on being able to conduct these types of attacks.

Another problem with data stored on systems is that it could come back to haunt you. For example, if 10 years ago you were involved in criminal behavior but have had your charges expunged, it will not matter when that data is found by prospective job search recruiters looking for viable candidates for an open position. This is a simple example of the many ways that data can be mined in hopes to conduct an attack.

Hacker Site Hacked

In 2014, the EC-Council website (http://www.eccouncil.org) was defaced to not only embarrass the organization itself but also in hopes to bring light to the fact that Edward Snowden was involved with them. Edward Snowden applied for the Certified Ethical Hacker credential and by doing so sent e-mails to EC-Council with personal information within it in hopes to bring notice to Ed's activities. Within that defacement activity, the hacker(s) posted private e-mails and even a snapshot of Edward Snowden's passport as seen in Figure 2.2.

Edward Snowden likely did not think that by sending his personal information to a reputable organization would ever wind up publically distributed; however, it did. Therefore, it's safe to say that because of Ed's worldwide fame, he increased his likelihood of becoming a target of information gathering and because its proven that most, if not all, data in transmission is stored or saved, that once it's found could be publically used evading that individuals privacy.

Examples of Privacy Invasion

There are many other examples of how privacy is no longer a guarantee. Consider a typical user of digital technology living in the world today. You leave your home in the morning and go to work. You go out for a lunch date and run an errand. You return to work and once the day is over, go back home. If you are using digital technology in the form of a mobile device and took it with you during these events, there could be a traceable footprint of where you went and at what time. You are under constant video surveillance just about anywhere you go, recording everything you do. Every location you went to likely had a video camera within or in the path to each destination. You paid by credit card when you had lunch. You placed seven phone calls on your mobile phone that day and sent 22 text messages. While at work, you made 19 phone calls and sent and received 120 e-mails.

As you can see, we can continue to flesh out this example by looking at what applications were used on the mobile device, and what systems and servers were used while at work or any other examples of digital technology used within

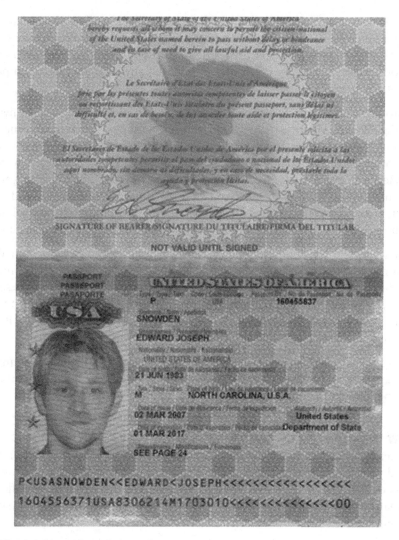

FIGURE 2.2 Edward Snowden's passport.

this specific time span; however, it should be enough to show you that your life is under surveillance and all of your actions are digitally recorded or traceable.

Outside of the digital world, it's possible that you could be watched by those with an interest in watching what you do. If you are the subject of someone under investigation you could be videotaped or photographed. If someone is stalking you, they could potentially follow you to see where you go, who you are with, and what you are doing.

In the physical and digital worlds, your privacy could be at risk and you could be the subject of damages by those who wish to do you harm. Harm can come in many forms. It may not be physical harm but what if while at the restaurant having lunch your credit card information was stolen? What if somehow your credit was damaged or if you used a debit card your bank account emptied? As you can see, invasion to your privacy could at any moment directly impact you at any time.

To protect yourself from being spied on you need to limit your exposure. By living in a digital world where you use your mobile phone and post pictures and engage in social media websites, you need to understand by doing so you subject yourself to exposure. Even if you attempt to mitigate attack by limiting exposure within each technology you use, you have to consider that you may miss something and/or someone you trust may expose you. You could use a credit card instead of a debit card or you could pay in cash. You could turn off your mobile phone if you did not wish to be tracked via cell towers. You could choose not to send an e-mail.

Also, we have focused on individuals; however, entities and groups could also be at risk. For example, let's assume that an attacker wants to spy on a company. They could gather information publically online using many sources such as a Who is database to pull Domain Name System (DNS) information that could potentially show personal information. They could use the Better Business Bureau website to gather information on a business track record.

All in all, it should be noted that maintaining privacy comes down to minimizing exposure and being aware of your activities. To exist in a digital world, it may be difficult to conceal your actions.

How to Gather Information

Gathering information can be quickly and easily done. Now that you understand your footprint, let's take a look at some of the ways your privacy can be evaded. There are many surveillance tools as well as those that do specific information gathering tasks and others that are manual tools where information can be collected and correlated.

In this section, we look at specific tools that can be used to conduct these tasks. Before we do we should generalize their use and impact and the reasons why they are so popular in the first place.

Data mining of information is not a new practice. As more and more data is centralized and tools evolve to do a better job of extracting key information for reporting and general use, the ability to use this for spying grows exponentially. Big data and informatics/analytics are major areas of technology growth today, where organizations need to tap their stored data to derive specific results from it. When considering how this type of data analysis can be used or misused, it's safe to say that regardless, the data is gathered, stored, and, if exploited, could be used against a target.

Information Gathering Tools

One of the most interesting tools to assist security professionals to come to light is called Backtrack. Backtrack is used to provide penetration testing analysts, a portfolio of security tools that can be used to test the security of a system, network, or service. If placed in the wrong hands, it can, in fact, be used to conduct surveillance of targets.

As an example, I have loaded Backtrack within Kali Linux as a virtual machine to demonstrate the product as seen in Figure 2.3. Once loaded, you can click on Applications and follow the path in the graphic to Information Gathering where you will find many tools that you can use that will collect, gather, and exploit data from a source.

Some of the tools within Backtrack such as Creepy will allow you to target Twitter accounts as well as Flickr accounts via Yahoo. We will get into more detail on how picture metadata can be used to exploit a target; however, for now, load up the tools and review what is offered within the toolset. Another interesting point to mention about Backtrack is how it uses network-level protocols such as DNS, Simple Network Management Protocol (SNMP), and Simple Mail Transfer Protocol (SMTP) to gather information from a target.

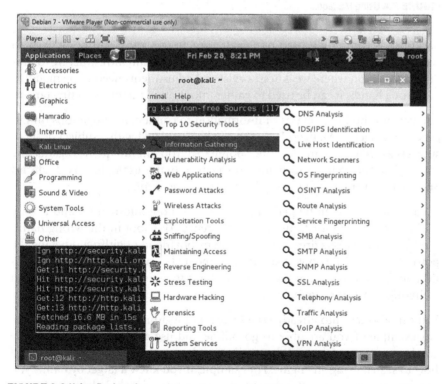

FIGURE 2.3 Using Backtrack.

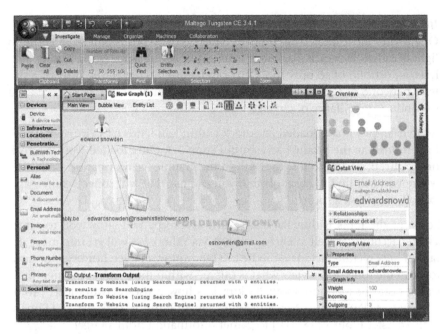

FIGURE 2.4 Using Maltego.

Backtrack is commonly used by Penetration Testers and Security Analysts to conduct security review of software, systems, services, and infrastructure to produce a report on where weaknesses exist and adjustments need to be made. In the wrong hands, it can be used to gather information on unsuspecting targets.

You can also build databases of information to conduct investigations on targets. A tool such as Maltego Tungsten can be populated with a subject or set of subjects as seen in Figure 2.4. Once populated, you can run queries against the source data and gather information on a target. In this example, I used Edward Snowden and attempted to map known e-mail accounts.

Data mining can then be performed to gather more information and a "case file" can be created for future use or reference. This tool in the wrong hands can become a stalkers dream. Imagine an ex-boyfriend or girlfriend having the power to create a file on you and keep it updated to track any known information about you. These are tools custom built to assist with data information gathering and are very good at it.

You can also tap into already established and legitimate tools to gather data. For example, if you are able to go online and use a search engine, you can conduct a large amount of data collection by understanding key words and how to search using an engine. For example, if you knew a target by name, you can then begin to add information after the name to include key words such

FIGURE 2.5 Searching online databases.

as "addresses," "phone number," and so on. There are literally hundreds of databases online that contain personal information that are freely searchable. A notable one could be the White Pages seen in Figure 2.5.

As we can see, you can also find address information and other personal information about a target without downloading and installing any tools. One point to mention is, as I used "John Smith" in my search, the more generic the name, the harder it is to search for their private information.

There are information gathering techniques that can also be used against an organization if that was your intended target. For example, here you can run a query against a domain name in a Who is database and find out contact information as well as location. By gathering this data, you could conduct a social engineering attack to gather more information. As seen in Figure 2.6, gathering data on a corporate entity to conduct an attack such as a social engineering attack could be done quickly using the Internet and a Who is database search.

As you can see, gathering information can be easily and quickly done and if you are organized and have a few pieces of key information to start with such as a name or a location of a target, you can map out information that can be used to conduct surveillance, such as the location of the target as an example.

Other paths can be used as we will see in the next section as we expand on information gathering; however, before we do, we must understand the legal and ethical concerns that are raised when performing such actions.

FIGURE 2.6 Conducting a Whois search.

ONLINE RECONNAISSANCE

As we learned in the last section, there is a lot of information you can gather on a target using the public Internet. Our focus in this part of this chapter is to show you just how easily it can be done. Online reconnaissance takes place when an attacker consciously decides to spy and conduct surveillance on a target using the Internet as their method of doing so. They do so with the intention of gathering intelligence and data on their target to plan an attack of some kind. The attacks are many; however, you can consider stalking being one of the most common. In this section of this chapter, we will look at the infrastructure that delivers the Internet as well as the applications, sites, pages, and other media that is used within it acting as resources and services. We will also take a look at the attacks that are performed and ways to mitigate them or lower your exposure to being attacked.

The Internet Threat

The public Internet is a goldmine for those conducting intelligence. When used in non-malicious ways, the Internet can be a source of a lot of information. Research on a homework assignment, locating the best travel path, or getting movie times are all simple examples of what can be done in seconds without having to leave your home or pick up your phone. When used for good reasons, the Internet can prove to be extremely helpful; however, when used for bad reasons, the Internet can be used to gather information to conduct attacks.

Another issue with the Internet is that once you put something on a server such as a blog post, a data file, or other source of data, it could remain there for a long time, possibly forever. Data backups collect data from servers and archive it.

Data can also be added without your knowledge. In the world of social media, it's common for people you connect to and with to "post" data such as an old picture of you. It can also be done in real time. For example, a favorite bar you frequently visit can quickly be online news if someone posts about it, tags a picture of you within it, or they post that you are in a group at a certain location. Attackers can use this information to ascertain your habits, favorite frequented places, and many other facts about you.

Data can also be doctored. Pictures can be digitally edited, words can be manipulated, and if someone has stolen your identity and posing (and posting) as you on the Internet, could cause serious issues for you.

Information is also added willingly, almost too willingly by many. Social media sites today encourage those who are part of them to post data, connect to others for no other reason other than to increase their numbers, and like things you normally wouldn't ever comment on outside of the digital world.

So, in sum, without any effort at all, your information can be added to the publically searchable Internet within seconds, stay within it indefinitely, and even if you think you have had it removed, it could still be archived somewhere for retrieval.

To add, this does not include the data that can be obtained from globally interconnected devices that can also provide those who seek information a source to get it. Servers cache data as an example to speed up Internet browsing and if this system was hacked, could reveal the browsing habits of an entire community as an example.

We should be concerned as a society, that if those who wish to do us harm need only to first have an Internet connection and second a "will" to be interested in gathering data on you, that all it takes is a few clicks of their mouse to obtain it.

Search Engines

Search Engines provide a wealth of information to those who know how to use it. As we just discussed, there is a public Internet full of information that is gathered *en masse*. Key word searches and refinement of topics as well as using specific tools and websites can give an attacker anything they need to begin surveillance on a target. As an example seen in Figure 2.7, you can search for anything within a search engine and it will attempt to show you data on your search query.

FIGURE 2.7 Searching for data with Google.

In this example, the search for Edward Snowden pulled up interesting articles, pictures (images), and many other pieces of information. This can also be refined by altering your key word search to include information such as "address," "phone number," or "contact" to narrow down what has been posted or placed on the Internet and as you search through the findings, you may just find it.

It should be noted that not all information found on the Internet is either relevant or factual. Just remember that if it is posted, it exists therefore you should not consider that all information you find is real. It just means it was tagged a certain way to be picked up by the search engines and based on "relevancy" will raise the most relevant to the top of the search findings.

Phishing

Phishing is an attack where an attacker is able to pose as a legitimate source on the Internet to trick you into believing they are the legitimate entities you are attempting to visit. When searching the Internet, you may find (or go directly to) a website where you want to conduct business. For example, let's use the example of logging into your bank account online to conduct a transaction.

If an attacker is able to manipulate that site either through manipulating DNS or through redirecting your browser, you would be brought to a site that you thought may be real, which in fact may be a phishing site. When you attach to it, you may put in your credentials and find out quickly that it is not in fact the site you wished to visit. That being said, the attacker has gathered information on you to be used to defraud you, steal from you, or conduct other attacks. If you use the same username and password for all of your sites, you have just given access to every site you have protected.

Protection against this attack can be found in most modern web browsers on the market today. Internet Explorer, for example, has a SmartScreen filter that runs a check against an online database to verify if a site is authentic as seen in Figure 2.8.

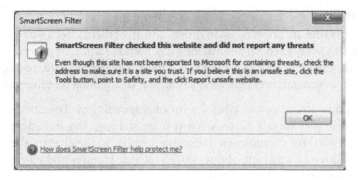

FIGURE 2.8 Content filtering.

Tracking

Another way you can be subject to information gathering is by websites that track who you are and where you come from. This can be used for marketing purposes; however, in the hands of those who wish to do harm, can be used to track you interests, location, your digital device (such as your PC), and your identity.

There are tools that allow you to block content, stop cookie usage, and other methods to stop personalized tracking of your digital footprint. You can use the Internet Explorer Tracking Protection options as seen in Figure 2.9 to ensure that you control what information is leaked out about you.

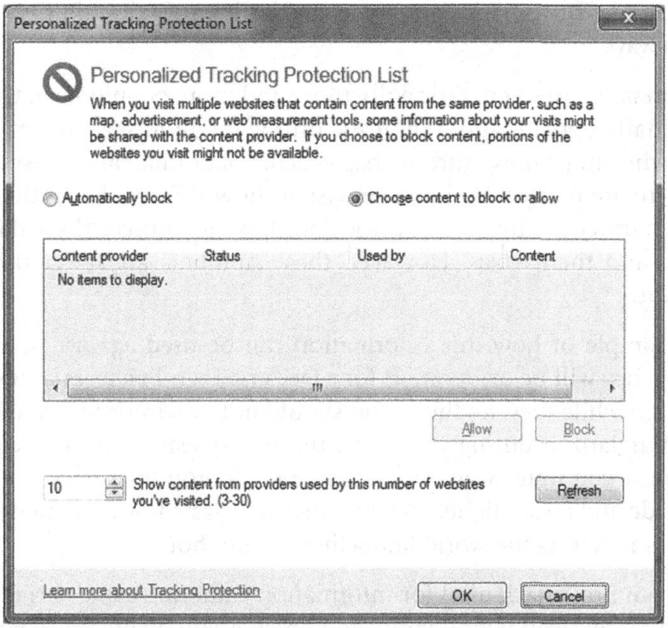

FIGURE 2.9 Microsoft tracking protection list.

Social Media

Social media sites are popping up in droves and all of them offer a way to connect and share. It's a way to socialize with long lost friends, family, or your co-workers. You can conduct business, share data, and meet new people, find new opportunities, and, in general, find new ways to connect to anything that interests you.

With this new found power comes a lot of responsibility. For one, you need to know who you are talking to, what you are sharing, and consider how this can impact you. For example, we mentioned earlier in the chapter that people you know can post anything about you, to include pictures and where you are physically located at any given time.

Also, when you join up for free social media sites such as Facebook, you have signed away your rights to your privacy. The owners of the site can use your data in any way they see fit based on the privacy policy you sign but probably do not read. As well, these site owners change this policy often and when they do, it's usually in ways to loosen up the restrictions that they place upon themselves in regard to protecting your identity and data.

More and more people join these sites daily and there does not seem to be a stop to using them, they only grow more important as they displace tradition TV and radio as sources of getting information. Just like the Internet, when used for good, they can be wonderful additions to the Internet in the form of allowing those who wish to connect and communicate forums to do so. In the hands of malicious users, however, it too becomes a goldmine for those who wish to conduct surveillance on targets and gather information to be used in malicious ways.

It's also amazing how generationally more and more people seem to feel; it's ok to put daily updates about their life online for all to see, pictures of what they do, who they know, and, worse, specific data that can be used against them. There are many who become wise to how this can harm them either by being harmed or by learning too late how to protect their data, their identities, and themselves. However, these numbers are fewer than those who do not.

A good example of how this information can be used against you is when people say they will be on vacation for a week and send pictures of themselves on the beach while they are there. You should not be surprised that when your home is burglarized during that time, the first question to be asked is, did anyone know you were away? These same people stop their mail delivery and leave outside and inside lights on while they are away; however, digitally show no restraint in letting the world know they are not home.

Another common attack used for information gathering using social media is when an attacker steals your identity and poses as you on the site. For example, an attacker can take a copy of your picture of your profile, set up a new profile, and add all of your friends. They can say, "Sorry, I accidently deleted my account and need to re-add you" and if you do not log into your account frequently (which can also be figured out by stalking you online), post as you, talk to your friends, and conduct any number of attacks while you are away.

In sum, safety should be something you consider when using social media sites. As you can see, there are quite a few ways in which you can be stalked, information can be gathered about you, and, in some cases, used against you.

Identify Theft

It may be funny in the movies, but not funny when it happens to you in real life (and it can). Identity theft, fraud, and other methods of acquiring and using your personal information against you consist of many legal issues today. Banks lose money, insurance rates rise, it costs individuals money, and criminals make a lot of money. Social security accounts are stolen and used, bank fraud takes place, and as we mentioned in social media earlier in this chapter, your personal identity can be used to impersonate you to gather more information.

You can limit exposure by considering what you post online. You can limit exposure by paying in cash instead of by credit card. There are many ways you can change your habits so that you can better protect your most valuable asset: you.

Scanning, Sniffing, and Mapping

Other ways to gather information rely on looking into lower levels of digital communications, primarily on the network. For example, you can use tools such as Wireshark, NMAP, and others to capture data and conduct packet-level analysis or port screening to gather and verify information about a target.

This type of information gathering requires you to be connected to a network and sometimes you will need to have access (or gain access) to unprivileged areas to conduct an attack; however, if you are able to you will be able to get the data you require. In this section, we look at using Backtrack to invoke NMAP to conduct information gathering on a host as seen in Figure 2.10.

In this attack, we simply load up NMAP and query the host we want to interrogate for information. It will reply back with specifics such as open ports. These open ports and IP addresses could potentially be manipulated for more information.

Although this is a simple example, more infiltration can be conducted as more information is learned. For example, an attacker may know that a specific port left opened may be something that they can penetrate and once they get to the next level of the attack, conduct another information gathering session to learn what else is open within the network.

FIGURE 2.10 Using NMAP.

Although this is information gathering at its lowest level, it should be considered a threat to you or anyone else because this is the same attack that can be conducted against any digital device using an IP address today. That means that any device you use that has an IP address can be probed for revealing information.

Wired and Wireless

Wired networks rely on cables and wireless networks rely on antennas using radio signals to attach to access points. Both eventually will connect to a higher level network that may ultimately connect to the Internet. That being said, let's look at the inherent strengths and weaknesses found in both technologies.

When considering wired networks, we consider networks and devices that are cabled together with either copper or fiber cabling. The types of networks are more difficult to gather information on because it is not easy to crack into a cable to extract information from it. By doing so, you can ruin the cable and terminate the signals carrying the information. This makes it more secure than wireless networks and generally produces a higher transmission speed. Its main weakness is that it requires cable to be run from source to destination and is generally costly and harder to maintain.

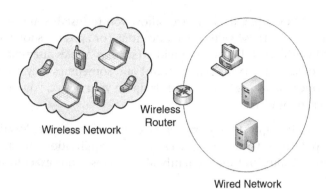

FIGURE 2.11 Wireless networking.

Wireless networks provide flexibility and the ability to roam between networks, and most devices today use this type of technology. Mobile devices, laptops, pads, and other handhelds rely on wireless to provide and maintain a network connection. There are, however, major weaknesses.

When wireless networks are used, they rely on radio signals that traverse through the air from source to destination and unless encrypted with strong encryption, they are easily captured, manipulated, and can be used for harm. Man in the Middle (MITM) attacks can be conducted where you can impersonate someone on the network. Information can be stolen and, in some cases, replayed against a destination system. A typical wireless network can be seen in Figure 2.11.

Infrastructure

Other concerns about keeping data private and safe revolve around the myriad of devices that your data transfers through. From your client–device (phone, laptop, PC), you can connect via a wireless access point, through multiple switches, servers, proxies, routers, security devices, and so on before your data reaches its destination. It is important to realize that every point in the network that your data traverses, that data can be stolen, read, intercepted, or manipulated. You would need to rely on the security teams entrusted to ensure your safety and privacy. This relies too much on the people in charge and is subject to human error.

Mobile Device Threat

The biggest trend today is the use of the mobile device. This includes (but not limited to) any device that you can use digitally that connects to a network for data. Global Positioning System (GPS) units, mobile phones, handhelds, pads, laptops, 2 in 1s, and many other devices today allow you to be flexible by being mobile. They rely on the ability to connect to networks (and thus the Internet) wirelessly and are as easy to manipulate by a malicious user because of their many flaws. For example, most devices allow you to install software on them from many sources. These software applications (or apps for short) are sometimes vetted by the mobile device provider (such as Apples attempting to provide a layer of security via the iTunes store) and sometimes they are not. That being said, once malicious software winds up on your device, you can likely be tracked, hacked, or worse.

Mobile devices use apps that allow for mapping of their exact location as an example. Apple uses Location Services to allow applications to provide additional functionality, but inadvertently also disclose your exact location at a specific time.

Data Threat (Metadata)

There is no bigger threat than being tracked online. You post a picture to Facebook and the next thing you know, you are a target. This can be done easily. For example, when using an Apple iPhone (or an Android device), you take pictures and information is stored in metadata without your knowledge. Again, when used for good, it serves as a way to archive your pictures and to know when and where you took them; however, when used for bad, it is a source for stalkers to pinpoint your exact location.

When considering the iPhone, you can adjust your privacy settings to turn Location Services off. An example can be seen in Figure 2.12.

FIGURE 2.12 Apple's location services.

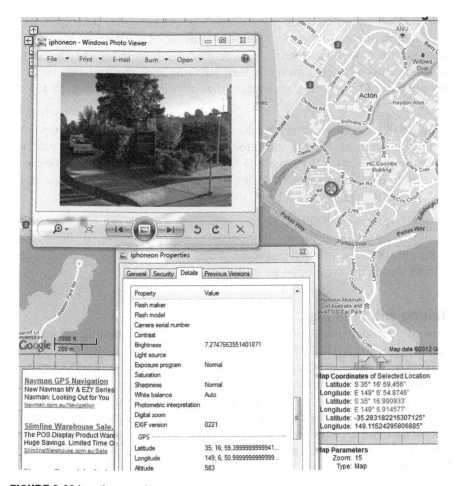

FIGURE 2.13 Location mapping.

If left on, or if someone takes a photo of you (or your children) with it on, you are in a situation where that picture if in the wrong hands could expose exactly where it has been taken. An example can be seen in Figure 2.13.

Here, if you look at the picture details, it will provide a GPS latitude and longitude recording that when plugged into Google map data, can provide an exact location of your whereabouts. A stalker across the world can find you and learn your location quickly and easily.

PHYSICAL RECONNAISSANCE

Our last section in the chapter will discuss physical reconnaissance and surveillance. Until now, we have discussed how infiltration, interception, and information gathering takes place within the digital world; however, some of the most successful attacks take place outside of it. There are many reasons for this – people are more overwhelmed and busy today and this could translate into not being aware of their surroundings, it could also be that people do not take into consideration that physical spying does in fact take place.

People will try evasive tactics to protect themselves online; however, they may not do so when traveling to work, for example. If they take the same path to work everyday, stop at the same 7-11 to get coffee, and park in the same spot, it's easy to discern patterns. This is how some private investigators learn how to "tail" their targets.

In this chapter, we will talk about how information can be gathered on a target by physically following them, talking to them, and/or intercepting phone calls. It should also be mentioned that some of these physical information gathering attacks sometimes cross boundaries into the digital world.

Tailing and Stalking

One of the oldest forms of investigation, information gathering, or stalking technique is to physically follow someone without their knowledge. Private investigators when conducting an information gathering session will generally use video and film footage gathered while following their intended targets. Law enforcement will do the same when conducting an investigation. Attackers will do so to gather information about a target. Stalking a target is considered tailing or following them sometimes to gather information, sometimes to do harm. There is generally no other good reason to follow and stalk someone.

There is no way to explain how this can be done without saying the key is to be inconspicuous (aka sneaky). You must remain out of site, but not so far out of site that you lose sight of your target. There is a balance that must be maintained and if that boundary is crossed, you risk being "made."

The only way to mitigate this danger is to be aware of your surroundings and change up your routine from time to time. Park somewhere different. Go to a different store. Take a different path. Practicing evasion when you pick up on someone tailing you is dangerous. You should not speed to get away and risk your life and those of others. If you are in danger, a trick is to drive to a police department or other location where you may be safe.

Social Engineering

Another tactic for information gathering revolves around a term called social engineering. What this means is, you trick someone through conversation to produce answers you need. For example, I place a call to you from a spoofed phone number that appears to you to be from a trusted source. I then tell you things that relate to you, us, or our conversation so that I can gain your trust. By asking specific questions and answers, I may be able to ascertain information from you needed to do another task, such as your account information to get into a personal website or bank account. This can then be leveraged into the digital world by exploiting the gathered information.

There are also software tools that can be used as seen in Figure 2.14. Here, Backtrack can load up social engineering programs that can assist you in performing such attacks.

There are other attacks too that can be used to gather information such as dumpster diving. This would be to sift through trash to gather up data you threw away that may contain personal information that can be used against you.

Another form of attack is shoulder surfing, which is simply looking over the shoulder of an unsuspecting victim to view what they are doing such as

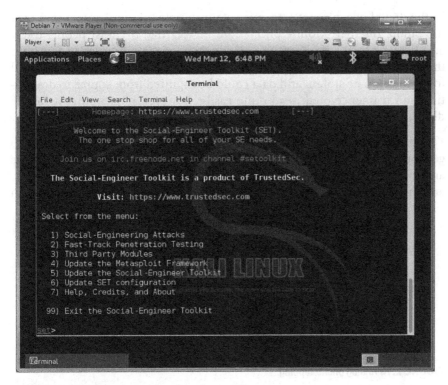

FIGURE 2.14 BackTrack's social engineering toolkit.

entering a password or texting someone to gather information about what they are doing.

Tapping

Phone conversations are easy ways to gather information. Even easier is the ability to "tap" a phone line to get information. Before the digital revolution, analog phones were used *en masse*. They still, however, are becoming a thing of the past as more and more people leverage digital cell phone technology. Before we review how to tap digital phones, we should cover how analog phones are tapped.

Wiretaps are nothing more than getting in between the phone source and destination and inserting a listening device in between. Since the phone system can be considered one long circuit from source to destination and creating a loop, all one would need to do is interject a load in that loop to tap it. An example of an older analog phone can be seen in Figure 2.15.

These copper wires contained in the phone and the loop itself are easily manipulated and information can be gathered rather quickly when conducting surveillance of a target.

In the digital age, phones transmit data over networks and sometimes over the public Internet. Mobile phones are now carried by most people today and because they are always in someone's possession, harder to tap from the client side. From the server side, voicemail servers can be hacked, cell tower logs can be stolen, and data could be captured from source to destination and if unencrypted, read quite easily; however, intercepting it can be difficult.

The easiest way to tap a digital device such as a mobile phone is to be able to get your hands on it. Once you do so, there are many software applications and tools as well as exploits that can be leveraged around it to listen in, track, and bug a device to gather information. Some tools, such as the one seen in

FIGURE 2.15 Analog phone tapping.

FIGURE 2.16 Recording iPhone calls.

Figure 2.16 called TapeACall can record a call without the recipient's knowledge for later playback.

It should be noted that there are other ways that law enforcement, government, spies, and attackers can "tap" into your phone conversations. Eavesdropping on calls is a quick way to gather information needed.

Legal and Ethical Concerns

In this section, we will cover a famous wiretapping case (case law and outcome) of how information gathering on a target online was brought into court and how it turned out.

The petitioner, Charles Katz, was charged with conducting illegal gambling operations across state lines in violation of federal law. In order to collect evidence against Katz, federal agents placed a warrantless wiretap on the public phone booth that he used to conduct these operations. The agents listened only to Katz's conversations, and only to the parts of his conversations dealing with illegal gambling transactions.

In the case of Olmstead v. United States (1928), the Supreme Court held that the warrantless wiretapping of phone lines did not constitute an unreasonable search under the Fourth Amendment. According to the Court, physical intrusion (a trespass) into a given area, and not mere voice amplification (the normal result of a wiretap), is required for an action to constitute a Fourth Amendment search. This is known as the "trespass doctrine." Partly in response to this decision, Congress passed the Federal Communications Act of 1933. This Act required, among other things, federal authorities to obtain a warrant before wiretapping private phone lines. In the case of Silverman v. United States

(1961), the Supreme Court refined the Olmstead trespass doctrine by holding that an unreasonable search occurs only if a "constitutionally protected area" has been intruded upon.

At his trial, Katz sought to exclude any evidence connected with these wiretaps, arguing that the warrantless wiretapping of a public phone booth constitutes an unreasonable search of a "constitutionally protected area" in violation of the Fourth Amendment. The federal agents countered by saying that a public phone booth was not a "constitutionally protected area," therefore, they could place a wiretap on it without a warrant.

Does the warrantless wiretapping of a public phone booth violate the unreasonable search and seizure clause of the Fourth Amendment to the United States Constitution?

RULING

Yes

REASONING

By a 7-1 vote, the U.S. Supreme Court agreed with Katz and held that placing of a warrantless wiretap on a public phone booth constitutes an unreasonable search in violation of the Fourth Amendment. The majority opinion, written by Justice Potter Stewart, however, did not address the case from the perspective of a "constitutionally protected area." In essence, the majority argued that both sides in the case were wrong to think that the permissibility of a warrantless wiretap depended upon the area being placed under surveillance. "For the Fourth Amendment protects people, not places. What a person knowingly exposes to the public, even in his own home or office, is not a subject of Fourth Amendment protection. ... . But what he seeks to preserve as private even in an area accessible to the public, may be constitutionally protected," the Court stated.

Building upon this reasoning, the Court held that it was the duty of the Judiciary to review petitions for warrants in instances in which persons may be engaging in conduct that they wish to keep secret, even if it were done in a public place. The Court held that, in the absence of a judicially authorized search warrant, the wiretaps of the public phone booth used by Katz were illegal. Therefore, the evidence against him gathered from his conversations should be suppressed.

Retrieved from:

http://www.uscourts.gov/educational-resources/get-involved/constitution-activities/fourth-amendment/wiretaps-cell-phone-surveillance/facts-case-summary.aspx

Katz v. United States - 389 U.S. 347 (1967)

U.S. Supreme Court

Katz v. United States, 389 U.S. 347 (1967)

Katz v. United States

No. 35

Argued October 17, 1967

Decided December 18, 1967

389 U.S. 347

CERTIORARI TO THE UNITED STATES COURT OF APPEALS

FOR THE NINTH CIRCUIT

Syllabus

Petitioner was convicted under an indictment charging him with transmitting wagering information by telephone across state lines in violation of 18 U.S.C. § 1084. Evidence of petitioner's
end of the conversations, overheard by FBI agents who had attached an electronic listening and
recording device to the outside of the telephone booth from which the calls were made, was introduced at the trial. The Court of Appeals affirmed the conviction, finding that there was no Fourth
Amendment violation, since there was "no physical entrance into the area occupied by" petitioner.

Held:

1. The Government's eavesdropping activities violated the privacy upon which petitioner justifiably
relied while using the telephone booth, and thus constituted a "search and seizure" within the
meaning of the Fourth Amendment. Pp. 389 U. S. 350-353.

(a) The Fourth Amendment governs not only the seizure of tangible items, but extends as well to
the recording of oral statements. Silverman v. United States, 365 U. S. 505, 365 U. S. 511. P. 389
U. S. 353.

(b) Because the Fourth Amendment protects people, rather than places, its reach cannot turn on
the presence or absence of a physical intrusion into any given enclosure. The "trespass" doctrine
of Olmstead v. United States, 277 U. S. 438, and Goldman v. United States, 316 U. S. 129, is no
longer controlling. Pp. 389 U. S. 351, 389 U. S. 353.

2. Although the surveillance in this case may have been so narrowly circumscribed that it could
constitutionally have been authorized in advance, it was not in fact conducted pursuant to the
warrant procedure which is a constitutional precondition of such electronic surveillance. Pp. 389
U. S. 354-359.

369 F.2d 130, reversed.

Page 389 U. S. 348

MR. JUSTICE STEWART delivered the opinion of the Court.

The petitioner was convicted in the District Court for the Southern District of California under
an eight-count indictment charging him with transmitting wagering information by telephone

from Los Angeles to Miami and Boston, in violation of a federal statute.[1] At trial, the Government was permitted, over the petitioner's objection, to introduce evidence of the petitioner's end of telephone conversations, overheard by FBI agents who had attached an electronic listening and recording device to the outside of the public telephone booth from which he had placed his calls. In affirming his conviction, the Court of Appeals rejected the contention that the recordings had been obtained in violation of the Fourth Amendment,

Page 389 U. S. 349

because "[t]here was no physical entrance into the area occupied by [the petitioner]." [2] We granted certiorari in order to consider the constitutional questions thus presented.[3]

The petitioner has phrased those questions as follows:

"A. Whether a public telephone booth is a constitutionally protected area so that evidence obtained by attaching an electronic listening recording device to the top of such a booth is obtained in violation of the right to privacy of the user of the booth."

Page 389 U. S. 350

"B. Whether physical penetration of a constitutionally protected area is necessary before a search and seizure can be said to be violative of the Fourth Amendment to the United States Constitution."

We decline to adopt this formulation of the issues. In the first place, the correct solution of Fourth Amendment problems is not necessarily promoted by incantation of the phrase "constitutionally protected area." Secondly, the Fourth Amendment cannot be translated into a general constitutional "right to privacy." That Amendment protects individual privacy against certain kinds of governmental intrusion, but its protections go further, and often have nothing to do with privacy at all.[4] Other provisions of the Constitution protect personal privacy from other forms of governmental invasion.[5] But the protection of a person's general right to privacy – his right to be let alone by other people[6] – is, like the

Page 389 U. S. 351

protection of his property and of his very life, left largely to the law of the individual States.[7]

[1] 18 U.S.C. § 1084. That statute provides in pertinent part:

[2] 369 F.2d 130, 134

[3] 386 U. S. 954. The petition for certiorari also challenged the validity of a warrant authorizing the search of the petitioner's premises. In light of our disposition of this case, we do not reach that issue.

[4] "The average man would very likely not have his feelings soothed any more by having his property seized openly than by having it seized privately and by stealth.. .. And a person can be just as much, if not more, irritated, annoyed and injured by an unceremonious public arrest by a policeman as he is by a seizure in the privacy of his office or home." Griswold v. Connecticut, 381 U. S. 479, 381 U. S. 509 (dissenting opinion of MR. JUSTICE BLACK).

[5] The First Amendment, for example, imposes limitations upon governmental abridgment of "freedom to associate and privacy in one's associations." NAACP v. Alabama, 357 U. S. 449, 357 U. S. 462. The Third Amendment's prohibition against the unconsented peacetime quartering of soldiers protects another aspect of privacy from governmental intrusion. To some extent, the Fifth Amendment too "reflects the Constitution's concern for. .. .. . the right of each individual "to a private enclave where he may lead a private life.""' Tehan v. Shott, 382 U. S. 406, 382 U. S. 416. Virtually every governmental action interferes with personal privacy to some degree. The question in each case is whether that interference violates a command of the United States Constitution.

[6] See Warren & Brandeis, The Right to Privacy, 4 Harv.L.Rev.193 (1890).

[7] See, e.g., Time, Inc. v. Hill, 385 U. S. 374. Cf. Breard v. Alexandria, 341 U. S. 622; Kovacs v. Cooper, 336 U. S. 77.

Because of the misleading way the issues have been formulated, the parties have attached great significance to the characterization of the telephone booth from which the petitioner placed his calls. The petitioner has strenuously argued that the booth was a "constitutionally protected area." The Government has maintained with equal vigor that it was not.[8] But this effort to decide whether or not a given "area," viewed in the abstract, is "constitutionally protected" deflects attention from the problem presented by this case.[9] For the Fourth Amendment protects people, not places. What a person knowingly exposes to the public, even in his own home or office, is not a subject of Fourth Amendment protection. See Lewis v. United States, 385 U. S. 206, 385 U. S. 210; United States v. Lee, 274 U. S. 559, 274 U. S. 563. But what he seeks to preserve as private, even in an area accessible to the public, may be constitutionally protected.

Page 389 U. S. 352

See Rios v. United States, 364 U. S. 253; Ex parte Jackson, 96 U. S. 727, 96 U. S. 733.

The Government stresses the fact that the telephone booth from which the petitioner made his calls was constructed partly of glass, so that he was as visible after he entered it as he would have been if he had remained outside. But what he sought to exclude when he entered the booth was not the intruding eye – it was the uninvited ear. He did not shed his right to do so simply because he made his calls from a place where he might be seen. No less than an individual in a business office,[10] in a friend's apartment,[11] or in a taxicab,[12] a person in a telephone booth may rely upon the protection of the Fourth Amendment. One who occupies it, shuts the door behind him, and pays the toll that permits him to place a call is surely entitled to assume that the words he utters into the mouthpiece will not be broadcast to the world. To read the Constitution more narrowly is to ignore the vital role that the public telephone has come to play in private communication.

The Government contends, however, that the activities of its agents in this case should not be tested by Fourth Amendment requirements, for the surveillance technique they employed involved no physical penetration of the telephone booth from which the petitioner placed his calls. It is true that the absence of such penetration was at one time thought to foreclose further Fourth Amendment inquiry, Olmstead v. United States, 277 U. S. 438, 277 U. S. 457, 277 U. S. 464, 277 U. S. 466; Goldman v. United States, 316 U. S. 129, 316 U. S. 134-136, for that Amendment was thought to limit only searches and seizures of tangible

Page 389 U. S. 353

Property.[13] But "[t]he premise that property interests control the right of the Government to search and seize has been discredited." Warden v. Hayden, 387 U. S. 294, 387 U. S. 304. Thus,

[8]In support of their respective claims, the parties have compiled competing lists of "protected areas" for our consideration. It appears to be common ground that a private home is such an area, Weeks v. United States, 232 U. S. 383, but that an open field is not. Hester v. United States, 265 U. S. 57. Defending the inclusion of a telephone booth in his list the petitioner cites United States v. Stone, 232 F. Supp. 396, and United States v. Madison, 32 L.W. 2243 (D.C. Ct.Gen.Sess.). Urging that the telephone booth should be excluded, the Government finds support in United States v. Borgese, 235 F.Supp. 286.
[9]It is true that this Court has occasionally described its conclusions in terms of "constitutionally protected areas," see, e.g., Silverman v. United States, 365 U. S. 505, 365 U. S. 510, 365 U. S. 512; Lopez v. United States, 373 U. S. 427, 373 U. S. 438-439; Berger v. New York, 388 U. S. 41, 388 U. S. 57, 388 U. S. 59, but we have never suggested that this concept can serve as a talismanic solution to every Fourth Amendment problem.
[10]Silverthorne Lumber Co. v. United States, 251 U. S. 385.
[11]Jones v. United States, 362 U. S. 257.
[12]Rios v United States, 364 U. S. 253.
[13]See Olmstead v. United States, 277 U. S. 438, 277 U. S. 464-466. We do not deal in this case with the law of detention or arrest under the Fourth Amendment.

although a closely divided Court supposed in Olmstead that surveillance without any trespass and without the seizure of any material object fell outside the ambit of the Constitution, we have since departed from the narrow view on which that decision rested. Indeed, we have expressly held that the Fourth Amendment governs not only the seizure of tangible items, but extends as well to the recording of oral statements, overheard without any "technical trespass under. .. local property law." Silverman v. United States, 365 U. S. 505, 365 U. S. 511. Once this much is acknowledged, and once it is recognized that the Fourth Amendment protects people – and not simply "areas" – against unreasonable searches and seizures, it becomes clear that the reach of that Amendment cannot turn upon the presence or absence of a physical intrusion into any given enclosure.

We conclude that the underpinnings of Olmstead and Goldman have been so eroded by our subsequent decisions that the "trespass" doctrine there enunciated can no longer be regarded as controlling. The Government's activities in electronically listening to and recording the petitioner's words violated the privacy upon which he justifiably relied while using the telephone booth, and thus constituted a "search and seizure" within the meaning of the Fourth Amendment. The fact that the electronic device employed to achieve that end did not happen to penetrate the wall of the booth can have no constitutional significance.

Page 389 U. S. 354

The question remaining for decision, then, is whether the search and seizure conducted in this case complied with constitutional standards. In that regard, the Government's position is that its agents acted in an entirely defensible manner: they did not begin their electronic surveillance until investigation of the petitioner's activities had established a strong probability that he was using the telephone in question to transmit gambling information to persons in other States, in violation of federal law. Moreover, the surveillance was limited, both in scope and in duration, to the specific purpose of establishing the contents of the petitioner's unlawful telephonic communications. The agents confined their surveillance to the brief periods during which he used the telephone booth,[14] and they took great care to overhear only the conversations of the petitioner himself.[15]

Accepting this account of the Government's actions as accurate, it is clear that this surveillance was so narrowly circumscribed that a duly authorized magistrate, properly notified of the need for such investigation, specifically informed of the basis on which it was to proceed, and clearly apprised of the precise intrusion it would entail, could constitutionally have authorized, with appropriate safeguards, the very limited search and seizure that the Government asserts, in fact, took place. Only last Term we sustained the validity of

Page 389 U. S. 355

such an authorization, holding that, under sufficiently "precise and discriminate circumstances," a federal court may empower government agents to employ a concealed electronic device "for the narrow and particularized purpose of ascertaining the truth of the. .. allegations" of a "detailed factual affidavit alleging the commission of a specific criminal offense." Osborn v. United States,

[14]*Based upon their previous visual observations of the petitioner, the agents correctly predicted that he would use the telephone booth for several minutes at approximately the same time each morning. The petitioner was subjected to electronic surveillance only during this predetermined period. Six recordings, averaging some three minutes each, were obtained and admitted in evidence. They preserved the petitioners end of conversations concerning the placing of bets and the receipt of wagering information.*

[15]*On the single occasion when the statements of another person were inadvertently intercepted, the agents refrained from listening to them.*

385 U. S. 323, 385 U. S. 329-330. Discussing that holding, the Court in Berger v. New York, 388 U. S. 41, said that "the order authorizing the use of the electronic device" in Osborn "afforded similar protections to those. .. of conventional warrants authorizing the seizure of tangible evidence." Through those protections, "no greater invasion of privacy was permitted than was necessary under the circumstances." Id. at 388 U. S. 57.[16] Here, too, a similar

Page 389 U. S. 356

judicial order could have accommodated "the legitimate needs of law enforcement"[17] by authoriz- ing the carefully limited use of electronic surveillance.

The Government urges that, because its agents relied upon the decisions in Olmstead and Gold- man, and because they did no more here than they might properly have done with prior judicial sanction, we should retroactively validate their conduct. That we cannot do. It is apparent that the agents in this case acted with restraint. Yet the inescapable fact is that this restraint was imposed by the agents themselves, not by a judicial officer. They were not required, before commencing the search, to present their estimate of probable cause for detached scrutiny by a neutral magis- trate. They were not compelled, during the conduct of the search itself, to observe precise limits established in advance by a specific court order. Nor were they directed, after the search had

[16]Although the protections afforded the petitioner in Osborn were "similar. .. to those. .. of conventional warrants," they were not identical. A conventional warrant ordinarily serves to notify the suspect of an intended search. But if Osborn had been told in advance that federal officers intended to record his conversations, the point of making such recordings would obviously have been lost; the evidence in question could not have been obtained. In omitting any requirement of advance notice, the federal court that authorized electronic surveillance in Osborn simply recognized, as has this Court, that officers need not announce their purpose before conducting an otherwise authorized search if such an announcement would provoke the escape of the suspect or the destruction of critical evidence. See Ker v. California, 374 U. S. 23, 374 U. S. 37-41. Although the protections afforded the petitioner in Osborn were "similar . . . to those . . . of conventional warrants," they were not identical. A conventional warrant ordinarily serves to notify the suspect of an intended search. But if Osborn had been told in advance that federal officers intended to record his conversations, the point of making such recordings would obviously have been lost; the evidence in question could not have been obtained. In omitting any requirement of advance notice, the federal court that authorized electronic surveillance in Osborn simply recognized, as has this Court, that officers need not announce their purpose before conducting an otherwise authorized search if such an announcement would provoke the escape of the suspect or the destruction of critical evidence. See Ker v. California, 374 U. S. 23, 374 U. S. 37-41. Although some have thought that this "exception to the notice requirement where exigent circumstances are present," id. at 374 U. S. 39, should be deemed inapplicable where police enter a home before its occupants are aware that officers are present, id. at 374 U. S. 55-58 (opinion of MR. JUSTICE BRENNAN), the reasons for such a limitation have no bearing here. However true it may be that "[i]nnocent citizens should not suffer the shock, fright or embarrassment attendant upon an unannounced police intrusion," id. at 374 U. S. 57, and that "the requirement of awareness . . . serves to minimize the hazards of the officers' dangerous calling," id. at 374 U. S. 57-58, these considerations are not relevant to the problems presented by judicially authorized electronic surveillance.
Nor do the Federal Rules of Criminal Procedure impose an inflexible requirement of prior notice. Rule 41(d) does require federal officers to serve upon the person searched a copy of the warrant and a receipt describing the material obtained, but it does not invariably require that this be done before the search takes place. Nordelli v. United States, 24 F.2d 665, 666-667.
Thus, the fact that the petitioner in Osborn was unaware that his words were being electronically transcribed did not prevent this Court from sustaining his conviction, and did not prevent the Court in Berger from reaching the conclusion that the use of the recording device sanctioned in Osborn was entirely lawful. 388 U. S. 41, 388 U. S. 57.
[17]Lopez v. United States, 373 U. S. 427, 373 U. S. 464 (dissenting opinion of MR. JUSTICE BRENNAN).

been completed, to notify the authorizing magistrate in detail of all that had been seized. In the absence of such safeguards, this Court has never sustained a search upon the sole ground that officers reasonably expected to find evidence of a particular crime and voluntarily confined their activities to the least intrusive

Page 389 U. S. 357

means consistent with that end. Searches conducted without warrants have been held unlawful "notwithstanding facts unquestionably showing probable cause," Agnello v. United States, 269 U. S. 20, 269 U. S. 33, for the Constitution requires "that the deliberate, impartial judgment of a judicial officer... be interposed between the citizen and the police.. .." Wong Sun v. United States, 371 U. S. 471, 371 U. S. 481-482. "Over and again, this Court has emphasized that the mandate of the [Fourth] Amendment requires adherence to judicial processes," United States v. Jeffers, 342 U. S. 48, 342 U. S. 51, and that searches conducted outside the judicial process, without prior approval by judge or magistrate, are per se unreasonable under the Fourth Amendment[18] – subject only to a few specifically established and well delineated exceptions.[19]

It is difficult to imagine how any of those exceptions could ever apply to the sort of search and seizure involved in this case. Even electronic surveillance substantially contemporaneous with an individual's arrest could hardly be deemed an "incident" of that arrest.[20]

Page 389 U. S. 358

Nor could the use of electronic surveillance without prior authorization be justified on grounds of "hot pursuit.[21] "And, of course, the very nature of electronic surveillance precludes its use pursuant to the suspect's consent.[22]

The Government does not question these basic principles. Rather, it urges the creation of a new exception to cover this case.[23] It argues that surveillance of a telephone booth should be

[18]See, e.g., Jones v. United States, 357 U. S. 493, 357 U. S. 497-499; Rios v. United States, 364 U. S. 253, 364 U. S. 261; Chapman v. United States, 365 U. S. 610, 365 U. S. 613-615; Stoner v. California, 376 U. S. 483, 376 U. S. 486-487.
[19]See, e.g., Carroll v. United States, 267 U. S. 132, 267 U. S. 153, 156; McDonald v. United States, 335 U. S. 451, 335 U. S. 454-456; Brinegar v. United States, 338 U. S. 160, 338 U. S. 174-177; Cooper v. California, 386 U. S. 58; Warden v. Hayden, 387 U. S. 294, 387 U. S. 298-300.
[20]In Agnello v. United States, 269 U. S. 20, 269 U. S. 30, the Court stated:
"The right without a search warrant contemporaneously to search persons lawfully arrested while committing crime and to search the place where the arrest is made in order to find and seize things connected with the crime as its fruits or as the means by which it was committed, as well as weapons and other things to effect an escape from custody, is not to be doubted."
Whatever one's view of "the longstanding practice of searching for other proofs of guilt within the control of the accused found upon arrest," United States v. Rabinowitz, 339 U. S. 56, 339 U. S. 61; cf. id. at 339 U. S. 71-79 (dissenting opinion of Mr. Justice Frankfurter), the concept of an "incidental" search cannot readily be extended to include surreptitious surveillance of an individual either immediately before, or immediately after, his arrest.
[21]Although "[t]he Fourth Amendment does not require police officers to delay in the course of an investigation if to do so would gravely endanger their lives or the lives of others,"
Warden v. Hayden, 387 U. S. 294, 387 U. S. 298-299, there seems little likelihood that electronic surveillance would be a realistic possibility in a situation so fraught with urgency.
[22]A search to which an individual consents meets Fourth Amendment requirements, Zap v. United States, 328 U. S. 624, but, of course, "the usefulness of electronic surveillance depends on lack of notice to the suspect." Lopez v. United States, 373 U. S. 427, 373 U. S. 463 (dissenting opinion of MR. JUSTICE BRENNAN).
[23]Whether safeguards other than prior authorization by a magistrate would satisfy the Fourth Amendment in a situation involving the national security is a question not presented by this case.

exempted from the usual requirement of advance authorization by a magistrate upon a showing of probable cause. We cannot agree. Omission of such authorization

"bypasses the safeguards provided by an objective predetermination of probable cause, and substitutes instead the far less reliable procedure of an after-the-event justification for the. .. search, too likely to be subtly influenced by the familiar shortcomings of hindsight judgment."

Beck v. Ohio, 379 U. S. 89, 379 U. S. 96. And bypassing a neutral predetermination of the scope of a search leaves individuals secure from Fourth Amendment

Page 389 U. S. 359

violations "only in the discretion of the police." Id. at 379 U. S. 97.

These considerations do not vanish when the search in question is transferred from the setting of a home, an office, or a hotel room to that of a telephone booth. Wherever a man may be, he is entitled to know that he will remain free from unreasonable searches and seizures. The government agents here ignored "the procedure of antecedent justification. .. that is central to the Fourth Amendment,"[24] a procedure that we hold to be a constitutional precondition of the kind of electronic surveillance involved in this case. Because the surveillance here failed to meet that condition, and because it led to the petitioner's conviction, the judgment must be reversed.

It is so ordered.

MR. JUSTICE MARSHALL took no part in the consideration or decision of this case.

"(a) Whoever being engaged in the business of betting or wagering knowingly uses a wire communication facility for the transmission in interstate or foreign commerce of bets or wagers or information assisting in the placing of bets or wagers on any sporting event or contest, or for the transmission of a wire communication which entitles the recipient to receive money or credit as a result of bets or wagers, or for information assisting in the placing of bets or wagers, shall be fined not more than $10,000 or imprisoned not more than two years, or both."

"(b) Nothing in this section shall be construed to prevent the transmission in interstate or foreign commerce of information for use in news reporting of sporting events or contests, or for the transmission of information assisting in the placing of bets or wagers on a sporting event or contest from a State where betting on that sporting event or contest is legal into a State in which such betting is legal."

We find no merit in the petitioner's further suggestion that his indictment must be dismissed. After his conviction was affirmed by the Court of Appeals, he testified before a federal grand jury concerning the charges involved here. Because he was compelled to testify pursuant to a grant of immunity, 48 Stat. 1096, as amended, 47 U.S.C. § 409(l), it is clear that the fruit of his testimony cannot be used against him in any future trial. But the petitioner asks for more. He contends that. his conviction must be vacated and the charges against him dismissed lest he be "subjected to [a] penalty. .. on account of [a]. .. matter. .. concerning which he [was] compelled. .. to testify.. .." 47 U.S.C. § 409(l). Frank v. United States, 347 F.2d 486. We disagree. In relevant part, § 409(l) substantially repeats the language of the Compulsory Testimony Act of 1893, 27 Stat. 443, 49 U.S.C. § 46, which was Congress' response to this Court's statement that an immunity statute can supplant the Fifth Amendment privilege against self-incrimination only if it affords adequate protection from future prosecution or conviction. Counselman v. Hitchcock, 142 U. S. 547, 142

[24]See Osborn v. United States, 385 U. S. 323, 385 U. S. 330.

U. S. 585-586. The statutory provision here involved was designed to provide such protection, see Brown v. United States, 359 U. S. 41, 359 U. S. 45-46, not to confer immunity from punishment pursuant to a prior prosecution and adjudication of guilt. Cf. Regina v. United States, 364 U. S. 507, 364 U. S. 513-514.

MR. JUSTICE DOUGLAS, with whom MR. JUSTICE BRENNAN joins, concurring.

While I join the opinion of the Court, I feel compelled to reply to the separate concurring opinion of my Brother WHITE, which I view as a wholly unwarranted green light for the Executive Branch to resort to electronic eavesdropping without a warrant in cases which the Executive Branch itself labels "national security" matters.

Neither the President nor the Attorney General is a magistrate. In matters where they believe national security may be involved, they are not detached, disinterested, and neutral as a court or magistrate must be. Under the separation of powers created by the Constitution, the Executive Branch is not supposed to be neutral and disinterested. Rather it should vigorously investigate

Page 389 U. S. 360

and prevent breaches of national security and prosecute those who violate the pertinent federal laws. The President and Attorney General are properly interested parties, cast in the role of adversary, in national security cases. They may even be the intended victims of subversive action. Since spies and saboteurs are as entitled to the protection of the Fourth Amendment as suspected gamblers like petitioner, I cannot agree that, where spies and saboteurs are involved adequate protection of Fourth Amendment rights is assured when the President and Attorney General assume both the position of "adversary and prosecutor" and disinterested, neutral magistrate.

There is, so far as I understand constitutional history, no distinction under the Fourth Amendment between types of crimes. Article III, § 3, gives "treason" a very narrow definition, and puts restrictions on its proof. But the Fourth Amendment draws no lines between various substantive offenses. The arrests in cases of "hot pursuit" and the arrests on visible or other evidence of probable cause cut across the board, and are not peculiar to any kind of crime.

I would respect the present lines of distinction, and not improvise because a particular crime seems particularly heinous. When the Framers took that step, as they did with treason, the worst crime of all, they made their purpose manifest.

MR. JUSTICE HARLAN, concurring.

I join the opinion of the Court, which I read to hold only (a) that an enclosed telephone booth is an area where, like a home, Weeks v. United States, 232 U. S. 383, and unlike a field, Hester v. United States, 265 U. S. 57, a person has a constitutionally protected reasonable expectation of privacy; (b) that electronic, as well as physical, intrusion into a place that is in this sense private may constitute a violation of the Fourth Amendment,

Page 389 U. S. 361

and (c) that the invasion of a constitutionally protected area by federal authorities is, as the Court has long held, presumptively unreasonable in the absence of a search warrant.

As the Court's opinion states, "the Fourth Amendment protects people, not places." The question, however, is what protection it affords to those people. Generally, as here, the answer to that question requires reference to a "place." My understanding of the rule that has emerged from prior decisions is that there is a twofold requirement, first that a person have exhibited an actual (subjective) expectation of privacy and, second, that the expectation be one that society is prepared to recognize as "reasonable." Thus, a man's home is, for most purposes, a place where he expects privacy, but objects, activities, or statements that he exposes to the "plain view" of outsiders are not "protected," because no intention to keep them to himself has been exhibited. On the other hand, conversations in the open would not be protected against being overheard, for the expectation of privacy under the circumstances would be unreasonable. Cf. Hester v. United States, supra.

The critical fact in this case is that "[o]ne who occupies it, [a telephone booth] shuts the door behind him, and pays the toll that permits him to place a call is surely entitled to assume" that his conversation is not being intercepted. Ante at 389 U. S. 352. The point is not that the booth is "accessible to the public" at other times, ante at 389 U. S. 351, but that it is a temporarily private place whose momentary occupants' expectations of freedom from intrusion are recognized as reasonable. Cf. Rios v. United States, 364 U. S. 253.

In Silverman v. United States, 365 U. S. 505, we held that eavesdropping accomplished by means of an electronic device that penetrated the premises occupied by petitioner was a violation of the Fourth Amendment.

Page 389 U. S. 362

That case established that interception of conversations reasonably intended to be private could constitute a "search and seizure." and that the examination or taking of physical property was not required. This view of the Fourth Amendment was followed in Wong Sun v. United States, 371 U. S. 471, at 371 U. S. 485, and Berger v. New York, 388 U. S. 41, at 51. Also compare Osborn v. United States, 385 U. S. 323, at 385 U. S. 327. In Silverman, we found it unnecessary to reexamine Goldman v. United States, 316 U. S. 129, which had held that electronic surveillance accomplished without the physical penetration of petitioner's premises by a tangible object did not violate the Fourth Amendment. This case requires us to reconsider Goldman, and I agree that it should now be overruled.* Its limitation on Fourth Amendment protection is, in the present day, bad physics as well as bad law, for reasonable expectations of privacy may be defeated by electronic as well as physical invasion.

Finally, I do not read the Court's opinion to declare that no interception of a conversation one-half of which occurs in a public telephone booth can be reasonable in the absence of a warrant. As elsewhere under the Fourth Amendment, warrants are the general rule, to which the legitimate needs of law enforcement may demand specific exceptions. It will be time enough to consider any such exceptions when an appropriate occasion presents itself, and I agree with the Court that this is not one.

MR. JUSTICE WHITE, concurring.

I agree that the official surveillance of petitioner's telephone conversations in a public booth must be subjected

Page 389 U. S. 363

*I also think that the course of development evinced by Silverman. supra, Wong Sun., supra, Berger, supra, and today's decision must be recognized as overruling Olmstead v. United States, 277 U. S. 438, which essentially rested on the ground that conversations were not subject to the protection of the Fourth Amendment.

to the test of reasonableness under the Fourth Amendment and that, on the record now before us, the particular surveillance undertaken was unreasonable absent a warrant properly authorizing it. This application of the Fourth Amendment need not interfere with legitimate needs of law enforcement.*

In joining the Court's opinion, I note the Court's acknowledgment that there are circumstances in which it is reasonable to search without a warrant. In this connection, in footnote 23 the Court points out that today's decision does not reach national security cases Wiretapping to protect the security of the Nation has been authorized by successive Presidents. The present Administration would apparently save national security cases from restrictions against wiretapping. See Berger v. New York, 388 U. S. 41, 388 U. S. 112-118 (1967) (WHITE, J.,

Page 389 U. S. 364

dissenting). We should not require the warrant procedure and the magistrate's judgment if the President of the United States or his chief legal officer, the Attorney General, has considered the requirements of national security and authorized electronic surveillance as reasonable.

MR. JUSTICE BLACK, dissenting.

If I could agree with the Court that eavesdropping carried on by electronic means (equivalent to wiretapping) constitutes a "search" or "seizure," I would be happy to join the Court's opinion For on that premise, my Brother STEWART sets out methods in accord with the Fourth Amendment to guide States in the enactment and enforcement of laws passed to regulate wiretapping by government. In this respect, today's opinion differs sharply from Berger v. New York, 388 U. S. 41, decided last Term, which held void on its face a New York statute authorizing wiretapping on warrants issued by magistrates on showings of probable cause. The Berger case also set up what appeared to be insuperable obstacles to the valid passage of such wiretapping laws by States. The Court's opinion in this case, however, removes the doubts about state power in this field and abates to a large extent the confusion and near-paralyzing effect of the Berger holding. Notwithstanding these good efforts of the Court, I am still unable to agree with its interpretation of the Fourth Amendment.

My basic objection is two-fold: (1) I do not believe that the words of the Amendment will bear the meaning given them by today's decision, and (2) I do not believe that it is the proper role of this Court to rewrite the Amendment in order "to bring it into harmony with the times," and thus reach a result that many people believe to be desirable.

*In previous cases, which are undisturbed by today's decision, the Court has upheld, as reasonable under the Fourth Amendment, admission at trial of evidence obtained (1) by an undercover police agent to whom a defendant speaks without knowledge that he is in the employ of the police, Hoffa v. United States, 385 U. S. 293 (1966); (2) by a recording device hidden on the person of such an informant, Lopez v. United States, 373 U. S. 427 (1963); Osborn v. United States, 385 U. S. 323 (1966), and (3) by a policeman listening to the secret microwave transmissions of an agent conversing with the defendant in another location, On Lee v. United States, 343 U. S. 747 (1952). When one man speaks to another, he takes all the risks ordinarily inherent in so doing, including the risk that the man to whom he speaks will make public what he has heard. The Fourth Amendment does not protect against unreliable (or law-abiding) associates. Hoffa v. United States, supra. It is but a logical and reasonable extension of this principle that a man take the risk that his hearer, free to memorize what he hears for later verbatim repetitions, is instead recording it or transmitting it to another. The present case deals with an entirely different situation, for as the Court emphasizes the petitioner "sought to exclude. .. the uninvited ear," and spoke under circumstances in which a reasonable person would assume that uninvited ears were not listening.

Page 389 U. S. 365

While I realize that an argument based on the meaning of words lacks the scope, and no doubt the appeal, of broad policy discussions and philosophical discourses on such nebulous subjects as privacy, for me, the language of the Amendment is the crucial place to look in construing a written document such as our Constitution. The Fourth Amendment says that

"The right of the people to be secure in their persons, houses, papers, and effects, against unreasonable searches and seizures, shall not be violated, and no Warrants shall issue, but upon probable cause, supported by Oath or affirmation, and particularly describing the place to be searched and the persons or things to be seized."

The first clause protects "persons, houses, papers, and effects against unreasonable searches and seizures.. . ." These words connote the idea of tangible things with size, form, and weight, things capable of being searched, seized, or both. The second clause of the Amendment still further establishes its Framers' purpose to limit its protection to tangible things by providing that no warrants shall issue but those "particularly describing the place to be searched, and the persons or things to be seized." A conversation overheard by eavesdropping, whether by plain snooping or wiretapping, is not tangible and, under the normally accepted meanings of the words, can neither be searched nor seized. In addition the language of the second clause indicates that the Amendment refers not only to something tangible so it can be seized, but to something already in existence, so it can be described. Yet the Court's interpretation would have the Amendment apply to overhearing future conversations, which, by their very nature, are nonexistent until they take place. How can one "describe" a future conversation, and, if one cannot, how can a magistrate issue a warrant to eavesdrop one in the future? It is argued that information showing what

Page 389 U. S. 366

is expected to be said is sufficient to limit the boundaries of what later can be admitted into evidence; but does such general information really meet the specific language of the Amendment, which says "particularly describing"? Rather than using language in a completely artificial way, I must conclude that the Fourth Amendment simply does not apply to eavesdropping.

Tapping telephone wires, of course, was an unknown possibility at the time the Fourth Amendment was adopted. But eavesdropping (and wiretapping is nothing more than eavesdropping by telephone) was, as even the majority opinion in Berger, supra, recognized,

"an ancient practice which, at common law, was condemned as a nuisance. 4 Blackstone, Commentaries 168. In those days, the eavesdropper listened by naked ear under the eaves of houses or their windows, or beyond their walls seeking out private discourse."

388 U.S. at 388 U. S. 45. There can be no doubt that the Framers were aware of this practice, and, if they had desired to outlaw or restrict the use of evidence obtained by eavesdropping, I believe that they would have used the appropriate language to do so in the Fourth Amendment. They certainly would not have left such a task to the ingenuity of language-stretching judges. No one, it seems to me, can read the debates on the Bill of Rights without reaching the conclusion that its Framers and critics well knew the meaning of the words they used, what they would be understood to mean by others, their scope and their limitations. Under these circumstances, it strikes me as a charge against their scholarship, their common sense and their candor to give to the Fourth Amendment's language the eavesdropping meaning the Court imputes to it today.

I do not deny that common sense requires, and that this Court often has said, that the Bill of Rights' safeguards should be given a liberal construction. This

Page 389 U. S. 367

principle, however, does not justify construing the search and seizure amendment as applying to eavesdropping or the "seizure" of conversations. The Fourth Amendment was aimed directly at the abhorred practice of breaking in, ransacking and searching homes and other buildings and seizing people's personal belongings without warrants issued by magistrates. The Amendment deserves, and this Court has given it, a liberal construction in order to protect against warrant-less searches of buildings and seizures of tangible personal effects. But, until today, this Court has refused to say that eavesdropping comes within the ambit of Fourth Amendment restrictions. See, e.g., Olmstead v. United States, 277 U. S. 438 (1928), and Goldman v. United States, 316 U. S. 129 (1942).

So far, I have attempted to state why I think the words of the Fourth Amendment prevent its application to eavesdropping. It is important now to show that this has been the traditional view of the Amendment's scope since its adoption, and that the Court's decision in this case, along with its amorphous holding in Berger last Term, marks the first real departure from that view.

The first case to reach this Court which actually involved a clear-cut test of the Fourth Amendment's applicability to eavesdropping through a wiretap was, of course, Olmstead, supra. In holding that the interception of private telephone conversations by means of wiretapping was not a violation of the Fourth Amendment, this Court, speaking through Mr. Chief Justice Taft, examined the language of the Amendment and found, just as I do now, that the words could not be stretched to encompass overheard conversations:

"The Amendment itself shows that the search is to be of material things -- the person, the house, his papers or his effects. The description of the warrant necessary to make the proceeding lawful, is

Page 389 U. S. 368

that it must specify the place to be searched and the person or things to be seized.. . ."

"* * * *"

"Justice Bradley in the Boyd case [Boyd v. United States, 116 U. S. 616], and Justice Clark[e] in the Gouled case [Gouled v. United States, 255 U. S. 298], said that the Fifth Amendment and the Fourth Amendment were to be liberally construed to effect the purpose of the framers of the Constitution in the interest of liberty. But that cannot justify enlargement of the language employed beyond the possible practical meaning of houses, persons, papers, and effects, or so to apply the words search and seizure as to forbid hearing or sight."

277 U.S. at 277 U. S. 464-465.

Goldman v. United States, 316 U. S. 129, is an even clearer example of this Court's traditional refusal to consider eavesdropping as being covered by the Fourth Amendment. There, federal agents used a detectaphone, which was placed on the wall of an adjoining room, to listen to the conversation of a defendant carried on in his private office and intended to be confined within the four walls of the room. This Court, referring to Olmstead, found no Fourth Amendment violation.

It should be noted that the Court in Olmstead based its decision squarely on the fact that wiretapping or eavesdropping does not violate the Fourth Amendment. As shown supra in the cited quotation from the case, the Court went to great pains to examine the actual language of the Amendment, and found that the words used simply could not be stretched to cover eavesdropping. That there was no trespass was not the determinative factor, and indeed the Court, in citing Hester v. United States, 265 U. S. 57, indicated that, even where there was a trespass, the Fourth Amendment does not automatically apply to evidence obtained by "hearing or

Page 389 U. S. 369

sight." The Olmstead majority characterized Hester as holding

"that the testimony of two officers of the law who trespassed on the defendant's land, concealed themselves one hundred yards away from his house, and saw him come out and hand a bottle of whiskey to another, was not inadmissible. While there was a trespass, there was no search of person, house, papers or effects."

277 U.S. at 277 U. S. 465. Thus, the clear holding of the Olmstead and Goldman cases, undiluted by any question of trespass, is that eavesdropping, in both its original and modern forms, is not violative of the Fourth Amendment.

While my reading of the Olmstead and Goldman cases convinces me that they were decided on the basis of the inapplicability of the wording of the Fourth Amendment to eavesdropping, and not on any trespass basis, this is not to say that unauthorized intrusion has not played an important role in search and seizure cases. This Court has adopted an exclusionary rule to bar evidence obtained by means of such intrusions. As I made clear in my dissenting opinion in Berger v. New York, 388 U. S. 41, 388 U. S. 76, I continue to believe that this exclusionary rule formulated in Weeks v. United States, 232 U. S. 383, rests on the "supervisory power" of this Court over other federal courts and is not rooted in the Fourth Amendment. See Wolf v. Colorado, concurring opinion, 338 U. S. 338 U.S. 25, 338 U. S. 39, at 40. See also Mapp v. Ohio, concurring opinion, 367 U. S. 367 U.S. 643, 367 U. S. 661-666. This rule has caused the Court to refuse to accept evidence where there has been such an intrusion regardless of whether there has been a search or seizure in violation of the Fourth Amendment. As this Court said in Lopez v. United States, 373 U. S. 427, 373 U. S. 438-439

"The Court has in the past sustained instances of 'electronic eavesdropping' against constitutional challenge when devices have been used to enable government agents to overhear conversations which would have been beyond the reach of the human ear [citing

Page 389 U. S. 370

Olmstead and Goldman]. It has been insisted only that the electronic device not be planted by an unlawful physical invasion of a constitutionally protected area. Silverman v. United States."

To support its new interpretation of the Fourth Amendment, which, in effect, amounts to a rewriting of the language, the Court's opinion concludes that "the underpinnings of Olmstead and Goldman have been. ... eroded by our subsequent decisions.. . ." But the only cases cited as accomplishing this "eroding" are Silverman v. United States, 365 U. S. 505, and Warden v. Hayden, 387 U. S. 294. Neither of these cases "eroded" Olmstead or Goldman. Silverman is an interesting choice, since there the Court expressly refused to reexamine the rationale of Olmstead or Goldman although such a reexamination was strenuously urged upon the Court by the petitioners' counsel. Also, it is significant that, in Silverman, as the Court described it, "the eavesdropping was accomplished by means of an unauthorized physical penetration into the premises occupied by the petitioners," 365 U.S. at 365 U. S. 509, thus calling into play the supervisory exclusionary rule of evidence. As I have pointed out above, where there is an unauthorized intrusion, this Court has rejected admission of evidence obtained regardless of whether there has been an unconstitutional search and seizure. The majority's decision here relies heavily on the statement in the opinion that the Court "need not pause to consider whether or not there was a technical trespass under the local property law relating to party walls." (At 365 U. S. 511.) Yet this statement should not becloud the fact that, time and again, the opinion emphasizes that there has been an unauthorized intrusion:

"For a fair reading of the record in this case shows that the eavesdropping was accomplished by means of an unauthorized physical penetration into the premises occupied by the petitioners."

(At 365 U. S. 509, emphasis added.) "Eavesdropping

Page 389 U. S. 371

accomplished by means of such a physical intrusion is beyond the pale of even those decisions.. . ." (At 365 U. S. 509, emphasis added.) "Here. .. the officers overheard the petitioners' conversations only by usurping part of the petitioners' house or office.. . ." (At 365 U. S. 511, emphasis added.) "[D]ecision here. .. is based upon the reality of an actual intrusion.. . ." (At 365 U. S. 512, emphasis added.) "We find no occasion to reexamine Goldman here, but we decline to go beyond it, by even a fraction of an inch." (At 365 U. S. 512, emphasis added.) As if this were not enough, Justices Clark and Whittaker concurred with the following statement:

"In view of the determination by the majority that the unauthorized physical penetration into petitioners' premises constituted sufficient trespass to remove this case from the coverage of earlier decisions, we feel obliged to join in the Court's opinion."

(At 365 U. S. 513, emphasis added.) As I made clear in my dissent in Berger, the Court in Silverman held the evidence should be excluded by virtue of the exclusionary rule, and "I would not have agreed with the Court's opinion in Silverman. .. had I thought that the result depended on finding a violation of the Fourth Amendment.. . ." 388 U.S. at 388 U. S. 79-80. In light of this and the fact that the Court expressly refused to reexamine Olmstead and Goldman, I cannot read Silverman as overturning the interpretation stated very plainly in Olmstead and followed in Goldman that eavesdropping is not covered by the Fourth Amendment.

The other "eroding" case cited in the Court's opinion is Warden v. Hayden, 387 U. S. 294. It appears that this case is cited for the proposition that the Fourth Amendment applies to "intangibles," such as conversation, and the following ambiguous statement is quoted from the opinion: "The premise that property interests control the right of the Government to search and seize has been discredited." 387 U.S. at 387 U. S. 304. But far from being concerned

Page 389 U. S. 372

with eavesdropping, Warden v. Hayden upholds the seizure of clothes, certainly tangibles by any definition. The discussion of property interests was involved only with the common law rule that the right to seize property depended upon proof of a superior property interest.

Thus, I think that, although the Court attempts to convey the impression that, for some reason, today Olmstead and Goldman are no longer good law, it must face up to the fact that these cases have never been overruled, or even "eroded." It is the Court's opinions in this case and Berger which, for the first time since 1791, when the Fourth Amendment was adopted, have declared that eavesdropping is subject to Fourth Amendment restrictions and that conversations can be "seized."* I must align myself with all those judges who up to this year have never been able to impute such a meaning to the words of the Amendment.

Page 389 U. S. 373

Since I see no way in which the words of the Fourth Amendment can be construed to apply to eavesdropping, that closes the matter for me. In interpreting the Bill of Rights, I willingly go as far as a liberal construction of the language takes me, but I simply cannot in good conscience give a meaning to words which they have never before been thought to have and which they certainly do not have in common ordinary usage. I will not distort the words of the Amendment in order to "keep the Constitution up to date" or "to bring it into harmony with the times." It was never meant that this Court have such power, which, in effect, would make us a continuously functioning constitutional convention.

With this decision the Court has completed, I hope, its rewriting of the Fourth Amendment, which started only recently when the Court began referring incessantly to the Fourth Amendment not so much as a law against unreasonable searches and seizures as one to protect an individual's privacy. By clever word juggling, the Court finds it plausible to argue that language aimed specifically at searches and seizures of things that can be searched and seized may, to protect privacy, be applied to eavesdropped evidence of conversations that can neither be searched nor seized. Few things happen to an individual that do not affect his privacy in one way or another. Thus, by arbitrarily substituting the Court's language, designed to protect privacy, for the Constitution's language, designed to protect against unreasonable searches and seizures, the Court has made the Fourth Amendment its vehicle for holding all laws violative of the Constitution which offend the Court's broadest concept of privacy. As I said in Griswold v. Connecticut, 381 U. S. 479,

"The Court talks about a constitutional 'right of privacy' as though there is some constitutional provision or provisions forbidding any law ever to be passed which might abridge the 'privacy'

Page 389 U. S. 374

of individuals. But there is not."

(Dissenting opinion, at 381 U. S. 508.) I made clear in that dissent my fear of the dangers involved when this Court uses the "broad, abstract and ambiguous concept" of "privacy" as a "comprehensive substitute for the Fourth Amendment's guarantee against unreasonable searches and seizures.' (See generally dissenting opinion at 381 U. S. 507-527.)

---

*The first paragraph of my Brother HARLAN's concurring opinion is susceptible of the interpretation, although probably not intended, that this Court "has long held" eavesdropping to be a violation of the Fourth Amendment and therefore "presumptively unreasonable in the absence of a search warrant." There is no reference to any long line of cases, but simply a citation to Silverman, and several cases following it, to establish this historical proposition. In the first place, as I have indicated in this opinion, I do not read Silverman as holding any such thing, and, in the second place, Silverman was decided in 1961. Thus, whatever it held, it cannot be said it "has [been] long held." I think my Brother HARLAN recognizes this later in his opinion when he admits that the Court must now overrule Olmstead and Goldman. In having to overrule these cases in order to establish the holding the Court adopts today, it becomes clear that the Court is promulgating new doctrine instead of merely following what it "has long held." This is emphasized by my Brother HARLAN's claim that it is "bad physics" to adhere to Goldman. Such an assertion simply illustrates the propensity of some members of the Court to rely on their limited understanding of modern scientific subjects in order to fit the Constitution to the times and give its language a meaning that it will not tolerate.

The Fourth Amendment protects privacy only to the extent that it prohibits unreasonable searches and seizures of "persons, houses, papers, and effects." No general right is created by the Amendment so as to give this Court the unlimited power to hold unconstitutional everything which affects privacy. Certainly the Framers, well acquainted as they were with the excesses of governmental power, did not intend to grant this Court such omnipotent lawmaking authority as that. The history of governments proves that it is dangerous to freedom to repose such powers in courts.

For these reasons, I respectfully dissent.

Retrieved from:

https://supreme.justia.com/cases/federal/us/389/347/case.html

As we can see from this case and others we will review, it is particularly important to consider the legal ramifications of cybercrime. With surveillance and reconnaissance in the digital world, there are enforceable laws that can be used to protect victims of related crimes.

SUMMARY

In sum, this chapter was written to open your eyes to the amount of ways in which information could be collected to conduct surveillance of a target. The digital footprint you leave everyday (you can't see it but it is there) could be enormous based on how much you interact in the digital realm.

Unfortunately, we cannot isolate ourselves from living and doing so carefully and with due diligence will keep us safe; however, the method of attack and the growing landscape expanding the attack vector puts everyone at risk. By practicing safe security practices such as being aware of your surroundings, being careful about leaving or losing devices or other personal information, and checking to see if your systems are free and clear of malware are all good ways to be safe.

Information gathering will take place; however, it's up to us to limit the amount of information that can be gathered. Stalkers gather information on targets, government agencies collect information on the public, their adversaries, and military targets, and corporations gather information on their competition – it is undeniable that this practice will not stop.

CHAPTER 3

Social Engineering

SOCIAL ENGINEERING

Security is built on the foundation of trust. You can secure your identity, computer, or access to your home, but you do give this information and access to those you trust. As an example, you hold the door for someone because you practice chivalry. Your kindness just thwarted the electronic badge system used to ensure that unauthorized users do not enter a facility. Attackers, hackers, and stalkers all hope that you let your guard down for this exact reason so that they can gain access to a trusted location. The main reason social engineering takes place is because it is easier to gain access to a trusted source by simply manipulating someone who can give you access instead of breaking in through technological means. This is the basic foundation of social engineering.

There are many definitions of social engineering. As we just discussed, manipulating a human control in order to gain unauthorized access is one of them. Another could be using a human to provide needed information to gain access to trusted resources. When considering technology specifically, it can sometimes be defined as malware used to trick a user into providing trusted data. In all of these examples, manipulation and trickery are key words used to define the basic underlying principles of social engineering.

In relation to information gathering, social engineering can be used to gain technical data such as passwords, physical and logical access to resources, and many other pieces of information that could be used to conduct a larger attack. Another example is that you trick someone through simple conversation to produce answers you need. For example, I place a call to you from a spoofed phone number that appears to you to be from a trusted source. I then tell you things that relate to you, us, or our conversation so that I can gain your trust. By asking specific questions and getting answers, I may be able to ascertain information from you needed to do another task, such as gather your account information to get into a personal website or bank account. This can then be leveraged into the digital world by exploiting the gathered information.

Am I Being Spied On?

In regard to social engineering, it's possible that you have been manipulated at points through your entire life and do not know that it happened to you. For example, someone you trusted could have gotten a phone number from you without your knowledge. Likely because you left the information out in the open and did not know it was being stolen. You could have been tricked on the playground at school in second grade. While growing up you may have manipulated your parents for information. It's very likely you yourself may be good at manipulating people for your own gain.

That being said, in regard to digital surveillance and reconnaissance, when considering your target, you may need to perform social engineering to gain access to trusted resources in hopes to attack your target directly or to gain more information about the target. Another example of a social engineering attack to gain information would be dialing a target by phone in hopes to trick them to release information you request. This provides cover and secrecy for the attack because you cannot see them. They can mask their voice as well as spoof their number providing even more cover for evasion purposes.

In Figure 3.1, we can see why social engineering is an attack that many malicious attackers find so desirable. Here, we have a corporate network accessible over the Internet and protected by a firewall. For an attacker to gain access to the trusted secure data, they would need to construct an attack over the Internet that may or may not penetrate the firewall. Firewalls are built to secure not only a network but also to log and alert the administrator to malicious activity such as a penetration attempt. An attacker would have to be very careful not to get caught. An easier path would be for them to place a call to a user inside the protected network and get information from them directly.

It is much easier to place a call and get the data directly. Most times, these attacks go completely undetected giving the attacker the ability to covertly gather information without getting caught. Many times, these attacks go undetected until the data is used in a way that draws attention, such as using a bank account number gathered over a phone or a social security number that is used to empty a bank account.

Scam Example

Gathering information leads to attacks. In the technical world, this can be done in many ways. An attacker can dial you on the phone. They can put software on your machine when you visit a website. They can e-mail you a uniform resource locator that looks similar to a legitimate website and take you to a malware site. Technically, anything is possible although the attack is the same – it is based on trickery.

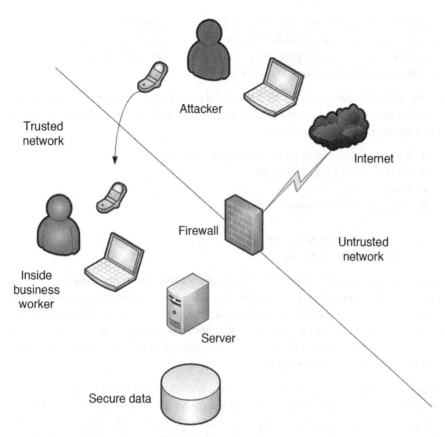

FIGURE 3.1 Protected and unprotected networks.

Phone scams take place everyday, thousands of times per day. An example of a phone scam used to gather information is as follows:

Attacker – *"[dials victim from a spoofed familiar phone number] Hello, we are running a survey today via the US Government to take a poll of who you may vote for in the next election, do you have a few minutes to answer a few brief questions?"*

Victim – *"[as victim looks up spoofed number and considers it safe] Yes, thank you. I have a lot of concerns about this nation's financial health and would love to answer a few questions."*

Attacker – *"Good, thank you. Before we continue, I would like to verify your identify for our records so we do not get duplicate responses that may taint the survey, can you verify the last 4 digits of your social security number?"*

Victim – *"Absolutely, it is 3928."*

Attacker – *"Thank you, and can you verify your current address?"*

For brevity's sake, we will stop here and review the issue with this transaction. While an attacker may be able to get some of this information online, in the cases where they cannot, you just provided them with what they may need to get into your personal bank account online.

In the following list, you will find the most common questions asked of someone that may be enough for a helpdesk to change the password for a personal account, such as a bank account.

- Last four digits of your social security number
- Your mother's maiden name
- Favorite pet
- One of the schools you attended
- Your zip code
- The street you grew-up on
- The last car you owned

What you can see from this list of examples is that there are data points that can be easily gathered without much effort. With this information, an attacker can easily thwart the controls put in place to protect your bank account and commit fraud. This is also a prime example of a social engineering attack. This is an information gathering technique that can be used very easily to gain access into your trusted resources.

Attackers can use this type of surveillance technique to build on information needed for a larger attack as well. For example, an attacker may be planning a larger attack and needs this type of information to track you. They may be interested in your patterns and habits, and finding out what your interests are and so on can all be obtained through casual conversation. This attack does not need to happen remotely either. Information can be obtained by overhearing someone talk at a party, an event, or a tradeshow.

How to Gather Information

As we discussed, social engineering is a way to gain unauthorized access to trusted resources. This intrusive behavior is done to penetrate defenses to gain information, data, or line of sight into a target. It's done to commit fraud or espionage. Another common attack is to gain access to commit identity theft. Other malicious behavior could be to cause harm or disruption. That being said, it is important that you learn to protect yourself and your interests carefully.

Before we learn how to mitigate this threat, we should discuss how attackers use social engineering to gather data. Earlier, we used a brief example of how an attacker may use a simple phone call to trick someone into providing trusted information. In the following examples, we will look at other ways attackers violate the sanctity of trust through social engineering and trickery.

Dumpster Diving

Dumpster diving is an interesting attack that produces an immense amount of information on an organization, firm, individual, or entity. You can learn a lot about a person or company from the trash they throw away. It's also extremely surprising how much personal and private information is thrown out for those to find. Generally, most dumpsters and trash receptacles do not come with locks, this would make it nearly impossible for regular trash collection services to dispose of it properly; however, other solutions are available to secure your trash.

For one, you should never throw anything out that has information contained on or within it without considering how it can be used against you. If you throw out bill statements and other paperwork that contain private information, you should consider burning it, shredding it, or any other way of destroying the information it contains.

In Figure 3.2, we can see an attacker digging through trash to locate useful information.

Cross cut shredders were created because it was proven that a bag of shredded paper that came from a normal straight cut shredder could be reassembled given enough time. Kevin Mitnick, president of Defensive Thinking, was originally a hacker who once caught, turned to good. He claims that

FIGURE 3.2 Dumpster diving.

social engineering is one of the biggest links and dumpster diving is a huge hole in security controls. A large amount of data can be assembled quickly by using paper shredders and enough time that can be used against you and/or an entity.

We tend to throw things away without considering the impact of them being recovered. We gleefully assume that because we put something in the trash, it is dutifully removed from the premise and destroyed adequately. If only that was the truth. Your trash can easily be recovered and used to gather information. Disk drives can be thrown out, and even if you attempted to destroy them, can be reassembled and/or fixed enough to get data off them. There are many secrets that can be uncovered in the trash; you should consider that next time before you throw something away.

Shoulder Surfing

Shoulder surfing is a seemingly harmless attack; however, your phone password, system password, or private and personal information can be gleaned quickly and easily most times without your knowledge. The quickest and the easiest surveillance attack that can be performed is glancing over someone's shoulder without their knowledge.

Unfortunately, this happens more than we would like to admit or believe. Many times just out of curiosity, people eavesdrop on others to learn about them, gather information, or just to be a part of what may be going on with them. Sitting on an airplane may be the best example of harmless curiosity that turns into an annoyance for a victim. You are sitting so close together that even if you wanted to maintain privacy, it's nearly impossible.

Eavesdropping seems harmless; however, it is also an information gathering technique used by those conducting surveillance and reconnaissance. In its worst form, shoulder surfing is useful in supplying an attacker with a lot of valuable information.

Sitting in a café, sitting in your cubicle at work, or on a bus or train in transit, you may be immersed in your work, reading, typing on your laptop or mobile, and not noticing someone looking inconspicuously at what you are doing, recording this information and transferring it for later use. They could even be secretly recording you without your knowledge. In Figure 3.3, we can see an example of someone shoulder surfing a victim without their knowledge, memorizing their keystrokes for a password, validating websites they are using, or reading the names and salaries off a payroll document.

A far more devastating attack comes from gleaning information that can be used quickly such as a bank ATM pin number. In Figure 3.4, we can see someone covering their pin as they enter it; however, someone who is trained well

FIGURE 3.3 Shoulder surfing.

to match your finger position to the 9 digits found on most commonly used keypads can quickly memorize what you typed. If they are successful at gaining access to your wallet or pocketbook without your knowledge, they can use this information as part of a larger attack.

Although banks are generally protected by cameras, someone trying to conceal their identity may not get caught. These pieces of information can be used for online access as well, as many re-use passwords and pins, gaining access to one may provide access to them all.

So, we have covered physical attacks that transcribe into digital attacks or larger attacks through simply spying on others, what they do and how they do. Sometimes what you don't know can hurt you. Take note that logical attacks that follow the same social engineering behaviors, but are leveraged in digital form.

Phishing

Phishing is an attack that falls along the lines of social engineering – thus, evading controls through trust. How is it done specifically? Well, if we followed

FIGURE 3.4 Pin theft.

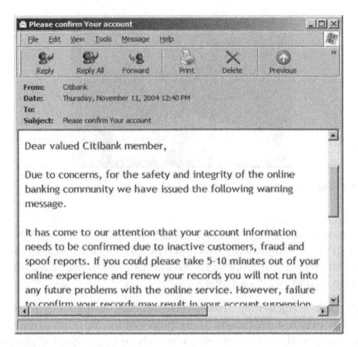

FIGURE 3.5 Phishing example.

the attacks listed earlier in this chapter where a phone call was used to glean valuable information, we can follow the same premise here within the digital domain. In recent years, phishing attacks have grown in number significantly. Why, you ask? Because of the simplicity in launching them and the successful information they produce.

In Figure 3.5, we can see an example of a common phishing scam. An attacker creates a form e-mail that looks professional. They may even make a copy of one used with company letterhead, images pulled from the site, and official-looking logos. They craft this e-mail with a malicious call to action and a payload. The call to action is based on fear.

The attacker tries to get you to produce information by clicking on a link (for example) that takes you to a malicious and fraudulent website. This website too contains official-looking information and, at times, is an exact replica of the site that you believe is legitimate. You may even enter your credentials that are recorded and used on the real site you thought you were visiting. This is one example of how phishing can be used to gather information.

Social Engineering Toolkit
The social engineering toolkit (SET), which is an open-source tool that comes by default with the Kali Linux distribution, can be found when you launch

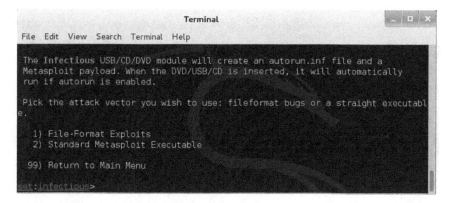

FIGURE 3.6 Using the SET with Backtrack to generate a payload.

Backtrack. As mentioned in a previous chapter, this tool can be used to gather information, conduct social engineering attacks, such as to send spoofed phishing texts to a victim's phone, as well as many other attacks such as spear-phishing attacks.

Spear-phishing requires an attacker to know a little bit about you. This is where phishing evolves into a larger attack. As we discussed earlier with our explanation and example on phishing, we use a "dear bank member" salutation, whereas when spear-phishing, the attack is less generalized and more formalized. For example, if your name is Sally, the e-mail or text sent may directly call you out by name. This allows the attacker to pinpoint who they are attacking and use information gathered from other sources to trick you into trusting them as a legitimate source.

When using the toolkit, you will also find the infectious media generator as one of the options. This tool allows you to create a payload that can be placed and then activated off removable media such as a USB drive or a DVD-ROM. In Figure 3.6, we can see an example of using a SET to generate a payload.

As you continue to make selections (such as creating a fire-format exploit) as seen in Figure 3.7, we can see just how easy it is to create an attack with Backtrack.

As you walk through the tool, you can then select specific attack formats such as creating an Adobe PDF file, a Zip file, and other formats. In Figure 3.8, we can see an example of the many different files you can create to launch your exploit.

In Figure 3.9, we can see how the payload can be deployed. In this example, we use a Windows meterpreter shell that can allow for a backdoor attack by using Internet protocol addresses and ports to make connections.

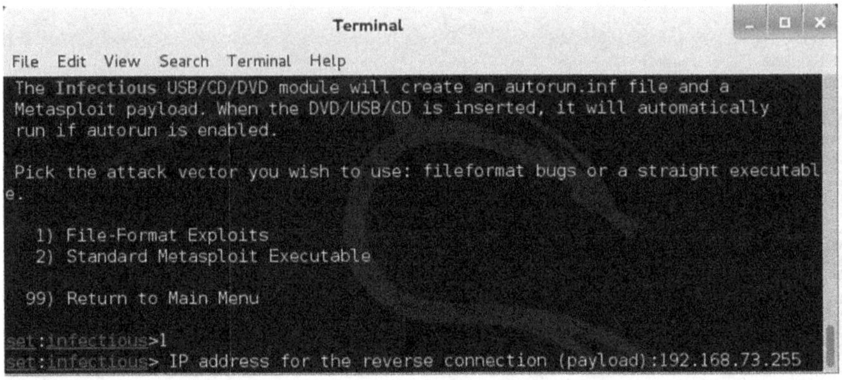

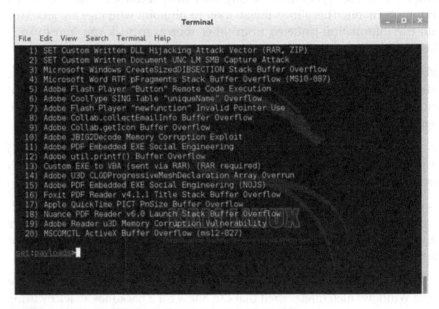

FIGURE 3.7 Using the SET with Backtrack to create an attack.

Finally, in Figure 3.10, we generate the payload by configuring the payload listener. You can find a copy of your payload in the path provided off the root directory. Once you have configured the attack, created the payload, and are ready, you can plot your attack.

This is but one example of one feature found on one tool of the hundreds of examples that can be provided when using this toolkit and Backtrack. Mass mailer attacks, SMS spoofing, and other attacks (such as those launched against wireless systems) can all be conducted with the SET. All of these (and more) are attacks that can be conducted with one toolkit. Other tools such as Maltego

FIGURE 3.8 Using the SET with Backtrack to launch your exploit.

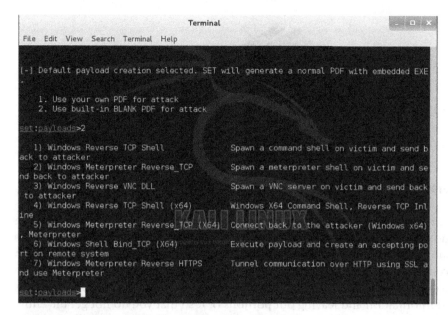

FIGURE 3.9 Using the SET with Backtrack to deploy the payload.

that we covered in Chapter 2 can be used in conjunction with the SET to build profiles on individuals and organizations you wish to attack.

The SET tool can also be downloaded online separately from Kali Linux and Backtrack by going to:

https://www.trustedsec.com/downloads/social-engineer-toolkit/

Bugging and Recording

Last on our list of attacks is bugging and recording. This is mentioned within social engineering because you can be manipulated in ways to incriminate

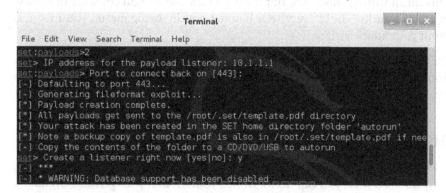

FIGURE 3.10 Using the SET with Backtrack to generate the payload by configuring the payload listener.

FIGURE 3.11 Surveillance tool.

yourself easily by an attacker. You can give up valuable information. Although not directly mapped to social engineering, many times your conversations are recorded and can be used against you. An attacker can easily conduct a conversation and record your voice, manipulate the audio, and use your own words to incriminate you. This is often done by the news media, taking clips of information and leaving out portions of it so that you do not get the entire context of what is being said to socially engineer a response from the public.

At a personal level, surveillance can be conducted to gather information on a victim. This can be done quickly and with ease using tools such as the one seen in Figure 3.11, where we can see an audio surveillance listening device that can be fitted with a SIM card and hidden without someone knowing it. It can be configured to call you directly (so you can listen) when someone triggers it above a certain decibel level.

We will drill down into this type of surveillance activity in upcoming chapters; however, for now, know that you can be manipulated by someone bugging, recording, tracking, and tricking you that all evade your trust and privacy. Does this mean trust no-one? No, but it does mean you should consider that these types of attacks "could" very well happen and by being aware, you may just limit your attack surface.

As you have learned, there are many ways to gather information without ever touching a computer terminal, a keyboard, or a device. There are many ways to conduct an attack or gather information without the need for a computer.

MITIGATION OF SOCIAL ENGINEERING

As we progress through this book, we learn not only how attacks are used and why but also what you can do to protect yourself and your privacy. Digital reconnaissance and surveillance techniques vary widely and, as you are learning, can be used in conjunction with other attacks to conduct larger more malicious attacks. In this section, we will highlight some of the most important things you should consider to limit your exposure to social engineering attacks, discuss privacy, and cover case law that shows how social engineering attacks are treated in the United States.

Mitigate Attack

It is difficult to mitigate social engineering attacks. It strikes at the very root of how human beings treat each other; defending against social engineering means that you need to be aware of your surroundings, who you are dealing with, and no, you cannot trust everyone you meet or know. In fact, social engineers scout for this overly trusting, gullible behavior in people in order to know who to manipulate and how to manipulate them. They are considered easy targets.

If you could openly trust everyone and everything, there would be no reason for security. No locks on doors and banks would leave their vaults wide open. The fact is that historically, this is not the case and security grows as an industry exponentially every year. As we have covered, there is a thin line between being overly safe and being paranoid. That does not mean you should not have faith in people and believe that you can trust them; it just means precautions are in order for your benefit and the benefit of your finances, your loved ones, and your safety.

You can remain safe by being aware. Be aware of your surroundings. Who are you talking to, who can be listening?

Are you typing something? Are you being recorded? If you remain aware and vigilant about your own personal security, you will understand how to mitigate social engineering attacks. Do not openly trust those you do not know and think about the actions of those you do.

When at work, take the security policies enforced in your organization seriously. No, do not hold the door open for someone you do not know to let them into your office suite. Yes, it's great manners; however, there have been dozens if not hundreds of penetration attacks conducted by allowing someone into an office suite by simply holding the door for someone to be nice, they do not need to use the biometrics or card reader and you have just been hacked.

Be aware of your actions. Do not allow someone to dig through your trash. Do not allow someone to watch over your shoulder. Shred or burn important papers you decide to trash and do not leave anything for the wolves. Do not sit somewhere with your back facing an open crowd; do not do personal or private work on your laptop or phone, mobile device, or pad if you cannot safeguard it from being overseen.

When you are talking to someone on the phone, be aware of your audience. Could you be on conference? Could the phone be tapped? Can the room you're in be bugged? Don't believe it can happen? Hopefully, by reading this book and others like it, you can start to realize that yes it does happen and it happens often.

When opening e-mails or receiving texts, take the extra time to perform a seconds worth of due diligence. Check the entire e-mail header, review the domain name in which the e-mail was sent, and validate with a phone call to the originator based on a trusted source (not from the e-mail itself) that this was in fact sent on purpose and not a scam.

Do not openly trust. Since this is tough to do, it's no question as to why this is one of the biggest attacks performed today and why it's the most difficult to mitigate. As you can see, there are many ways to mitigate this form of attack but it comes down to not trusting everything you see and hear and trusting everyone you do or do not know. It simply comes down to verifying and validating things and, if possible, ensuring that they are safe.

Information Privacy

Now that we have learned about the many ways that an attacker can socially engineer a situation to gather information and ways to attempt to prevent it, we should briefly discuss the importance of information privacy. If you want something to remain safe, it's best not to talk about it, record it, or write it down.

An old saying, "If you want to keep a secret, never tell anyone."

This is incredibly difficult to do. There are things that we must simply record and write. Since the digital domain grows everyday, it's almost impossible to record it. You're on video camera, your actions are logged, you work on a laptop for 8 h a day ... how do you keep your information private?

To keep your information private, you need to secure it the best way possible. Although this book does not go deep into the realm of encryption, it's mentioned here so that you can further research it if needed. Today, there are literally dozens of encryption methods, algorithms, and security features that attempt to keep your transmissions, data, and privacy encrypted. As encryption grows in strength, so does the ability for hackers to crack it. For example, wireless communications were originally thought to be safe using wired equivalent privacy and it was thwarted. It led the way for Wi-Fi Protected Access (WPA) and Wi-Fi Protected Access II (WPA2). What this means is although you believe encryption can save your privacy, it does not guarantee it.

Reverse Social Engineering

Are there times when you find yourself manipulated and want to counterattack? Should or shouldn't you just try to get out of the situation? Reverse social engineering (RSE) is considered a counterattack to social engineering. An example could be, let's say someone called your place of business and had been asking questions and you immediately knew you were being tricked. What if you played into it and fed false information back? What would happen if you countered the move by getting the authorities involved real time and they conducted a trace of the phone call, manipulating the attacker to stay on the line to close the trace?

For sake of argument, we should disclose here that unless you are a trained professional, you should not counterattack. You do not know the stability of those you are dealing with and you do not want to antagonize them.

LEGAL AND ETHICAL CONCERNS

There are many legal and ethical concerns revolving around social engineering attacks. For one, they are used for tricking good people into divulging useful information to be used against them and/or the entities they work for. One of the most commonly known social engineering attacks took place in the 1990s that allowed Kevin Mitnick to perform an advanced persistence threat against a target.

WEDNESDAY, FEBRUARY 15, 1995 (202) 514-2008

TDD (202) 514-1888

FUGITIVE COMPUTER HACKER ARRESTED

IN NORTH CAROLINA

WASHINGTON, D.C. – FBI agents and the Raleigh-Durham Fugitive Task Force today arrested Kevin Mitnick, a well-known computer hacker and federal fugitive on charges he violated probation, the Department of Justice announced.

The arrest occurred at 1:30 a.m. after an intensive two-week electronic manhunt, which led law enforcement agents to Mitnick's apartment in Raleigh, North Carolina.

Mitnick, 31, was convicted by federal authorities in 1988 in Los Angeles for stealing computer programs and breaking into corporate networks. He received a one-year sentence in that case, and a federal warrant was later issued following Mitnick's violation of probation.

In this most recent incident, Mitnick is alleged to have electronically attacked numerous corporate and communications carriers located in California, Colorado, and North Carolina where he caused damage and stole proprietary information.

Mitnick's capture represents a coordinated effort by law enforcement and private industry, including system administrators and security representatives from companies allegedly attacked by Mitnick. One of these sites, the San Diego Supercomputer Center (SDSC), and Tsutomu Shimomura, a Senior Fellow at SDSC, provided significant assistance to law enforcement personnel during the investigation.

Mitnick also is under investigation by state law enforcement authorities in California and Washington State for separate activities there.

As is typical in such interstate computer cases, many FBI offices, U.S. Attorneys' offices, and other law enforcement agencies have coordinated their efforts. These offices include the FBI's National Computer Crime Squad at the Washington Metropolitan Field Office, as well as FBI and U.S. Attorneys" Offices in Raleigh and Greensboro, North Carolina; San Diego, Los Angeles and San Francisco, California; and Denver, Colorado.

Members of the Raleigh-Durham Task Force which made the arrest included the U.S. Marshals Service, the North Carolina State Bureau of Investigation, and the local sheriffs' offices.

Legal and technical assistance is also being provided by the Criminal Division's Computer Crime Unit in Washington, D.C.

Retrieved from:

http://www.justice.gov/opa/pr/Pre_96/February95/89.txt.html

As we learned, Mitnick was under investigation by state law enforcement and once caught, was held accountable for his acts. This opened the door for legal issues to be better understood by those practicing cyberlaw.

More Legal Issues

In the next example, we discuss the legal (and ethical issues) revolving around world of spying, surveillance, reconnaissance, and cybercrime. In the next case that we will review, we have a potential victim and an attacker disputing charges of cybercrime.

Although the Gioconda Law Group PLLC and Arthur Wesley Kenzie settled the dispute that had been pending before the New York federal district court, involving the misspelled domain name GIOCONDOLAW.COM, there is still a disagreement about the methods used where interception, social engineering, and cybersquatting were involved. In this case, other issues such as reconnaissance tactics, social engineering, and other attacks are mentioned and should be reviewed so that you are aware that these attacks can and will be held accountable in a court of law if you are found guilty.

Plaintiff Gioconda Law Group PLLC alleges cybersquatting, trademark infringement unlawful interception and disclosure of electronic communications, and related state law claims against Defendant Arthur Wesley Kenzie. The Plaintiff filed a partial motion for judgment on the pleadings with respect to Defendant's alleged violation of the Anti-cybersquatting Consumer Protection Act (ACPA).

As an information security researcher, Kenzie believes that he conferred numerous benefits on Plaintiff and on the public by drawing attention to a significant vulnerability. He noted there was no evidence that he gained economic profit from his actions, made any other commercial use of the infringing domain name (IDN), or attempted to sell the IDN back to the Plaintiff.

The reasons listed above are why the court cannot find that Arthur Wesley Kenzie acted in "bad faith intent to profit" (which is a prerequisite to an ACPA violation), therefore denying the motion for judgment on the pleadings of Gioconda Law Group PLLC.

UNITED STATES DISTRICT COURT

SOUTHERN DISTRICT OF NEW YORK

GIOCONDA LAW GROUP PLLC,

Plaintiff,

-against-

ARTHUR WESLEY KENZIE,

Defendant.

12 Civ. 4919 (JPO)

MEMORANDUM AND

ORDER

J. PAUL OETKEN, District Judge:

Plaintiff Gioconda Law Group PLLC alleges cybersquatting, trademark infringement, unlawful interception and disclosure of electronic communications, and related state law claims against Defendant Arthur Wesley Kenzie. Plaintiff has filed a partial motion for judgment on the pleadings with respect to Defendant's alleged violation of the Anticybersquatting Consumer Protection Act (ACPA). For the reasons that follow, Plaintiff's motion is denied.

I Standard of Review

Federal Rule of Civil Procedure 12(c) provides that "[a]fter the pleadings are closed – but early enough not to delay trial – a party may move for judgment on the pleadings." Under Rule 12(c), "a party is entitled to judgment on the pleadings only if it has established that no material issue of fact remains to be resolved and that [it] is entitled to judgment as a matter of law." *Bailey v. Pataki*, No. 08 Civ. 8563, 2010 WL 234995, at *1 (S.D.N.Y. Jan. 19, 2010) (quotation marks and citations omitted). "The standard for granting a Rule 12(c) motion for judgment on the pleadings is identical to that of a Rule 12(b)(6) motion for failure to state a claim." *Patel v. Contemporary Classics of Beverly Hills*, 259 F.3d 123, 126 (2d Cir. 2001) (citations omitted). "In both postures, the district court must accept all allegations in the [non-movant's pleadings] as true and draw all inferences in the non-moving party's favor." *Id.* (citation omitted). As a leading treatise explains:

[A] Rule 12(c) motion is designed to provide a means of disposing of cases when the material facts are not in dispute between the parties and a judgment on the merits can be achieved by focusing on the content of the competing pleadings, exhibits thereto, matters incorporated by reference in the pleadings, whatever is central or integral to the claim for relief or defense, and any facts of which the district court will take judicial notice. The motion for a judgment on the pleadings only has utility when all material allegations of fact are admitted or not controverted in the pleadings and only questions of law remain to be decided by the district court.

5C Charles Alan Wright & Arthur R. Miller, et al., Federal Practice and Procedure, § 1367 (3d ed. 1998) (footnotes omitted); *accord Juster Associates v. City of Rutland, Vt.*, 901 F.2d 266, 269 (2d Cir. 1990). Thus, "[i]n considering motions under Federal Rule 12(c), district courts frequently indicate that a party moving for a judgment on the pleadings impliedly admits the truth of its adversary's allegations and the falsity of its own assertions that have been denied by that adversary." Fed. Prac. & Proc. § 1370. Because "hasty or imprudent use of this summary procedure by the courts violates the policy in favor of ensuring to each litigant a full and fair hearing on the merits of his or her claim or defense," federal courts are "unwilling to grant a motion under Rule 12(c) unless the movant clearly establishes that no material issue of fact remains to be resolved and that he is entitled to judgment as a matter of law." Fed. Prac. & Proc. § 1368. In considering Rule 12(c) motions, district courts may take notice of "the facts alleged in the complaint, documents attached to the complaint as exhibits, and documents incorporated by reference in the complaint." *Piazza v. Florida Union Free Sch. Dist.*, 777 F. Supp. 2d 669, 677 (S.D.N.Y. 2011) (quotation marks and citations omitted).

II Background[1]

A. Facts Taken as True For Purposes of this Motion

Plaintiff is a professional limited liability company duly organized under the laws of the State of New York. It is engaged in the authorized practice of law with a particular focus on brand protection and intellectual property, and has focused significant energies in recent years on combating piracy and counterfeiting on the Internet. Defendant is a sophisticated computer programmer with multiple advanced degrees in computer programming, including a Bachelor of Technology Degree in Computer Systems from BCiT with majors in Network Security Administration and Network Security Development. His principal place of business is in Vancouver, British Columbia, Canada, and he identifies himself on LinkedIn as a "Cyber Security and Mobile App Developer."

Plaintiff's general allegation is that "[t]his case presents the Court with an identifiable Internet domain name cybersquatter and hacker who has intentionally intercepted e-mail traffic intended for the plaintiff, a New York law firm which focuses on anti-counterfeiting and brand protection litigation." Defendant denies this particular allegation. Plaintiff alleges that "[d]omain name typosquatting is a well-known form of cybersquatting that is usually used to capture web traffic when an Internet user accidentally misspells a legitimate domain name in his web browser." Defendant agrees that this description is "essentially correct," though he emphasizes that the purpose of typosquatting can be either malevolent or benevolent.

Defendant registered GIOCONDOLAW.COM ("the Infringing Domain Name" or "IDN") and explains that he did so "within the broader context of his responsible, good faith information security research into a significant e-mail vulnerability that is not currently well understood."

---

[1] *This background reflects application of the Rule 12(c) standard of review to the pleadings.*

Defendant registered the IDN from third-party Internet Registrar GoDaddy, Inc. on January 19, 2012. When Plaintiff discovered Defendant's conduct, it sent e-mails to the addresses info@giocondolaw.com and joseph.gioconda@giocondolaw.com; it used a registered receipt e-mail system to conclude that both of these e-mail messages were received by active mailboxes capable of receiving misdirected messages. When he registered the IDN, Defendant used the Domains by Proxy domain privacy service, "but not for the alleged sole purpose of concealing his identity." Defendant then intentionally redirected Internet web browser users to Plaintiff's legitimate web site – the Gioconda Law Group PLLC Website" – but not for the alleged sole purpose of avoiding detection." After Plaintiff contacted Defendant and informed him of the Complaint, Defendant replied, in part, as follows:

> As for starting litigation against me, I am not clear what has caused you to assume that I would not be amenable to resolving your concerns and claims. My intentions with the domain name you are concerned about are transparent and above board, as they are part of my research into an email vulnerability that I have been studying since September 2011 and which I have been publicly discussing on my website. ... I am doing nothing to cause any injury to your firm or any trademark rights you have, and would be glad to discuss those issues with you. ... I have no objections to facilitating a transfer of the domain to you."[2]

Defendant has also registered the following eight domain names: rnastercard.com, rndonalds.com, nevvscorp.com, rncafee.com, rnacvvorld.com, rnonster.com, pcvvorld.com, andqvvest.com.[3] He admits that he directed that each of these Internet domain names redirect to the legitimate third parties' websites, "but not for the alleged sole purpose of avoiding detection."

Defendant was recently the subject of a Uniform Domain Name Resolution Policy ("UDRP") proceeding in a Complaint brought by Complainant Lockheed Martin, for the Defendant's similar registration of the confusingly similar Internet domain names LockheedMarton.com and LockheedMartun.com. The UDRP Panel concluded that "no one could provide unsolicited service or subject a third party to a research programme without its consent and by using typos variation of a protected trademark."[4] The Panel added that "[i]t is obvious that the Respondent intentionally created the possibility to receive the so-called 'Black Hole' correspondence of the Complainant. ... the Respondent itself [] created the alleged vulnerability of the Complainant's trademark, and his purpose was to offer services to the Complainant, looking for financial gain."

On April 17, 2012, Plaintiff received from the U.S. Patent and Trademark Office a registration number, indicating federal registration of the Service Mark "Gioconda Law Group PLLC" in International Class 45 for "providing information in the field of intellectual property."

Plaintiff's First Claim for Relief invokes the ACPA and alleges that "[t]he Infringing Domain Name that the Defendant has registered is virtually identifiable to, and/or confusingly similar to the Gioconda Law Service Mark, which was distinctive at the time that the Defendant registered the Infringing Domain Name." Defendant admits this allegation. Plaintiff further alleges that

---

[2] This text is taken from Pl. Ex. 3, the authenticity of which is acknowledged in Defendant's Answer at 12.
[3] Plaintiff alleges, though Defendant denies, that these domain names are meant to mimic, respectively, mastercard.com, mcdonalds.com, newscorp.com, mcafee.com, macworld.com, monster.com, and pcworld.com, qwest.com.
[4] This opinion is incorporated by reference in the Complaint and, in any event, would be a proper subject of judicial notice under Federal Rule of Evidence 201.

"[t]he Defendant registered and is using the Infringing Domain Name with bad-faith intent to profit from the Gioconda Law Service Mark," that "[t]he Defendant has no bona fide noncommercial or fair use of the Gioconda Law Service Mark," and that "on information and belief, the Defendant intends to divert consumers away from the Plaintiff for unlawful commercial gain, by creating a likelihood of confusion as to the source, sponsorship, affiliation or endorsement of the Infringing Domain Name, and related e-mail addresses." Defendant expressly denies these allegations. Plaintiff adds, and Defendant denies, that Defendant's "acts have caused and will continue to cause irreparable injury to the Plaintiff and to the public."

In his Answer, Defendant asserts a number of "Defenses." Many of these "Defenses" are not affirmative defenses in the technical sense of the term. Rather, they are statements of fact that deny specific allegations set forth in the Complaint (all of which are denied by Defendant in the responsive section of his Answer). Defendant also elaborates on the nature of his conduct. He states that his actions "have been only for good faith, non-commercial, legitimate purposes, solely for the Plaintiff's benefit," adding that "[t]here have been no actual damages suffered by the Plaintiff, nor any damages intended, and only good faith, non-commercial, legitimate purposes intended by the Defendant." He explains that his good faith purposes "have been for information security research into an e-mail vulnerability the Defendant initially called the 'Black Hole' e-mail vulnerability. ... there appears to be very little awareness of this vulnerability, which is the primary reason the Defendant was motivated to undertake this research." Because "this vulnerability can be almost trivially exploited to covertly and passively undertake reconnaissance on a vulnerable organization," it opens entities like Plaintiff to "social engineering attacks." The benefit Defendant confers, in his view, is that he prevents a malevolent entity from exploiting this gap in e-mail security and informs companies about the need for protection by posting about how to defend against the vulnerability on his blog. Defendant states that if he does receive e-mails intended for an entity like Plaintiff, he "ensure[s] that the contents of vulnerable e-mails [are] never read or disclosed to third parties." He adds that he has "arranged for vulnerable domain names to be transferred to subject organizations so that they could take their own responsibility for protecting themselves." Defendant states that he concealed his activities so that other members of the public would not learn which companies are vulnerable and then target those entities.[5]

III Discussion

A. Legal Standard

"To successfully assert a claim under the ACPA, a plaintiff must demonstrate that (1) its marks were distinctive at the time the domain name was registered; (2) the infringing domain names complained of are identical to or confusingly similar to plaintiff's mark; and (3) the infringer has a bad faith intent to profit from that mark." *Webadviso v. Bank of Am. Corp.*, 448 F. App'x 95, 97 (2d Cir. 2011) (citing 15 U.S.C. § 1125(d)(1)(a)). Because Defendant expressly admits Plaintiff's allegation that the IDN registered by Defendant "is virtually identical to, and/or confusingly similar to the Gioconda Law Service Mark, which was distinctive at the time that the Defendant registered the Infringing Domain Name," the only issue is whether Defendant acted with "bad faith intent to profit from that mark."

---

[5] *In the "Defenses" section of his Answer, Defendant critiques the UDRP, invokes Professor Orin Kerr's scholarship on the Wiretap Act to illuminate the nature of his security research agenda, raises a number of defenses and arguments applicable to Plaintiff's unlawful interception and disclosure of electronic communications claim, and critiques American privacy law. He also raises a Rule 11 "defense" and a "defense" based on the New York Rules of Professional Conduct, which the Court interprets as motions for sanctions and denies as meritless.*

15 U.S.C. § 1125(d)(1)(A)(i).[6] At this stage in the case, accepting as true only facts admitted by Defendant in the pleadings, a determination of "bad faith intent to profit" raises important questions about the ACPA's scope. An overview of the statute's purpose and the doctrine designed to implement it reveals the potential difficulties of applying traditional bad faith analysis to a case like this one.

1 The ACPA

"Cybersquatting involves the registration as domain names of well-known trademarks by non-trademark holders who then try to sell the names back to the trademark owners. Since domain name registrars do not check to see whether a domain name request is related to existing trademarks, it has been simple and inexpensive for any person to register as domain names the marks of established companies. This prevents use of the domain name by the mark owners, who not infrequently have been willing to pay 'ransom' in order to get 'their names' back." *Sporty's Farm L.L.C. v. Sportsman's Mkt., Inc.*, 202 F.3d 489, 493 (2d Cir. 2000). In other words, "[c]ybersquatting is the Internet version of a land grab. Cybersquatters register well-known brand names as Internet domain names in order to force the rightful owners of the marks to pay for the right to engage in electronic commerce under their own name." *Interstellar Starship Services, Ltd. v. Epix, Inc.*, 304 F.3d 936, 946 (9th Cir. 2002). This practice "is considered wrong because a person can reap windfall profits by laying claim to a domain name that he has no legitimate interest in or relationship to." *Harrods Ltd. v. Sixty Internet Domain Names*, 302 F.3d 214, 238 (4th Cir. 2002).

Alarmed by a rising wave of cybersquatting in the 1990s, and concerned by the apparent inadequacy of preexisting laws, Congress enacted the ACPA in 1999. This law was passed "to protect consumers and holders of distinctive trademarks from 'cybersquatting.' *Webadviso*, 448 F. App'x at 97 (quoting *Sporty's Farm*, 202 F.3d at 493). As the Senate Judiciary Committee explained, the ACPA was designed to "protect consumers and American businesses, to promote the growth of online commerce, and to provide clarity in the law for trademark owners by prohibiting the bad-faith and abusive registration of distinctive marks as Internet domain names with the intent to profit from the goodwill associated with such marks. ... ." S. Rep. No. 106-140, at 4 (1999); *see also id.* at 9 (noting that the law aims squarely at "intent to trade on the goodwill of another's mark").

2 The ACPA's Requirement of "Bad Faith Intent to Profit"

A key element of any ACPA violation is "bad faith intent to profit." *See Interstellar Starship Services*, 304 F.3d at 946 ("A finding of 'bad faith' is an essential prerequisite to finding an ACPA violation."). The Second Circuit has "expressly note[d] that 'bad faith intent to profit' are terms of art in the ACPA and hence should not necessarily be equated with 'bad faith' in other contexts." *Sporty's*

---

[6] *Because these allegations are admitted in the Answer, the Court does not conduct an independent examination of whether they would withstand more careful scrutiny. It is settled, however, that registrations with the U.S. Patent Trademark Office can support a finding that a mark is distinctive and famous. See TCPIP Holding Co. v. Haar Communications Inc., No. 99 Civ. 1825, 2004 WL 1620950, at *5 (S.D.N.Y. July 19, 2004). By the same token, registration of domain names that constitute slight variations of a registered mark, including domain names that differ by one or two characters, often satisfies the requirement of confusing similarity. See, e.g., Sporty's Farm L.L.C. v. Sportsman's Mkt., Inc., 202 F.3d 489, 497-98 (2d Cir. 2000); TCPIP Holding, 2004 WL 1620950, at *5; Spear, Leeds, & Kellogg v. Rosado, 122 F. Supp. 2d 403, 406 (S.D.N.Y. 2000) aff'd sub nom. Spear, Leeds & Kellogg v. Rosado, 242 F.3d 368 (2d Cir. 2000). Indeed, courts have expressly held that the ACPA covers typosquatting. See, e.g., S. Co. v. Dauben Inc., 324 F. App'x 309, 312 n.2 (5th Cir. 2009); Green v. Fornario, 486 F.3d 100, 103 n.5 (3d Cir. 2007); Shields v. Zuccarini, 254 F.3d 476, 483 (3d Cir. 2001) ("Zuccarini argues that registering domain names that are intentional misspellings of distinctive or famous names (or 'typosquatting,' his term for this kind of conduct) is not actionable under the ACPA. ... This argument ignores the plain language of the statute and its stated purpose.. . ."); Verizon California Inc. v. Navigation Catalyst Sys., Inc., 568 F. Supp. 2d 1088, 1094 (C.D. Cal. 2008).*

Farm, 202 F.3d at 499 n.13. To that end, the ACPA enumerates nine factors relevant to the bad faith inquiry:

(I) the trademark or other intellectual property rights of the person, if any, in the domain name;

(II) the extent to which the domain name consists of the legal name of the person or a name that is otherwise commonly used to identify that person;

(III) the person's prior use, if any, of the domain name in connection with the bona fide offering of any goods or services;

(IV) the person's bona fide noncommercial or fair use of the mark in a site accessible under the domain name;

(V) the person's intent to divert consumers from the mark owner's online location to a site accessible under the domain name that could harm the goodwill represented by the mark, either for commercial gain or with the intent to tarnish or disparage the mark, by creating a likelihood of confusion as to the source, sponsorship, affiliation, or endorsement of the site;

(VI) the person's offer to transfer, sell, or otherwise assign the domain name to the mark owner or any third party for financial gain without having used, or having an intent to use, the domain name in the bona fide offering of any goods or services, or the person's prior conduct indicating a pattern of such conduct;

(VII) the person's provision of material and misleading false contact information when applying for the registration of the domain name, the person's intentional failure to maintain accurate contact information, or the person's prior conduct indicating a pattern of such conduct;

(VIII) the person's registration or acquisition of multiple domain names which the person knows are identical or confusingly similar to marks of others that are distinctive at the time of registration of such domain names, or dilutive of famous marks of others that are famous at the time of registration of such domain names, without regard to the goods or services of the parties; and

(IX) the extent to which the mark incorporated in the person's domain name registration is or is not distinctive and famous within the meaning of subsection (c) of this section.

15 U.S.C. § 1125(d)(1)(B)(i). A leading treatise on the law of trademarks notes that "[t]he first four factors suggest circumstances tending to indicate an absence of bad faith intent to profit from the goodwill of the mark, the next four tend to indicate that such bad faith does exist and the last factor points in either direction, depending on the degree of distinctiveness and fame of the mark." 4 McCarthy on Trademarks and Unfair Competition § 25:78 (4th ed.).

3 The Scope of "Bad Faith Intent to Profit"

Because the ACPA has the potential to encompass a broad array of online conduct, courts are "reluctant to interpret the ACPA's liability provisions in an overly aggressive manner." *Virtual Works, Inc. v. Volkswagen of Am., Inc.*, 238 F.3d 264, 270 (4th Cir. 2001); *see also id.* ("The ACPA was not enacted to put an end to the sale of all domain names.").[7] This is particularly true of the bad faith intent to profit requirement.

[7] *This point also extends to some of the indicia of bad faith, which are just that: indicia. See, e.g., 4 McCarthy on Trademarks and Unfair Competition § 25:78 (4th ed.) ("[C]aution must be exercised, for the mere registration of multiple domain names for resale does not per se mark one as a cybersquatter. One may be in a justifiable business of reserving many domain names. For example, in one case defendant legitimately registered thousands of domain names for resale as 'vanity' e-mail addresses which consisted of common surnames, names of hobbies, careers, pets, sports interests, and music. The fact that some of these resembled prominent trademarks did not make defendant a cybersquatter." (footnote omitted)).*

Courts have struggled to define the boundaries of "bad faith intent to profit" because the ACPA expressly allows consideration of factors *beyond* the nine enumerated indicia. *See* 15 U.S.C. § 1125(d)(1)(B)(i) (noting that courts "may consider factors such as, but not limited to" the nine enumerated indicia). Courts have taken that grant of discretion to heart. *See Sporty's Farm*, 202 F.3d at 498 ("[W]e are not limited to considering just the listed factors when making our determination of whether the statutory criterion has been met. The factors are, instead, expressly described as indicia that 'may' be considered along with other facts."). As the Fourth Circuit has explained, "[w]e need not. .. march through the nine factors seriatim because the ACPA itself notes that use of the listed criteria is permissive." *Virtual Works*, 238 F.3d at 269.

Thus, a number of courts – including the Second Circuit – have departed from strict adherence to the statutory indicia and relied expressly on a more case-specific approach to bad faith. *See Sporty's Farm*, 202 F.3d at 499 ("The most important grounds for our holding that Sporty's Farm acted with a bad faith intent. .. are the *unique circumstances of this case*, which do not fit neatly into the specific factors enumerated by Congress but may nevertheless be considered under the statute." (emphasis added)); *see also Interstellar Starship Services*, 304 F.3d at 946-47. As part of that analysis, courts look to a defendant's whole course of conduct, including conduct during ACPA litigation. *See, e.g., Storey v. Cello Holdings, L.L.C.*, 347 F.3d 370, 385 (2d Cir. 2003) ("Congress intended the cybersquatting statute to make rights to a domain-name registration contingent on ongoing conduct rather than to make them fixed at the time of registration.").

This "unique circumstances" approach to the bad faith inquiry is logical and in accord with the plain language of the ACPA. *See Sporty's Farm*, 202 F.3d at 499. It allows courts to secure the ACPA's core purpose even where a defendant has sidestepped the nine indicia. *See Newport News Holdings Corp. v. Virtual City Vision, Inc.*, 650 F.3d 423, 436 (4th Cir. 2011) *cert. denied*, 132 S. Ct. 575 (2011) (refusing to apply a "formalistic approach" to application of the enumerated factors and noting that doing so could "undermine the purpose of the ACPA, which seeks to prevent the bad-faith and abusive registration of distinctive marks as Internet domain names with the intent to profit from the goodwill associated with such marks" (quotation marks and citations omitted)). But this "unique circumstances" analysis must be undertaken with caution. As the House Report explained with respect to the nine indicia, "[t]hese factors are designed to balance the property interests of trademark owners with the legitimate interests of Internet users and others who seek to make lawful uses of others' marks, including for purposes such as comparative advertising, comment, criticism, parody, news reporting, fair use, etc." Quoted in 2 Federal Unfair Competition: Lanham Act 43(a) Appendix H. Given that the ACPA reflects a careful assessment of the dangers presented by unduly broad application of the ACPA's liability provisions, courts are well served to tread carefully in identifying additional "unique circumstances" that reveal bad faith intent to profit.[8]

That inquiry must be guided by an assessment of how close a defendant's conduct falls to the ACPA's heartland. The clearest case for a finding of bad faith intent to profit typically arises when a defendant "register[s] a domain name of an established entity in bad faith" and then "offer[s] to sell the domain name to the entity at an exorbitant price." *Target Adver., Inc. v. Miller*, No. 01 Civ. 7614, 2002 WL 999280, at *10 (S.D.N.Y. May 15, 2002); *see also TCPIP Holding*, 2004 WL 1620950, at *5 (finding bad faith intent to profit where a defendant "submitted no less than three offers to sell back various packages of domain names (the vast majority of which [he] acquired after he received Plaintiff's cease and desist letter) for exorbitant demands of approximately half a

---

[8] *The ACPA expressly creates another safe haven from unduly broad application of the bad faith inquiry by providing that "[b]ad faith intent. .. shall not be found in any case in which the court determines that the person believed and had reasonable grounds to believe that the use of the domain name was a fair use or otherwise lawful." 15 U.S.C. § 1125(d)(1)(B)(ii).*

million dollars"). Thus, courts have identified two "quintessential example[s]" of bad faith: where a defendant "purchases a domain name very similar to the trademark and then offers to sell the name to the trademark owner at an extortionate price," and where a defendant "intend[s] to profit by diverting customers from the website of the trademark owner to the defendant's own website, where those consumers would purchase the defendant's products or services instead of the trademark owner's." *Utah Lighthouse Ministry v. Found. for Apologetic Info. & Research*, 527 F.3d 1045, 1058 (10th Cir. 2008); *see also Ford Motor Co. v. Catalanotte*, 342 F.3d 543, 549 (6th Cir. 2003) ("Registering a famous trademark as a domain name and then offering it for sale to the trademark owner is exactly the wrong Congress intended to remedy when it passed the ACPA."). In those situations, the case for bad faith is at its peak.

In cases that vary too much from the specific evil contemplated by the ACPA, however, some courts have looked skeptically at claims of bad faith. On occasion, they have even refused to find an ACPA violation. As the Sixth Circuit noted in a 2004 decision:

> The paradigmatic harm that the ACPA was enacted to eradicate – the practice of cy-bersquatters registering several hundred domain names in an effort to sell them to the legitimate owners of the mark – is simply not present in any of [Defendant's] actions. In its report on the ACPA, the Senate Judiciary Committee distilled the crucial elements of bad faith to mean an "intent to trade on the goodwill of another's mark." S.Rep. No. 106-140, at 9. *See also Ford Motor Co. v. Catalanotte*, 342 F.3d 543, 549 (6th Cir. 2003) ("Registering a famous trademark as a domain name and then offering it for sale to the trademark owner is exactly the wrong Congress intended to remedy when it passed the ACPA."). There is no evidence that this was [Defendant's] intention when she registered the Lucas Nursery domain name and created her web site. It would therefore stretch the ACPA beyond the letter of the law and Congress's intention to declare anything to the contrary.

Lucas Nursery & Landscaping, Inc. v. Grosse, 359 F.3d 806, 810 (6th Cir. 2004).

One year later, the Fifth Circuit adopted a similar approach while assessing an ACPA claim aimed at a site designed to "inform potential customers about a negative experience with [a] company." *TMI, Inc. v. Maxwell*, 368 F.3d 433, 439 (5th Cir. 2004). That court examined the nine statutory indicia of bad faith, then added that "we particularly note that Maxwell's conduct is not the kind of harm that ACPA was designed to prevent." *Id.* at 440; *see also id.* (noting the absence of bad faith after "analyzing the statutory factors and ACPA's purpose").

The Eleventh Circuit joined this line of precedent in 2009. Emphasizing that "'bad faith' is not enough" and that "[a] defendant is liable only where a plaintiff can establish that the defendant had a 'bad faith *intent to profit*,'" the Eleventh Circuit saw no bad faith intent to profit under the ACPA where a plaintiff accused the defendant "not of a design to sell a domain name for profit but of a refusal to sell one." *S. Grouts & Mortars, Inc. v. 3M Co.*, 575 F.3d 1235, 1246-47 (11th Cir. 2009) (citations omitted) (emphasis in original). It added that:

> The Senate Report accompanying the Anticybersquatting Consumer Protection Act bol-sters our understanding that a "bad faith intent to profit" is the essence of the wrong that the Act seeks to combat. That report defines cybersquatters as those who: (1) regis-ter well-known brand names as Internet domain names in order *to extract payment* from the rightful owners of the marks; (2) register wellknown marks as domain names and warehouse those marks *with the hope of selling them* to the highest bidder; (3) register well-known marks *to prey on* consumer confusion by misusing the domain name to

divert customers from the mark owner's site to the cybersquatter's own site; (4) target distinctive marks *to defraud consumers,* including to engage in counterfeiting activities. The report says nothing about those who hold onto a domain name to prevent a competitor from using it.

Id. at 1246 (quotation marks and citations omitted) (emphasis in original).

Although cases arising from attempts to suppress consumer commentary sites have afforded many of the occasions for courts to warn against over-broad application of the ACPA's bad faith inquiry, *see Lamparello v. Falwell,* 420 F.3d 309, 320 (4th Cir. 2005); *Mayflower Transit, L.L.C. v. Prince,* 314 F. Supp. 2d 362, 370-71 (D.N.J. 2004), the core insight of these rulings remains generally applicable in other ACPA contexts, *see Lewittes v. Cohen,* No. 03 Civ. 189, 2004 WL 1171261, at *8 (S.D.N.Y. May 26, 2004) ("[O]n the whole, the allegations set forth in the Complaint do not even remotely suggest that defendants perpetrated the core activities that threaten to result in the paradigmatic harm that the ACPA was enacted to eradicate." (quotation marks and citations omitted)).

Of course, this logic does not entail the conclusion that an extortionate demand, or use of the improperly registered domain name in commerce, is always necessary to a violation of the ACPA, which sets out a more expansive list of indicia that may support a finding of bad faith intent to profit. *See, e.g., Bosley Med. Inst., Inc. v. Kremer,* 403 F.3d 672, 681 (9th Cir. 2005) ("[O]ne of the nine factors listed in the statute that courts must consider is the registrant's "bona fide noncommercial or fair use of the mark in a site accessible under the domain name." This factor would be meaningless if the statute exempted all noncommercial uses of a trademark within a domain name. We try to avoid, where possible, an interpretation of a statute that renders any part of it superfluous and does not give effect to all of the words used by Congress." (quotation marks and citations omitted)); *Hamptons Locations, Inc. v. Rubens,* 640 F. Supp. 2d 208, 221 (E.D.N.Y. 2009) ("[A] review of the case law from other jurisdictions indicates that the prevailing view is that the ACPA does not require a plaintiff to demonstrate defendant's use in commerce."). Rather, these cases caution that where extortionate demands and use in commerce are absent, and the other indicia do not point toward bad faith, courts must step carefully in relying on a more general bad faith inquiry to conclude that a defendant violated the ACPA.

B. Application

The only issue at this stage in the litigation is whether, on the pleadings and materials of which the Court may take notice, Plaintiff can prove enough facts to show that Defendant acted with "bad faith intent to profit" as that term is defined by the ACPA. Where Defendant has not admitted a fact and Plaintiff has not proven it through other means, the Court reads the absence of that information in the light most favorable to Defendant. In other words, for purposes of this motion for judgment on the pleadings, the Court will not assume that facts favor Plaintiff where there is simply no undisputed evidence about those facts based on the pleadings.

This analysis begins with the nine indicia of "bad faith intent to profit" enumerated in the statute. *See* 15 U.S.C. § 1125(d)(1)(B)(i). There is no evidence either way concerning Defendant's rights in the domain name (Factor I), whether the domain name consists of a name that is commonly used to identify Defendant (Factor II), Defendant's prior use of the domain name in connection with the bona fide offering of any goods or services (Factor III), Defendant's bona fide noncommercial or fair use of the mark in a site accessible under the domain name (Factor IV), and Defendant's provision of true contact information (Factor VII). The absence of any admitted facts in the pleadings regarding five of the nine indicia strongly augurs at this preliminary stage against a finding of bad faith intent to profit.

Factor V fits the facts awkwardly. On the one hand, Defendant *did* intend to demonstrate his ability to lure consumers away from Plaintiff's site and e-mail system, thereby exposing a potential vulnerability in Plaintiff's online presence. On the other hand, there is no evidence that Plaintiff did so in a manner that could harm the goodwill represented by Plaintiff's mark or otherwise damage the mark. To the contrary, anybody who visited the site maintained by Defendant would be immediately redirected to Plaintiff's site. It is possible that the diversion of e-mails from Plaintiff to Defendant has caused problems of a sort that would trigger the application of Factor V, particularly if Defendant replied to those e-mails in a manner that could have damaged Plaintiff's mark, but at this stage in the case there are not enough facts for the Court to conclude that Factor V indicates bad faith intent to profit.

Factor VI cuts against a finding of bad faith intent to profit, at least for purposes of this Rule 12(c) motion. Although it appears that Defendant has not, and does not intend to, use the IDN in the bona fide offering of any goods or services, there is no evidence in the pleadings that Defendant has offered to sell the disputed IDN to a third party. Nor is there evidence that he has attempted to sell it to Plaintiff, the mark owner. Rather, in his e-mail to Plaintiff, Defendant said that "I am doing nothing to cause any injury to your firm or any trademark rights you have, and would be glad to discuss those issues with you. ... I have no objections to facilitating a transfer of the domain to you." The Court's analysis of this factor might look different on a summary judgment record, depending on the evidence presented, but at this stage in the litigation it cuts in Defendant's favor.[9]

Factors VIII and IX support a finding of bad faith. Defendant admits that he has acquired at least eight other domain names with an intent similar to that which motivated his acquisition of the IDN. He also admits that Plaintiff's mark is famous and distinctive.

Reviewing the factors set forth in the ACPA, the Court concludes that only two of the nine weigh in favor of a finding of bad faith intent to profit. That is not enough. Accordingly, Plaintiff can prevail on this motion for judgment on the pleadings only if a more general assessment of the "unique circumstances" of this case demands a finding of bad faith. *See Sporty's Farm*, 202 F.3d at 499. That inquiry is guided by the analysis set forth above, which concluded that courts stand on firmer ground when they use "unique circumstances" analysis to enforce the core purpose of the ACPA, and that courts are more skeptical of such reasoning when a defendant's conduct falls outside the heartland of conduct contemplated by Congress in promulgating the ACPA.

Defendant alleges that his conduct is part of a security-focused research agenda into a vulnerability in e-mail systems of the sort used by Plaintiff. He states that he undertook this activity for good faith, noncommercial reasons, and that he has arranged for domain names and e-mails to be transferred back to other entities situated similarly to Plaintiff.[10] As an information security researcher, he believes that he is conferring numerous benefits on Plaintiff and on the public by drawing attention to a significant vulnerability. He notes that there is no evidence that he has gained economic profit from his actions, made any other commercial use of the IDN, or attempted to sell the IDN back to Plaintiff. Although a UDRP panel has condemned his behavior, it does not follow that Defendant's conduct therefore runs afoul of the ACPA.

The ACPA is designed principally for cases where a defendant either forces a markholder to purchase a domain name at an extortionate price or diverts customers from the markholder's website to the defendant's own website. *See Utah Lighthouse*, 527 F.3d at 1058. On the factual record

---

[9] *For example, Defendant denies in his Answer that a proposed transfer of the IDN to Plaintiff contemplates any payment by Plaintiff, a fact taken as true for purposes of this motion.*
[10] *Defendant does not explain why he has not yet transferred the IDN to Plaintiff. That bare omission, however, does not suffice to justify a finding of commercial intent or extortionate demands.*

that the Court must adopt for purposes of a Rule 12(c) motion, this case is not within those "core" ACPA scenarios. Defendant's alleged ideological, scholarly, and personal motives for squatting on the IDN, while perhaps idiosyncratic, do not fall within the sphere of conduct targeted by the ACPA's bad faith requirement. If anything, given that Defendant aims both to influence Plaintiff's behavior and shape public understanding of what he perceives to be an important vulnerability in cyber security systems, this case arguably falls closer to cases involving parody and consumer complaint sites designed to draw public attention to various social, political, or economic issues. *Cf. Lamparello*, 420 F.3d at 320; *TMI*, 368 F.3d at 439.

The ACPA is not an all-purpose tool designed to allow the holders of distinctive marks the opportunity to acquire any domain name confusingly similar to their marks. *See Schmidheiny v. Weber*, 319 F.3d 581, 582 (3d Cir. 2003) ("The purpose of the [ACPA] is to curtail *one form of cybersquatting –* the act of registering someone else's name as a domain name for the purpose of demanding remuneration from the person in exchange for the domain name." (quotation marks and citations omitted) (emphasis added)). The requirement of bad faith intent to profit imposes an important limit that cabins the statute's scope and ensures that the ACPA targets only the specific evils that Congress sought to prevent. This third element thus leaves untouched conduct that might annoy or frustrate mark holders, but that Congress shielded from liability by enumerating indicia of the sort of bad faith it had in mind. *See, e.g., S. Grouts & Mortars*, 575 F.3d at 1246-47; *TMI*, 368 F.3d at 439; *Lewittes*, 2004 WL 1171261, at *8. Thus, on the facts taken as true for purposes of this motion, the Court cannot find that Defendant acted with the "bad faith intent to profit" prerequisite to an ACPA violation.

IV Conclusion
For the foregoing reasons, Plaintiff's motion for judgment on the pleadings is DENIED. The Clerk of Court is directed to close the motion at Dkt. No. 26.

SO ORDERED.

Dated: New York, New York

April 23, 2012

Retrieved from:

http://law.justia.com/cases/federal/district-courts/new-york/nysdce/1:2012cv04919/398351/47

As we have learned from this case, the court of law will review specifics of the attack and make decisions based on the fact and evidence. In this case, we can also see that some attacks also lead to others depending on the target and what is to be gained. Remember, all crimes have the potential to leave a trace and these digital bread crumbs could be used as evidence in the court of law.

SUMMARY

As we have learned, the use of social engineering seems to trick or fool a trusted party into providing information to get around security controls that are in place to protect data, privacy, and so on. Social engineering can be used for tricking an individual into divulging information about information systems, networks, or other operational details that may contribute to the reconnaissance phase of a cyberwarfare attack. They can be used to influence an individual to bypass physical security controls, granting an attacker access to a physical facility where he or she might undertake offensive cyberwarfare operations. They can also be used to convince an individual to disable electronic security controls, such as bypassing a firewall or allowing a Virtual Private Network (VPN) connection from an unauthorized source.

Tricking an insider into installing software on a computer within the organization's protected network, secretly creates a back door that allows the attacker to gain access to the network.

These types of threats often leverage social engineering as part of a comprehensive attack on an organization or a person. Attackers may use these techniques to perform intelligence gathering, influence user behavior to facilitate an attack, or cover their tracks after an attack takes place.

CHAPTER 4

Mobile Phone Tracking

PHONE TRACKING

In the previous chapters, we covered how dangerous a phone can be, whether it be an old public switched telephone network (PSTN)-based phone or a new digital mobile phone. Although the chapter focuses on mobile phone attacks, it should be considered that just about every device with network connectivity these days can place you at the scene of the crime. It is also very disturbing that with mobile technology, devices are carried with you and not left in your home, placing you directly at the scene of the crime. That being said, your movements are being tracked and recorded and you should be aware.

When you are tracked with your mobile phone (or device), you are essentially giving your exact geographical position away to your telecommunications carrier. The radio towers that you use to obtain and maintain your signal are also used as reference to your exact position. Global positioning system (GPS) technology also aids in placing your location that we will discuss further in this chapter. Carriers can also track movement based on technology called location-based services (LBS). This technology can be used to assess specific coordinates as you use your mobile device. We will also discuss this technology further within this chapter.

In this chapter, we will also address how the US government is taking advantage of an outdated law on privacy and technology to track Americans. If you use your mobile phone, it will register its position with cell towers every few minutes, whether the phone is being used or not – and mobile carriers are retaining location data on their customers. As the government collects and uses this data, a record of your movements is being kept without your permission or knowledge.

Before we get into the specifics of how mobile devices are used for surveillance and reconnaissance, gathering information, tracking, and misuse, we must first understand the specifics of mobile technology and which types are most commonly used.

Mobile Phones

Since this book is about digital surveillance and reconnaissance and how to defend against attacks, we will not get too deep into the architecture of the devices themselves; however, we will cover the specific phone types and the specific attacks leveraged against them. It's important to know how they are used to track your movements and how they can be used against you.

Why is spying on mobile devices so important to understand? If you are a victim, let's look at what could be at risk:

- View SMS messages – Applications can record all SMS activities from the target phone. All sent and received messages can be recorded in an online account, even if the messages are deleted from the mobile phone.
- View call logs – Each call can also be logged by the application that will also be uploaded to your online account. This provides the caller and the time of call.
- Track GPS location – GPS tracking can provide your location at any time and be recorded to an online account.
- View photos and videos – All photos and videos taken can be recorded and sent to an online account.
- View contact list – A contact list of phone numbers can also be viewed and sent to an online account.
- Website URL logs – This can show that websites are visited and sent to an online account.
- Call recording – Your calls and messages can be recorded and retrieved and sent to an online account.

As you can see, with a simple application, your privacy is no longer secure and everything you say and do as well as where you go can be tracked.

Apple iPhone

Proprietary hardware, tightly controlled software, and a tightly controlled application store called iTunes makes up the Apple iPhone experience. This does not mean that you're safe from surveillance, far from it. It just means that it's less likely that malware will immediately infect your phone and allow you to be tracked.

As seen in Figure 4.1, the Apple iPhone is a handheld computer/phone that allows you to collaborate via applications, texts, e-mails, and phone conversations.

Tools and software (specifically Cydia) can be used to "crack" into the phone so that you can use it more freely; however, by doing so you open yourself up to more possibilities of being infected with malware. Regardless, many applications are available to load on the phone to track others beyond how they are already tracked via location services and tower acknowledgments.

FIGURE 4.1 Apple iPhone.

Any mobile device can be tracked in numerous ways; however, those that are more commonly used (such as the iPhone) have more applications developed for that specific purpose.

Google Android

Open Source driven, Linux-based Google Android phones are widely used next to Apple iPhones. Having multiple hardware vendors and a variety of operating system types, Android is extremely flexible. Google Play allows for application download and installation and many applications are available for tracking and reconnaissance of the phone.

As seen in Figure 4.2, the Android platform is highly customizable and if you are a professional at mobile phone development, many options exist to place a tracker on the phone without your knowledge. Also subject to malware attacks, the mobile devices produced can be easily tracked.

Android (as well as iPhone) allows for an attacker to download applications from their application stores to use for tracking such as Spying Droid that covertly allows an attacker to use one Android device as a camera unit and another Android device to view live audio and video from the first device. If conveniently placed, it could provide covert surveillance for information gathering. Another app that can be downloaded is called Couple Tracker, which allows an attacker to spy on another person such as a spouse for the purposes to get their location, see their messages, or to verify their location.

FIGURE 4.2 Google Android.

Just like iPhone, you may need a higher privilege level on your phone that may require you to root it or use super user access.

Windows Phone

Similar to Apple and Google, Microsoft has a mobile device called Windows Phone. The marketplace is where you can get applications for your mobile device and among them are the same spy applications that are available for all other major phones. It is susceptible to the exact same surveillance risks associated with Apple and Google devices.

As seen in Figure 4.3, Windows Phone is Microsoft's line of mobile phone devices. Recently, Microsoft acquired Nokia who is the primary maker of Windows Phone hardware and the merger has rebranded these companies as Microsoft Mobile.

Although it's a different company, it's the same exact set of risks, problems, and concerns associated around privacy.

Blackberry

An older mobile device type that has significantly evolved is the Blackberry from RIM Research in Motion (RIM). As seen in Figure 4.4, the Blackberry offers many of the same features as does Apple, Google, and Microsoft; however, the Blackberry has predominately been used in the business world of enterprise

FIGURE 4.3 Windows phone.

FIGURE 4.4 Blackberry phone.

companies and generally married to a Blackberry Enterprise Server that allows for advanced functionality. In the past few years, the Blackberry has undergone significant graphic user interface changes and enhancements in order to stay competitive with the other device offerings from Apple and others.

That being said, it too can be hacked and tracked just as easily as the others. Other devices exist and can be tracked as well. Following the same concepts as we covered, anything that works by providing an Internet protocol (IP) address, an assigned phone number, or an e-mail account can be easily tracked. Other device types and software packages allow for tracking ability. GPS devices, pads, and other mobile devices can be tracked. Microsoft's XBOX game console can not only be tracked but also can be viewed by an attacker inside your home through its sensor.

You should be concerned because what we just briefly covered is only half of the story. The other half is how the mobile devices you use give your location away without any application usage of any kind.

Phone Tracking

Phone tracking can be simply done by carrying your phone with you as you go about your day. So how is it done?

When a mobile device connects to a cell network, it registers with the carrier. When your mobile device is powered on, it emits a signal that is picked up by multiples towers. Your phone is triangulated by its distance from multiple towers. GPS receivers provide tracking information as well. Wireless signals can also be tracked in the same fashion. Shockingly, even if it is powered off, it may still be susceptible. In foreign countries, viruses (malware) have been distributed to keep the phone on enough to produce a signal for tracking.

As seen in Figure 4.5, when you carry your phone, it emits a signal that works with carrier cell towers and/or GPS satellites that provide you with the service, but also keep a log of your location within the system. This means that government agencies, law enforcement, or, if hacked, an attacker can also verify and validate your position at any time.

There are ways to also review these logs to trace your movements. So, if you travel from New York to New Jersey five days a week, your path to and from could be articulated from review logs at tower locations along that path. Of course, this is all deemed to be legal unless misused, but as we have learned, the government is collecting data to track the behaviors of suspected terrorists. They do this by collecting all data and then filtering on what they need. What seems to evade our private lives is that the information is in fact captured and available. It could be misused if an opportunity arose.

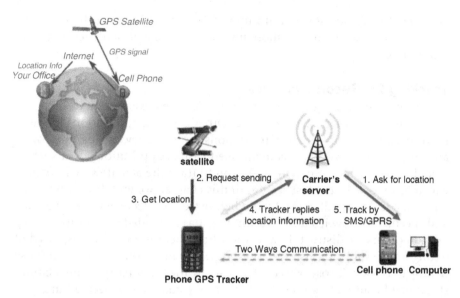

FIGURE 4.5 Example of phone tracking.

The Patriot Act

Immediately after the September 11 attack on the United States, the Congress passed the Patriot Act. The Patriot Act is an expansion of the surveillance laws allowing the government to spy on its citizens while reducing the oversight required to do so, fairly and with accountability. The bill was sent to vote without time for review, debate, or discussion and the threat of attacks was used to create a fear vote.

This act was created to expand surveillance laws by the government so that it had expanded record searching ability held by third parties (such as a telecom carrier), secret searches of private property without the need to inform the owner, and other expanded intelligence searches.

MALICIOUS TRACKING

As we can see, tracking can be done without your knowledge and at many different levels. Your mobile device although helpful and a needed fixture of your person, is now a mobile tracking device that can be used to find you, evade your privacy at any moment, or as a tracking tool for another malicious user, stalker, attacker, or threat.

Before we get into how to track a phone by example, it's important to understand the first steps to protecting yourself as much as possible. First, do not leave your phone unattended. Do not leave it unlocked. Do not leave it without a password. Use a strong password scheme. Make sure nobody is shoulder surfing you when you use your phone. In Chapter 8, mitigation strategies will be covered in detail; however, it's important to note here that by practicing simple security steps, such as those just listed, you significantly lessen the attack surface.

Tracking for Reconnaissance

Not all phone tracking is bad. Many applications exist today to help you find a lost or a stolen mobile device. Other tracking applications are used to keep tabs on children you are responsible for. They can be (and often are) used for wrongdoing. As mentioned earlier, applications exist such as Google Play's Track Your Wife by Tryfon to track the activities of a possible cheating spouse. In the last section of this chapter, we will discuss how this type of action is handled legally but before we do, let's review why it's done and specifically how it's done. Technology has expanded our ability to keep tabs on others we distrust. In a relationship where someone is suspected of wrongdoing, applications exist to validate this malicious behavior to those willing to track it. Those who track it, usually the other party in the relationship, may be able to ascertain facts that they had first suspected but could not prove.

A tool that can be (and is commonly) used is one that does not appear on the phone itself, if hidden, is MSpy. This is a great tracking tool that once installed will basically give you all of the information about anyone's mobile device use. Although this tool can be used for good, such as tracking a child by phone, it can also be used to secretly spy on someone without their knowledge. Some of the features included with MSpy are:

- Dashboard tool – Overall dashboard used to get an overview of the tracked mobile device.
- Listen to incoming and outgoing calls – This will allow you not only see incoming and outgoing calls but also listen to them.
- Run SMS tracking – You can track all incoming and outgoing SMS text messages.
- Read e-mails – This tool allows you to see and read all e-mails associated with the target device.
- Perform GPS tracking of the target device – You can track the device via GPS and show locations via map.
- View photos and videos – You can view all digital media photos and videos on the target device.
- See calendar events and contacts – You can see all calendar-related information on the target device.
- Read chat and Instant Message (IM) conversations – Review all chat and IM conversations specifically via text.
- Track browsing history – You can see what websites are being used on the target device.

- View Skype messages – You can track all Skype data on the target device.
- Monitor WhatsApp messages – You can track all WhatsApp data on the target device.

You can also track Facebook data, Viber data, and much more. That being said, privacy is no longer an option to the unsuspecting user of the mobile device with a product such as MSpy configured on it. Again, it can also be used for good security reasons when you give a child a mobile device so that you can track usage as well as location. You can also restrict data being used on the target device with MSpy. However, when considering the surveillance that can be done especially without your knowledge, it could be worrisome to someone who does not know it is there.

As seen in Figure 4.6, we will begin to prepare an Apple iPhone for surveillance tracking. First, if you are attempting to track someone, you need to get access to the device itself. To do so, you can get access to the device in many ways. In this example, we will look at what many users are attempting to do as of the writing of this book – track a significant other or spouse. First, get the device and if password protected, you can either crack the password, of shoulder surf to get it. There are many ways to easily bypass the password of an Apple iPhone. Once you do, you need to jailbreak the phone. Jailbreaking a phone is done

FIGURE 4.6 Jailbreaking and prepping a phone for tracking.

FIGURE 4.7 Installing and configuring MSpy.

quickly and easily, by downloading a package online that matches your iOS version, you can run the program, the phone will reboot and you will have full access to the phone.

Once Cydia is installed (part of Jailbreaking routine), you can open it and install and configure MSpy. You will have to purchase a subscription for their services and they can assist you with this process as well. Once you get a subscription and register the phone, you can configure the phone for tracking.

As seen in Figure 4.7, installing MSpy is quick and painless. You download the package and it installs on your phone and will drop an icon on the iPhone home page; however, it will be removed once the registration is completed.

Once MSpy is installed and you have registered the service, you can begin to customize the mobile device so that it can be tracked. As seen in Figure 4.8, you will need to turn on location services for MSpy in order to physically track the phone.

As seen in Figure 4.9, you can then hide the applications on the home page so whoever is using the device does not see the applications installed. This can be helpful so that once the victim uses the phone, they will not know that MSpy is installed on it. There is no visual existence so it can be hidden and kept secret.

FIGURE 4.8 Turning on location services.

Once MSpy is installed, you can access the online dashboard to view all of the data and track the phone.

As seen in Figure 4.10, the dashboard can be used to view call logs (shown), text messages, listen to calls, track movement, and so on. As you can see, whoever is being tracked will not know and all interactions on the phone will be logged for viewing by the attacker.

It is possible that a very savvy user who knows how to go into the settings of their phone and nose around may stumble across the changes; however, it can be easily played off as an update from Apple as an example. It's rare that these changes are found unless the person who you are victimizing really know what to look for.

Lastly, for safety and possible furthering the attacks on the target phone, you should change the default password.

As seen in Figure 4.11, it is recommended that you change the default Apple password of Alpine as well as the default mobile password on your device. This

FIGURE 4.9 Hiding the applications on the system.

can be done, obviously, for security, but it can also be used to configure an Secure Shell (SSH) tool for remote access into the device from your personal computer.

You can of course use other tools such as StealthGenie and Mobile Spy instead of MSpy; however, MSpy provided the features needed for this example.

FIGURE 4.10 Using the MSpy dashboard.

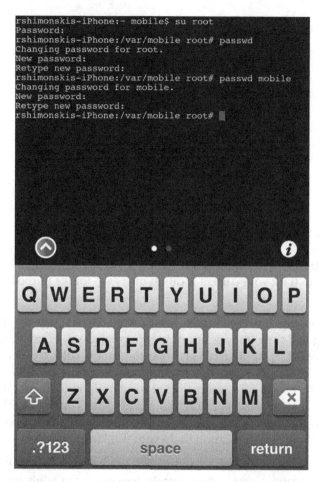

FIGURE 4.11 Changing the passwords on your mobile phone.

As well, although we configure this tool for use on an Apple iPhone, you can also configure this system on mobile devices from Microsoft, Google, and others; however, the services are the same and the outcome is similar, your privacy has been evaded.

Location-Based Services

Embedded within the mobile phones technology is a service called LBS. This allows location data to assist with providing enhanced functionality. The applications are developed so that you do not have to input information; the information required is simply queried from your device.

With Apple's iPhone, the operating system (iOS) is deployed with a standard LBS functionality that allows applications to be able to track where you are and

"Maps" Would Like to Use
Your Current Location
Don't Allow
OK

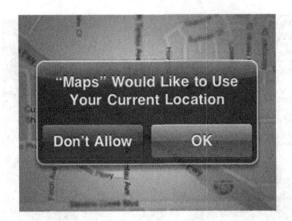

FIGURE 4.12 Using LBS.

report it to the querying application. For example, as seen in Figure 4.12, Maps can use LBS to track your current location on a map for the purpose of making your life easier.

This functionality, however, evades your privacy. When you use LBS, Apple is collecting real-time tracking location information on its user base. Privacy policies released by Apple have said that the data is collected anonymously; however, how do you know this to be factual? And even if it was collected anonymously, it could be reconstructed to identify individuals. Why would Apple need this information in the first place? When considering the amount of questions that come up about protecting privacy, it's easier to opt out and simply not allow any application to do your thinking for you.

Other legal concerns are raised about LBS. For example, with LBS enabled, someone who gains access to your mobile device could possibly use the device to trace back your steps through your social media accounts that also use this technology to "map" your traveling habits. As seen in Figure 4.13, other applications such as Google Maps also attempt to track your location through LBS.

It should be clear that your privacy is affected when you choose to allow software to track you; it should not come as a surprise that this data and the data

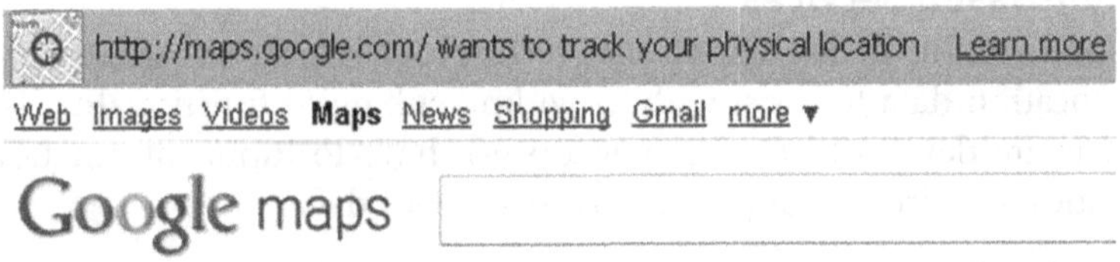

http://maps.google.com/ wants to track your physical location
Learn more
Web Images Videos Maps News Shopping Gmail more ▼
Google maps

FIGURE 4.13 Google Map tracking.

FIGURE 4.14 SIM chips.

stored on the servers that collect the data could be used to track you and gather information about your habits.

Tracking a SIM

Each mobile device used as a phone will have a subscriber identity module (SIM) card installed that uniquely identifies the device. The SIM card (or chip) will store information and allows the device to be tracked. The SIM will send out a signal to the carrier network in order to be used on the carrier network, but can also be misused. For good purposes, you can track your phone if stolen or lost. However, a phone can also be tracked maliciously through the SIM. As seen in Figure 4.14, SIM chips are commonly used in most if not all mobile phone devices.

To track a SIM easily, report your device stolen and contact your service provider or carrier. They may be able to track your device for you. You can also install GPS software (covered in the next section) to pinpoint the devices location via satellite. Apple uses a program called MobileMe that is a cloud-based solution to back up your phone; however, it can also be used to track your phone if lost. You can also install a SIM tracker application on a phone so that the movements of the phone can be tracked both in real time and historically.

Global Positioning System and Geolocation

A GPS is used to pinpoint the physical device location directly or through triangulation. As discussed earlier in this chapter, a GPS can use a satellite or a series of satellites to track movement of a device. For good purposes, GPS can provide you with mapping data for trips as well as to find a lost device. However, for

FIGURE 4.15 Yahoo Map tracking with latitude.

malicious purposes, GPS can show an attacker your exact position worldwide. Geolocation data can also be used to track device usage; however, it does so using information from other sources as well. TCP/IP can be used to assist with Geolocation. As seen in Figure 4.15, other applications such as Yahoo maps provide Geolocation data.

Google Mapping
Another major issue with the tracking of location by applications is the possible abuses that can take place with Google Latitude. In line with Geolocation tracking, Latitude can (with your permission of course) pinpoint your exact location on the Earth. Used in conjunction with Google Maps, Latitudes friend finder location-aware tool for your phone also combines with your Google Talk phone service.

As seen in Figure 4.16, Google Maps with latitude provide Geolocation data. Google LBS provide those with accounts the ability to track "friends"; however, if we were able to gain access to this data, we would be able to track victims without their knowledge.

What may seem worse is, Google has access to this data as well. Another concern would be, although privacy policies state that this data is not used in illicit ways, one can only guess what would happen if someone were to get their hands on this data for malicious purposes. The point here is it's still "collected."

FIGURE 4.16 Google Map tracking.

Other tools that can be used on mobile devices are iLocalis, InstaMapper, and many, many more. As you can see, there is no shortage for phone tracking utilities in the market and if an attacker were to get their hands on the data they collect, it could be used for malicious purposes.

Google Glass Tracking?

As we move into the world of Google Glass and other wearable technology, one has to ask – how safe is this technology? How can it invade my privacy? The answer is simple – it is nearly identical to the mobile device you carry, except these are mobile devices you wear. As seen in Figure 4.17, Google Glass is a wearable mobile device that allows you to access the Internet and applications through a pair of glasses.

As technology develops and privacy and security risks are not addressed, more and more personal data will be collected and stored that can be used by those who may wish to track you. A large number of attacks can be launched aside from gathering of information through tracking. Man in the middle attacks can take place where an attacker can inject themselves between the source and the destination and pollute the conversations with false data. Eavesdropping attacks can take place where information is gathered and other attacks may be launched, for example, if bank account information is intercepted.

At a higher level, the governments we are supposed to trust with our security and safety are gathering data and analyzing it for patterns. Is it possible that someone could be falsely accused of a crime they didn't commit by simply being within the "pattern?" What about your ability to keep your life private? Where does privacy end and safety and security pick up? All of these questions

FIGURE 4.17 Google Glass.

need to be answered by those who are concerned about rights to privacy being stripped away; however, the digital age keeps us bound to the technological landscape in which we now live.

LEGAL AND ETHICAL CONCERNS

There are many legal and ethical concerns revolving around mobile phone tracking. For one, it is unethical to simply attempt to spy on another and evade their privacy either for malicious intent or otherwise. Marketing purposes in the opinions of many do not count ... you should not be tracked.

The Location Privacy Protection Act of 2012 (S.1233) was introduced by Senator Al Franken (D-MN) in order to regulate the transmission and sharing of user location data in the USA. It is based on the individual's one-time consent to participate in these services (Opt In). The bill specifies the collecting entities, the collectable data, and its usage. The bill does not specify, however, the period of time that the data collecting entity can hold on to the user data (a limit of 24 h seems appropriate since most of the services use the data for immediate searches, communications, etc.), and the bill does not include location data stored locally on the device (the user should be able to delete the contents of the location data document periodically just as he would delete a log document). The bill that was approved last month by the Senate Judiciary Committee would also require mobile services to disclose the names of the advertising networks or other third parties with which they share consumers' locations.

In January 2009, a special report by the Department of Justice revealed that based on 2006 data, approximately 26,000 persons are victims of GPS stalking annually, including by cell phone. In December 2010, an investigation by the

Wall Street Journal revealed that of 101 top smartphone apps, 47 disclosed a user's location to third parties, typically without user consent. In April 2011, iPhone and Android devices were found to be sending Apple and Google location data, even when users were not using location apps and even though Apple users had no way to stop this. In June 2011, Nissan Leaf drivers discovered that their cars automatically transmitted their vehicles' location, speed, and destination to many third party websites accessed through the car's computer.

In September 2011, users of Windows Phone 7 smartphones discovered that their phones sent their location to Microsoft when the camera was on – even that app was denied permission to access location. Later that month, OnStar told its customers that it would continue to track their cars' speed and GPS locations "for any purpose, at any time" – even if those customers had ended their OnStar service plans. In November 2011, consumers learned that smartphones were sending location and other information to a firm called Carrier IQ – even though they had never heard of the company and had no way to stop this. In May and October 2012, the Federal Communications Commission (FCC) and Government Accountability Office (GAO) issued separate reports finding that mobile companies were giving their customers too little information about how their location information was used and disclosed to third parties. The GAO also found that industry self-regulation had been unclear and inconsistent. Unfortunately, most of these activities are entirely legal. Even after Jones, every time you use the Internet on your smartphone, companies are legally free to give or sell your location information to almost anyone they want – without your consent. While the Communications Act prohibits wireless companies offering phone service from freely disclosing their customers' whereabouts, an obscure section of the Electronic Communications Privacy Act of 1986 explicitly allows smartphone companies, app companies, and wireless companies offering Internet service to give their customers' location information to nongovernmental third parties – without their customers' permission.

The Location Privacy Protection Act of 2012 (S. 1223), sponsored by Senator Al Franken and cosponsored by Senators Richard Blumenthal, Chris Coons, Bernard Sanders, Richard Durbin, Robert Menendez, and Dianne Feinstein, will fix this outdated federal law to require companies to (1) get a customer's permission before collecting his or her location data or (2) sharing it with nongovernmental third parties. The bill will also (3) raise awareness and help investigations of GPS stalking and (4) criminalize the knowing and intentional operation of "stalking apps" to violate federal antistalking and DV laws. This bill does not concern or affect law enforcement location tracking, which is addressed in other legislation.

The bill was introduced with the support of a coalition of consumer privacy and antidomestic violence groups, including the Center for Democracy and Technology, Consumer Action, Consumers Union, the Minnesota Coalition for

Battered Women, the National Association of Consumer Advocates, the National Center for Victims of Crime, the National Consumers League, the National Network to End Domestic Violence, the National Women's Law Center, and the Online Trust Alliance.

Retrieved from:

http://www.franken.senate.gov/files/docs/LPPA_one_pager.pdf

and

http://thomas.loc.gov/cgi-bin/query/L?c112:./list/c112s.lst:1201

An interesting case of People versus Hall is a classic case on how tracking and mobile technology can be used in the court of law, the outcome, and the effect of using such technology. The defendant Alexander Hall was indicted for one count of murder in the second degree, four counts of assault in the first degree, and one count of criminal possession of a weapon in the second degree allegedly committed on October 12, 2005 outside a New York City Night Club.

Detective Rivera of the New York City Police Department conducted the investigation when one of the other defendant's disclosed his cell phone number. The cell records were then subpoenaed in hopes of being able to track the location the of the defendant's whereabouts to iron out the inconsistencies in each of their stories. T-Mobile's system automatically records the identity of the towers the second a call starts until it is disconnected that pinpoints exact locations. Information such as the cell customer's account information, name, date of birth, social security number, and call detail is already being retained for ordinary business purposes that were obtained by the People from T-Mobile Cellular.

Hall sought to suppress records obtained on the ground that such subpoena was issued without probable cause and in violation of Hall's constitutional rights. Hall also sought suppression of identification evidence obtained subsequent to the issuance of the subpoena. The evidence Hall wanted suppressed consisted of records relating to Hall's cellular telephone.

The people met their burden to establish their compliance with the Federal Stored Communications Act (SCA) (18 USC § 2703) that they contend provides authorization for the subpoena and the receipt of the subpoenaed information, but Hall argues they fell short of the constructional requirements for retrieval of cell site data and under this cases circumstances was used as a "tracking device." Under ECPA, cells are not considered tracking devices.

The court finds that the subpoenaed material was properly obtained.

There is no fourth amendment violation as the records obtained and the information gathered was property of T-Mobile and belongs to them for legitimate business purposes.

Hall's motion was denied.

People v Hall

People v Hall 2006 NY Slip Op 26427 [14 Misc 3d 245] October 17, 2006 Stone, J. Supreme Court, New York County Published by New York State Law Reporting Bureau pursuant to Judiciary Law § 431. As corrected through Wednesday, January 24, 2007

[*1] The People of the State of New York, Plaintiff,

v

Alexander Hall, Defendant.

Supreme Court, New York County, October 17, 2006

APPEA RANCES OF COUNSEL

Frederick Hafetz, Priya Chaudhry and Louis Freeman for defendant. Linda Ford for plaintiff.

OPINION OF THE COURT

Lewis Bart Stone, J.

On December 2, 2005, defendant Alexander Hall was indicted for one count of murder in the second degree (Penal Law § 125.25 [2]), four counts of assault in the first degree (Penal Law § 120.10 [3], [4]), and one count of criminal possession of a weapon in the second degree (Penal Law § 265.03 [2]), allegedly committed on October 12, 2005. Hall now seeks to suppress records obtained on November 4, 2005 by the District Attorney's office through a grand jury subpoena issued by the Honorable Michael Ambrecht, on the ground that such subpoena was issued without probable cause and in violation of Hall's constitutional rights, and also seeks to suppress identification evidence obtained subsequent to the issuance of the subpoena.

The evidence sought to be suppressed consists of records relating to Hall's cellular telephone (the cel) obtained by the People from T-Mobile Cellular, the carrier for the cel. At the hearing held on June 26, 2006, the People called three witnesses, Sue Johnson, custodian of records for T-Mobile, Police Detective Kevin Rivera of the 34th Precinct Detective Squad, and Assistant District Attorney Al Peterson of the New York County District Attorney's office. I find all such witnesses credible. The defense called no witnesses. After the evidentiary hearing, the court reviewed the written memoranda of law submitted by the parties and thereafter heard oral arguments. Findings of Fact.

On October 12, 2005, at approximately 4:11 a.m., outside of Club Viva located at 4168 Broadway, in Manhattan, three people were shot, one of whom, Tabitha Perez, was killed. The investigation conducted by detectives of the New

York City Police Department (NYPD) led to Hall and three of his friends, [*2] Sabin Abad, Christopher Ulanga, and Javier Gonzalez, all of whom had earlier been ejected from the club and had been involved in an altercation with the club's bouncers. Following the altercation, the four left in two separate vehicles, which had been parked in the adjacent parking garage. Shortly, thereafter, the People contend, Hall returned in one of the vehicles and shot and killed Tabitha Perez and wounded the other two victims.

Rivera, an NYPD detective, was assigned to investigate the case. An attendant from the parking garage provided Rivera with the license plate number of one of the vehicles allegedly used by one of the persons fleeing the altercation. The vehicle matching such plate number was a blue Acura, registered to Ulanga's grandfather. Ulanga was interviewed at the 34th Precinct on October 12, 2005 and he told Rivera that he was at the club with a friend named Mark, and that after they were there for a while he observed some type of dispute and thereafter left in the Acura with his friend Jay and went home. Ulanga disclosed his cell phone number to Rivera.

Following this interview, the People subpoenaed Ulanga's cell phone incoming/outgoing call records in order to identify Mark, Jay, or other people Ulanga was in contact with that night as possible witnesses or suspects. After receiving the records of calls from Ulanga's cell phone, the People then subpoenaed subscriber information for the phone numbers that Ulanga's phone had made or received around the time of the shooting and the hours immediately following. This investigation led to cell phones belonging to Hall, Gonzalez, and Abad, each of whom were subsequently interviewed.

Gonzalez, who was interviewed by Rivera on October 23, 2005, stated that on the evening in question, he was at the club with Abad, Ulanga, and Hall, and was involved in the altercation and that afterward he drove to the Bronx and dropped off Abad.

Abad, who was interviewed by Rivera on October 25, 2005, stated that he was in the club with Gonzalez, Ulanga, and Hall that evening and he was escorted out when he tried to light a cigarette inside the club and that during the dispute outside the club he was injured on the head, and then drove to the Bronx with Gonzalez.

Hall, in the presence of counsel, was interviewed by Rivera on October 28, 2005, at which time he stated that he was at the club with Ulanga, Abad, and Gonzalez, and stated that during the dispute he grabbed Abad and told him "don't worry about it, we will see him later." Hall claimed that after the dispute, the four went to the garage to retrieve their vehicles and all four went directly to the vicinity of Hall's apartment on West 96th Street. Gonzalez stayed and slept on the couch and Ulanga and Abad left. Hall stated that he was not in the vicinity of the club at the time of the shooting.[*3]

Following the Hall interview and recognizing the conflict between the stories of the four as to where each was at the relevant times, the People obtained a court order for cell site records for each of the four cell phone numbers, to enable them to determine the general location of where calls were made from the cell telephones of each of the four men between the time the four left the club and the time of the shooting. T-Mobile's system automatically records the identity of the antenna tower to which a particular cell phone was connected at the beginning and end of each call made or received by that phone.

Based on the affidavit of an assistant district attorney attesting to the facts gleaned in the investigation, Honorable Michael Ambrecht, sitting as the grand jury judge, issued subpoenas to T-Mobile for such cell site information for the cell phones of the four suspects (including the cel), between October 10 and October 13, 2005. T-Mobile, which had recorded such information in the ordinary course of its business and retained such records for its own business purposes, complied, providing subscriber information for the cel showing Hall's account number, name, address, social security number, date of birth, and home telephone number and call detail records from October 10 to October 13, 2005, the dates requested in the subpoena. These records show the start time, end time, and duration of each call made or answered by the cel for the specified dates as well as cell tower records identifying which T-Mobile cell tower received the signal from the cel at the beginning and end of each call, thus, identifying the approximate location of the cel when completed calls to or from it were begun and ended that evening and identifying the telephone number of the caller or recipient of the call. These records provide no information by which the location of the cel may be ascertained other than in connection with completed actual calls made or received. It is this cell site information that Hall seeks to suppress.

Cellular telephone or "wireless" networks, operated by T-Mobile,[1] are divided into geographic coverage areas, or "cells." Each T-Mobile cell contains an antenna tower that sends a signal to cellular phones on the T-Mobile network through which such telephones may transmit and receive calls while located in such coverage area. The size of a particular T-Mobile cell is determined by a number of factors, including, but not limited to, the radio reception range, the topography of the surrounding land, the presence of buildings, and prevailing weather patterns, and the expected cellular [*4]telephone traffic in the area. T-Mobile cell size ranges from several hundred feet[2] in some urban locations, such as portions of Manhattan, to more than 15 miles in suburban and rural areas.

---

[1] The testimony was specific to T-Mobile's operations and records. As this case relates solely to the Hall's motion to suppress the specific T-Mobile records obtained, this court does not find on the basis of this hearing that all cell phone carriers systems operate in a similar manner as to lead to the same result had the records of a different carrier been in question.

[2] A city block between numbered streets in Manhattan is, for example, traditionally about 200 feet.

Generally, each T-Mobile antenna tower provides 360 degrees of coverage. As a T-Mobile cell phone and its user move from place to place during a call, the system automatically switches the connection to the T-Mobile cell antenna tower that provides the best reception. For this process to function correctly, each cell phone using the T-Mobile network must periodically transmit a unique identification code to register its presence within each T-Mobile cell. T-Mobile then uses this unique number, together with information identifying the antenna tower to which the cell phone is currently connected, and in many cases, the 120-degree portion or "sector" of the tower facing the cell phone, to route calls to and from the cell phone. Each T-Mobile cell tower is assigned a unique number that is automatically used to route calls and that is recorded in the case of completed calls to indicate the starting and ending cell involved in such call.

Although T-Mobile cellular phones turned on by the user regularly emit signals that are received by the nearest tower, even when no call is being made, unless the subscriber makes a completed call or a completed call is made to such subscriber, T-Mobile's system does not automatically make or keep any records of such signals or which cell site received such signals and did not, in the case of the cel, make or keep any such records where calls were not made or recorded during the period relevant to this case.

The T-Mobile system has the capacity, however, to allow "pinging" of a T-Mobile telephone that has been turned on by its subscriber, even if the subscriber is not making a call, to determine the cell in which such phone is located at the time of the "ping." To do so, T-Mobile would have to expressly act to cause its network to do so, but cannot reconstruct such information for periods to when such action was taken. The subpoena neither called upon T-Mobile to "ping" the cel nor is there any evidence that T-Mobile "pinged" the cel to generate the records, or information in question here. Thus, the information which Hall seeks to suppress did not arise from "pinging."

The People contend that they have met their burden to establish their compliance with the federal Stored Communications Act (SCA) (18 USC § 2703) which they contend provides authorization for the subpoena and the receipt of the subpoenaed information. Hall does not dispute that the People have established [*5]compliance with the SCA, which requires "specific and articulable facts showing that there are reasonable grounds to believe that the … records or other information sought[ ] are relevant and material to an ongoing investigation" (18 USC § 2703 [d]), but argues instead both that such statutory standard falls short of constitutional requirements for the retrieval of cel site data, and further that the cel under the circumstances of this case was a "tracking device," and that, as a result, the People have not met their obligations under a different federal statute, the Electronic Communications Privacy Act of 1986 (ECPA) (18 USC § 3117 [b]). Under ECPA, the People must seek prior court approval based on probable cause, before they may use a "tracking device." As a third contention, Hall claims that by obtaining the cell site records, the People invaded the privacy of Hall's home, as "warrantless monitoring of an electronic tracking device in a private residence which is not open to visual inspection, violates the Fourth Amendment."

Central to Hall's second and third contentions is that the cel is a "tracking device." The People do not contend that they have complied with ECPA, but instead assert that the cel is not a "tracking device" under ECPA and, as a result, compliance with ECPA's higher standard was unnecessary. As to the claim that obtaining cell site records represented a warrantless monitoring of an electronic tracking device in a private residence, the People counter both that the cel was not a tracking device, and that there was no "monitoring in a private residence."

As the parties' positions as to Hall's second and third contentions turn mainly on whether the cel was a "tracking device," it is necessary to address such contentions. Hall's claim under ECPA must be analyzed under the definition of a tracking device in ECPA. Hall's Fourth Amendment claim, however, being constitutional, cannot rest alone on such statutory definition of tracking device, as Congress in enacting ECPA may have, as a discretionary matter, balanced privacy interests of individuals against law enforcement's interest in a way more favorable to privacy concerns than those mandated by the Constitution. Similarly, if, as the People contend, the monitoring of broadcasts to and from cellular phones recorded outside of a person's home is a matter of federal statutory concern, rather than a constitutional principle (as will be discussed below), Congress may, in its definition of a tracking device in ECPA, set a balance that would have been short of the constitutional balance in favor of privacy mandated by the Fourth Amendment with respect to tracking devices placed in a suspect's home.

Under ECPA, a tracking device is an electronic device that permits the tracking of a person or thing. Case law has expanded the definition to include devices that fit the definition, although they were not originally designed or intended to track movement. The ECPA is designed to prevent police authorities from tracking movement through such a device without obtaining prior court approval based on a [*6]probable cause standard. The record here does not establish that the cel was designed or intended to be a tracking device but was designed to be a cellular telephone to be used on the T-Mobile network that retained and recorded information within its system, in the regular course of business for billing purposes, which information was disclosed pursuant to the subpoena.

It is also clear that the cel could be transformed into a portion of a device to track the cell in which the cel was located but only if the T-Mobile network was directed to "ping" the cel, so long as the cel was on, and that no such direction or pinging took place. However, the record is also clear that in the T-Mobile network, only the nearest cell tower would register the presence of the pinged cell,[3] thus determining the location of the cell only within an area the size of such cell, and could not determine the direction or speed of the person carrying the cel unless and until that person finished the call in another cell.

To determine what is a tracking device for the purpose of ECPA, it is necessary to look to the purpose of ECPA, its legislative history, cases, and the ordinary meaning of words. The ECPA was enacted in 1986, which although only 20 years ago, represents an almost antediluvian age with respect to present technology and communications systems. The United States Senate report accompanying adoption of the ECPA, in its glossary of terms, defined an "electronic tracking device" as a one-way radio communication device that emits a signal on a specific radio frequency. This signal can be received by special tracking equipment and allows the user to trace the geographical location of the transponder. Such "homing" devices are used by law enforcement personnel to keep track of the physical whereabouts of the sending unit, which might be placed in an automobile, on a person, or in some other item.[4]

This almost quaint definition essentially defined the classic "bug" that the police would surreptitiously attach to a car or a person's clothing to enable them to be followed in real time. It is not surprising that the courts, faced with a more generic statutory definition, were able to extend the concept to two-way devices such as cellular telephones which the police now often use to perform the same function as a [*7]"bug" placed by them.

Such federal courts routinely require a showing of probable cause under the ECPA as a condition of allowing the police to use cellular telephones as tracking devices on a prospective basis, that is, to gain future information relating to a suspect's movements. These cases do not address certain differences between the cellular telephone and the classic bug, that is the fact that in most cases, the phone subscriber, being aware of his possession of the phone, would not necessarily take it with him at all times and might turn it off for short or extended periods. The courts seem instead to assume that a cell phone owner will keep his telephone on and with him as a general matter, thus making a cellular telephone rigged to show the functional location equivalent of a bug. Because technology has changed the state of the art far from the classic bug, the courts are not of the same mind as to how to interpret ECPA and the results vary

---

[3] While there was testimony that during some periods of high cellular telephone usage, a call may be routed through an adjacent tower, rather than through the nearest, Johnson's testimony made it clear that the times the relevant calls were made in the middle of the night were not periods of high use, and accordingly only the nearest tower would be recorded as handling actual calls.

[4] S Rep No. 541, 99th Cong, 2d Sess (1986).

among courts. The consensus seems to be that prospective tracking through a suspect's cellular telephone requires a finding of probable cause under ECPA.

In re Application for Pen Register and Trap/Trace Device with Cell Site Location Auth. (396 F Supp 2d 747 [SD Tex 2005] [hereafter cited as Texas I]), cited by both parties here in support of their positions, the court described the tracking device in such case as follows: "Tracking devices have progressed a long way. Most agencies now have sophisticated tracking devices that use cell site towers or satellites … These types of tracking devices are usually monitored from the law enforcement agency's office. Through the use of computers, a signal is sent to the tracking device (it is pinged), and the tracking device responds. The signal is picked up using cellular telephone cell sites or satellites. The location of the tracker, and therefore the vehicle, is determined through triangulation and a computer monitor at the agency office shows the location of the vehicle on a map. These tracking devices are very accurate, and can differentiate between a vehicle traveling on an interstate highway or the feeder (service) road. The tracking devices will also provide the direction of travel and the speed the vehicle is traveling." (Id. at 754.)

Using the technology described above, the cellular telephone in question together with the computer, cell sites, and satellites and the use of triangulation, the location of the cellular telephone can be tracked in real time. There is no question that the combination of these factors made the operation addressed by the court in Texas I one involving a tracking device.

The record here shows the cel to fall far from this level of convergence with the "bug" problem that ECPA addressed. The record here shows that the T-Mobile [*8]system would only, upon "pinging," determine the single cell tower nearest to the cel, thus precluding any possibility of triangulation that is the basis for all GPSs and the court's decision in Texas I. Even assuming the factual conclusion that a governmental agency had the capacity, using its own computers through the T-Mobile network, to monitor the location of the cel in real time, the facts established at this hearing show that T-Mobile could not, at the time in question, actually have done so and there has been no preservation of data to permit even such a capable governmental agency of now tracking Hall's movements as so described in Texas I. As the Texas I court said (at 751), "By a process of triangulation from various cell towers, law enforcement is able to track the movements of the target phone, and hence locate a suspect using the phone." Here, such scenario did not create the information that Hall seeks to suppress.[5]

---

[5] While it is clear that federal government agencies have the capacity to triangulate from "pinging" cell phones, carriers are not required to have such a capacity. (See United States Telecom Assn. v Federal Communications Commn., 227 F3d 450 [DC Cir 2000] [discussing that the New York City Police Department request to the Federal Communications Commission (FCC) to require cellular telephone carriers to have the ability to triangulate was rejected].)

In expanding the concept of a tracking device from the original transponder "bug" to cases where cellular telephones are involved to reflect changes in technology, the courts have determined that, where the cell phone, satellites, or cell antennas, and the carrier's system and computers located at law enforcement offices to "ping," triangulate, and analyze data work together to create the functional equivalent of a bug, the parts may each be treated as a "tracking device."[6]

The information in question arose from the ordinary use and operation of the cel, and not its putative possible secondary function of a tracking device had the government pinged and triangulated (which it would not have done on the evening of the alleged crime as the police had not ascertained the phone number of the cel until many days later). Thus, for the purposes of ECPA, the cel was not a tracking device.

With respect to the Fourth Amendment concerns as to the "intrusion" into Hall's [*9]home, the question is easier. For the same reasons set forth above, the cel could not, on the evening in question, be analogized to a bug, thus differentiating the cel from cases where the People may have bugged a defendant's home. As there was no triangulation, the subpoenaed records can no more than show that Hall was, at certain times when he used the cel, in the vicinity of his home, and cannot even show whether he was inside or outside of his home at the time of any call. On the other hand, had Hall used a landline from his home, his telephone records would have more accurately shown his whereabouts at home[7] and such records could have clearly been obtained by subpoena without the showing of a probable cause. This argument is at best a makeweight, and is hereby rejected. The Constitutional Standard of the Stored Communications Act.

Hall concedes that the People have met the standard that the SCA provides for a subpoena thereunder, but asserts that, as to the cell tower information which Hall seeks to suppress, the SCA is constitutionally insufficient under the Fourth Amendment standards. The US Constitution Fourth Amendment, adopted in the eighteenth century, when there were neither telephones, cellular telephones, nor an understanding of electronics,[8] provides: "The right of

---

[6] Some courts also require the government to provide the cellular telephone to bring such a system under the ECPA. (See In re Application of United States for Order for Disclosure of Telecommunications Records & Authorizing Use of Pen Register & Trap & Trace, 405 F Supp 2d 435 [SD NY 2005].) Such case, which Hall claims was wrongfully decided, is the only reported federal case in the district in which this court sits. If such case controls, Hall's contentions would fail as Hall provided his own cellular telephone. It is therefore not surprising that Hall asserts this case to be wrongfully decided. This court need not determine the correctness of such case as the issue there involved prospective data collection and not historical data from which triangulation site information could not be ascertained, as is the case here.

[7] Perhaps, if he used a portable telephone, he might even have been outside of his home.

[8] Benjamin Franklin may have had some understanding of electricity.

the people to be secure in their persons, houses, papers, and effects, against unreasonable searches and seizures, shall not be violated, and no Warrants shall issue, but upon probable cause, supported by Oath or affirmation, and particularly describing the place to be searched, and the persons or thing to be seized."

While additions to the judicial gloss on this amendment are constant, certain aspects seem to have evolved over time as they relate to this case. An initial inquiry is whether the papers (and an attendant information) in question are the property of the person seeking to protect them (including those papers, which another holds for them) under circumstances where there is a reasonable expectation of privacy or whether such papers or information belong to someone else.

It is well settled, for example, that a defendant has no legitimate expectation of privacy and no cognizable Fourth Amendment interest in bank records and, therefore, lacks standing to challenge a subpoena for them. (United States v White, 401 US 745 [1971]; see United States v Miller, 425 US 435 [1976]; Matter of Cappetta, 42 NY2d 1066 [1977]; Matter of Shapiro v Chase Manhattan Bank, N.A., 53 AD2d 542 [1976]; Cunningham[*10]& Kaming v Nadjari, 53 AD2d 520 [1976]; Matter of Democratic County Comm. of Bronx County v Nadjari, 52 AD2d 70 [1976].)

The same principle has been applied to the records of a telephone company relating to a person's account. (See Smith v Maryland, 442 US 735 [1979]; People v Di Raffaele, 55 NY2d 234 [1982].) On a parallel track, the electronic emanations from telephones, intercepted or tapped or overheard outside of a person's house, have not received constitutional protection under the Fourth Amendment. As the Fourth Amendment in the nineteenth century could never have contemplated the interception of electronic waves, where there was no intrusion into a house, it was left to the Congress to address the new technology. The Congress did, by adopting a series of laws to regulate privacy issues in the electronic and telecommunications areas, and continues to readdress this issue from time to time as technology changes. Central to this regulatory scheme have been the Federal Communications Act enacted in 1934, the ECPA enacted in 1986, the Communications Assistance for Law Enforcement Act of 1994, which strictly regulated the disclosure of the content of electronic communications, and the SCA, enacted in 2006. The Congress is at present holding hearings on pretexting and related matters such as the use of data brokers that may lead to further legislation in this area. Hall cites a press report of issues raised at these hearings.

Over the period where Congress has regularly legislated in this area, balancing disclosure and access issues, and expressly providing for stronger privacy rights than in the Fourth Amendment standards under the FCC, rights equal to the Fourth Amendment standards in the ECPA and weaker than the Fourth Amendment standards in the SCA, Congress has acted with the assumption that the Fourth Amendment is irrelevant because of the nature of electronics and telephones, relegating the appropriate determination of balancing to the Congress to do so by statute, under its powers to regulate interstate commerce.

To support his broad constitutional challenge to the long-standing statutory scheme and understanding of the Congress in areas where it has been regularly revisiting issues and legislation, Hall cites a recent Indiana District Court case. (In re United States, 2006 WL 187684, 2006 US Dist LEXIS 45643 [ND Ind 2006].)[9]

In such case, the federal District Court for the Northern District of Indiana upheld a decision of a magistrate, as not being clearly erroneous. The magistrate found that the People had sought both prospective and historical data. The court, [*11]after reviewing the federal statutes, concluded that a request under the SCA combined with a request under the pen register statute (which authorized a real-time future recording) could not bypass the probable cause requirement. Although there was broad language, the case does not expressly address what historic information may be obtained without showing of probable cause under the SCA in the absence of a pen register and trap-and-trace device having triangulation capacity.

Thus, this court finds that there is no Fourth Amendment infirmity to the SCA. The Fourth Amendment does not apply to disclosures thereunder because the information, having been gathered by T-Mobile for its own legitimate business purposes, belongs to T-Mobile, not Hall, and because the Fourth Amendment does not apply to the interception of electromagnetic waves outside of a person's home, so as to constitute the acquisition of such information as a search or seizure. As Hall concedes that the People have followed the standards in the SCA for the subpoena, Hall's objection to such information is rejected.

As this court finds that the subpoenaed material was properly obtained, no analysis is necessary regarding the subsequent identification evidence nor is it necessary to determine whether there was an independent source to provide the basis for Hall's arrest.

Hall's motion is denied.

Retrieved from:

http://law.justia.com/cases/new-york/other-courts/2006/2006-26427.html

---

[9] Otherwise, Hall concedes, as the People have urged, that the federal cases address subpoenas for prospective information and do not address constitutional questions of the quantum of support required for a subpoena for historical data, the issue here.

SUMMARY

As we have learned, tracking is done quite simply because of our wanting (and needing) to carry a mobile device with us everywhere we go. We can be mapped, tracked, followed, and stalked with ease because of our devices. In this chapter, we discussed how to track movement and activity through a user's mobile phone. All major mobile platforms were covered to include iPhone and Windows Phone devices. We looked at apps that can be used to track our movements on a dashboard.

The government is taking advantage of outdated laws on privacy and technology to track Americans like never before. As long as it is turned on, your mobile phone registers its position with cell towers every few minutes, whether the phone is being used or not, and mobile carriers are retaining location data on their customers. We discussed how you can take care to ensure that you limit how you are tracked.

CHAPTER 5

Physical Device Tracking

PHYSICAL TRACKING

In the previous chapter, we covered the fundamentals of tracking and focused on the mobile device that is likely to be your cell phone, although we find ourselves carrying it or within devices that can also be tracked, such as your car. We carry our cell phones everywhere we go, which basically gives those with access a clear line of sight into your movement, activities, communications, and more. However, beyond the cell phone, we use many other products, services, devices, and applications that also track our behavior. In this chapter, we will look at not only the mobile phone but also other mobile devices that can be tracked. We will also look at other devices that you may not know can be tracked, such as your vehicle.

Another interesting trend emerging in today's technology is the "physical tracking" of items with devices. Other devices also exist that help those who are forgetful. New devices are coming to market that allow you to place trackers on items you would normally misplace, for example, a set of keys. More commonly, tools are being sold to "track your pets" with sensors that only operate with Bluetooth and can only be tracked so far; some offerings can track you within larger radiuses. Another growing trend is with wearable technology where a new market has opened. This technology allows tracking and the data collected is used with an application so that you can track your health, diet, and medical condition. As shown in Figure 5.1, the number of devices coming to market to "track" a plethora of things, such as health, is increasing exponentially.

Other physical tracking such as finding a lost phone has been around for some time now; however, the technology has been evolving. By registering a device online, offerings such as Apple's MobileMe (iCloud) allows for the recovery of a lost or stolen device by tracking it. Our vehicles are now coming equipped from the factory with tracking devices installed in them. LoJack, which has been around for years, is also another form of advanced anti-theft device that allows tracking and recovery of a stolen car. LoJack can also be used with other devices such as laptops. Surveillance gear to track someone physically is also

FIGURE 5.1 Health Tracker

emerging, such as universal serial bus (USB) devices, that can be placed within a car or on a person (perhaps in a pocketbook) to track movement of an individual without their knowledge.

As you can see, tracking is nothing new and it's growing at an alarming rate. It's growing in availability and ease of use. It's being offered as a service for the forgetful and appearing as a standard feature in devices everywhere. This goes beyond the tracking being done without your knowledge. Within the chapter, we will also make reference to tracking without technology, stalking, etc.; however, the bulk of this chapter will revolve around the technical tracking devices used to physically bug you with or without your knowledge.

■ Historical Examples

The government spy agencies, militaries, and other covert operation teams have been using physical tracking devices for a long time. Although this seems archaic compared with today's technology, spying has been taking place for a long time and tracking a target is not a new topic. We have also seen them in spy movies, where a physical bug was placed on a car, a person, or an object to "track" the movement of a target, most notably in movies such as *Mission Impossible*. Again, although this is a movie, the technology is real and used by military, agencies, and governments – and now the consumer! As we will learn in this chapter, placing a tracking device on a target can now be done as easily as ordering a device online and using it out of the box.

Device Fingerprint

When you are charged with a crime and go through the process of getting fingerprinted, your details are added to a database so that you can be tracked. As fingerprints are unique to an individual, it seems likely that if you are caught after being fingerprinted, you can be a possible target of investigation if your prints show up at another crime scene. Similar to physical human fingerprinting, devices can also leave a unique mark.

With technology, you need to understand that there are unique characteristics that pinpoint or associative you to a device.

- Username – when you log into a device with a set of credentials (username and password), you are leaving a logical fingerprint logged in a system.
- Internet protocol (IP) address – when you use a device that uses TCP/IP, your IP address leaves a fingerprint that can be tracked.
- Phone number – your phone number assigned by your carrier is another logical fingerprint that associates you to your mobile device or location.
- Mac address – it is a burned in address that denotes the Network Interface Card (NIC) manufacturer and a unique hex number that leaves a unique fingerprint that maps to a device.
- Serial number – serial numbers leave a fingerprint that maps something physical or logical to a unique number.
- SIMM – your SIMM has a unique fingerprint associated with it.
- Barcode – a barcode can be unique and allow tracking of whatever is associated with it.

As you can see, tracking is done every day, in many ways so that devices you use, places you go, and things you buy can all be tracked. It is possible that when you leave your home in the morning and go to work – go out to lunch and then back to work and return home – your entire day and everything you have done can be tracked. The credit cards you used, the calls you made, and the ticket you got on a busy intersection can all be used to track your patterns, your movements, and your ultimate location.

The lines can blur as well; fingerprint device can be used to access systems through biometrics. Although this topic is outside the range of topics we cover in this book, it should be noted that biometric devices use fingerprint data, as shown in Figure 5.2, where the biometric device can be seen in a Windows Device Manager.

This is a way to mitigate your device being accessed, which will only allow you access into it based on your biometric credentials.

Tracking for Reconnaissance Today

As we can see, tracking can be done without your knowledge and at many different levels. Your mobile device, although helpful and a needed fixture of your person, is now a mobile tracking device that can be used to find you, evade your privacy at any moment, or as a tracking tool for another malicious user, stalker, attacker, or threat.

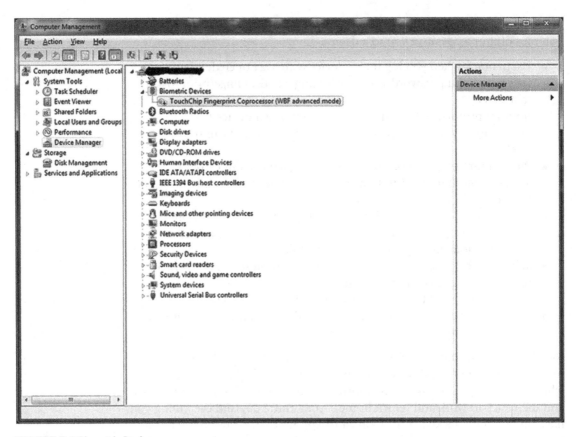

FIGURE 5.2 Biometric Device

Before we get into how to track a phone, for example, it's important to understand the first steps to protecting yourself as much as possible. First, do not leave your phone unattended. Do not leave it unlocked. Do not leave it without a password. Use a strong password scheme. Make sure that nobody is shoulder surfing you when you use your phone. In Chapter 8, mitigation strategies will be covered in detail; however, it's important to note here that by practicing simple security steps, such as those listed above, you lessen the attack surface significantly.

Before we get to mitigation, let's recapitulate what we have learned in earlier chapters about why someone would track you in the first place. Tracking is done for good reasons and on purpose. As a company, we need to know how many units we sold this quarter for financial statements. We track the units, the progress, and so on. This can be manipulated, however, for example, if we wanted to see what demographic purchased specific units and then

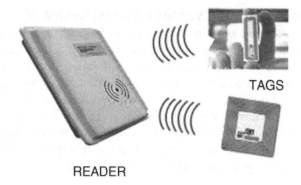

TAGS

READER

FIGURE 5.3 RFID Tracking

we build a campaign to market to the specific demographic. This is good but questionable. This is a good example of simple tracking for logistical purposes turned into a marketing campaign. Another good reason would be hospitals that do bed tracking to keep inventory of their patients. They can use chips such as radio-frequency identification (RFID) to do this tracking. We also have to consider patient security and confidentiality. We can encrypt or secure this data to ensure safety. What if this information got into the wrong hands? Now we can start to see how good tracking can be further manipulated into a danger zone. As shown in Figure 5.3, the number of devices using RFID is increasing and allowing for advanced tracking of devices.

How can this type of tracking be used for bad? It can be turned into malicious intent when the tracking is used for surveillance and reconnaissance of targets such as people simply using their mobile phones. They may turn on location tracking so that they can allow applications on their devices to assist with finding things and giving specific directions, for example, but what if that location-based service (LBS) was used to further exploit buying patterns. What if it was used to track location? What if it got into the wrong hands?

Bad reasons … and there are many, need to be considered when you think about how to safeguard your identity and privacy. Reconnaissance and surveillance techniques used to gather information about a target are nothing more than the exploitation of information that can be gathered through the myriad of ways available. The ability to track a target today is exponentially growing easier as more and more users move to mobile devices and more and more devices come to market to allow for tracking abilities. A rule of thumb is to limit your exposure. Only use what you need and be cautious. Think about why you want to use a service, device, or application before using it and consider the risks. Also apply common sense to every situation you are in.

Application Installation Versus Physical Device

There are also different ways in which you can be tracked; some ways are application specific and others are physical device specific. If you access a server to download files, you likely do this via an IP-based device that then connects to another IP-based device. Yes, the addressing can be spoofed; however, this can be easily mitigated if you know what to look for. Also, you need to consider that every movement you make in an application-centric world can be logged, which allows system administrators to look through logs and review activity. If you are at work and visit a questionable website against company policy, it's likely that you can and will be found doing so.

So what about physical devices? In this section, we will review some of the devices that you can use to track things; however, some of them can also track you!

As shown in Figure 5.4, the number of devices coming to market that people are wearing and carrying is becoming a concern to those who want to maintain privacy. With physical devices, you find that they can be clipped anywhere and can perform functions such as tracking your blood pressure or how far you have walked; however, it is when it is married to an application that the concern should set in.

As shown in Figure 5.5, the physical devices (such as ones people may put on their pet) can be tracked through the Internet (the cloud) to a computer of mobile device. Once it does so, it can then be tracked with all of the fingerprinting information we mentioned earlier.

Physical and application tracking is beginning to blur. You can, in fact, place a physical tracking device in the car of an unsuspected person (perhaps your significant other) to track their whereabouts, but it's not until this device is viewed in an application console or the device is linked to an application that you can view the tracking information. Therefore, it should be noted that

FIGURE 5.4 Physical Tracking Devices

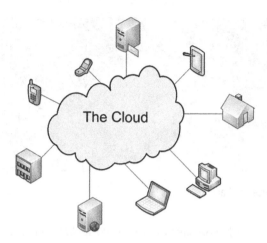

FIGURE 5.5 Tracking Through the Cloud

physical and application-based (or logical) tracking go hand in hand when tracking targets today.

Physical Device Tracking

There are many ways tracking can be accomplished. If the device is Bluetooth-based, it will emit a signal to other devices and those can be tracked by the system. If wireless, it will use 802.11-based technologies to be tracked by the central system. A global positioning system (GPS) is used to pinpoint the physical device location directly or through triangulation. As discussed earlier in this chapter, a GPS can use a satellite or a series of satellites to track movement of a device. For good purposes, GPS can provide you with mapping data for trips as well as to find a lost device. However, for malicious purposes, GPS can show an attacker your exact position worldwide. Geolocation data can also be used to track device usage by using information from other sources. TCP/IP can be used to assist with Geolocation. IP addresses can be tracked if it's an IP-based system.

As shown in Figure 5.6, the devices that can be used for tracking may use different technologies to allow for target tracking. For example, some are USB devices that, once placed, need to be retrieved. Some use GPS technology to communicate with a server that can allow it to be tracked and mapped.

Physical device tracking is a concern for those who are being stalked. For example, if an attacker is interested in learning your location, where you go and what you do, and wants to track you, they simply need to place a tracking device on you or in something you own, such as your car. You may never find it if it is placed in your car. An example could be, if a significant other wanted to see

FIGURE 5.6 Wireless Tracker

where you go on while you say you are at work. Are you stopping by a motel during the day? The physical tracker could give your location.

Some technologies are used for purposes of locating trucks in a fleet, as shown in Figure 5.7. Asset tracking is used to ensure that a fleet of trucks can be mapped and monitored for many purposes, one being to be able to give the customer accurate shipping information. It can also be used in emergencies.

As we can see, tracking is only bad when maliciously used but it's hard to control. It really depends on who uses the technology and why they use it – are they using it for the wrong reason? Then it is considered a problem. That being said, we really need to understand the fundamentals of being safe with the technical landscape growing toward allowing ourselves to be tracked.

You should always consider that you can and will be tracked. This should give you the edge you need to check yourself for tracking devices. Consider that you should always review what "tracking" you will allow of yourself with tracking technology. For example, if you use a health tracker, does it contain sensitive information you do not want to share? If this device connects to an application, do you want it to save this information? Where is it saved? On a central

FIGURE 5.7 Fleet Location Tracking

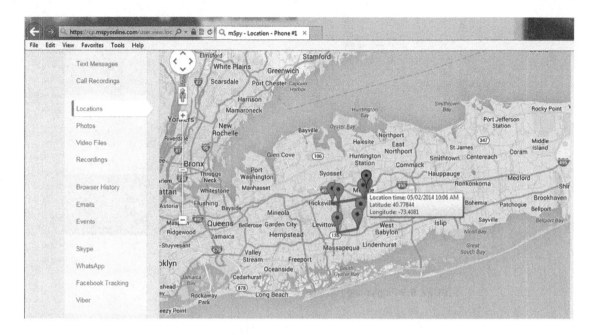

FIGURE 5.8 Physical Location Tracking Via Console

database server? Who has access to this data? As shown in Figure 5.8, the devices that map your location are always targets of misuse. You can quickly use a device on your phone that allows the tracking of your exact location at all times.

When using LBS, GPS, or any other application that uses a positioning and locating system, you can quickly become the target of another person or group. We discussed in earlier chapters how the government can track your activity and location, so consider it possible that others can too. When you sign on to Facebook, it tracks the device in which you signed in to it with. Facebook calls it security; however, it can be considered privacy infringement.

As shown in Figure 5.9, the mapping that can be done when you are being tracked is significant. For example, you can be tracked based on pattern. Your work routine, where you shop, and what main roads you take. As an example, it could be found that you take the same major road to work every day and are usually in the location at a specific time.

This level of tracking is concerning. What if this information got into the wrong hands? What if someone is doing this without your knowledge? These are all the reasons why you should always consider the risks when using tracking devices. You can always review your devices (or choose not to use them) for tracking. Yes, your phone could still be tracked, we made this clear; however,

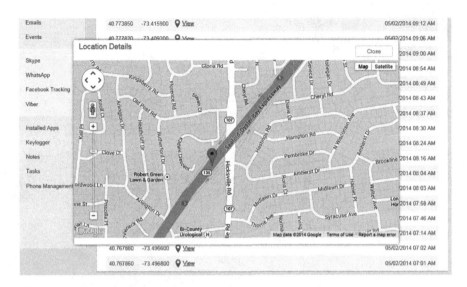

FIGURE 5.9 Pinpointing Location

you could also check for extra applications or services (such as LBS) that can help track you.

The best way to stay anonymous is, if you do not want to be tracked, leave your mobile device (and all tracking devices) at home when you leave the house. Consider that you will be on video camera and you could be tracked in your vehicle (license plate is a fingerprint), for example; however, you could take the bus. Disguise yourself. Sounds pretty crazy, doesn't it? That's because it is – you literally have to strip yourself of any traceable devices and travel in disguise to remain anonymous!

The only way to mitigate this threat is to limit exposure. Consider and weigh the risks of using tracking technology. Do not leave your car unlocked and do not leave your purse out of sight. Do spot checks. Leave your phone locked and on your person. Be slightly paranoid to remain safe.

Safe Devices Used Against You

Although we have talked about how physical devices used for good can be used maliciously, we have not talked about the new breed of technology that is also becoming more prevalent. Wearable technology is becoming more than a fad; it's becoming what we will be using in the future almost exclusively. As wearable technology starts to increase in popularity and becomes more important in our work and our personal lives, as security professionals we need to prepare for the coming storm.

FIGURE 5.10 Wearable Technology

As shown in Figure 5.10, the devices that track your heart rate, what you ate for lunch, how far you have walked, and what your emotional state was today are being developed into wearable technology fused with application-specific back-ends that manipulate this data.

As with any new technology, we must always be considerate of accidental or malicious access, leak, or corruption of data. Wearable technology is today's mobile laptop from years ago. When laptops first came to light and "going mobile" seemed brand new, laptop drives were fully encrypted. Now we make sure that we do so in case the laptop is stolen. We will be able to do this as well with wearable technology; however, what is more concerning is its ability to "track" your location, which is our focus. Pedometer use is growing as more people become health conscious. This means that an application tracks where you go and how long it took you to get there. This is data that in the wrong hands could be used against you. As shown in Figure 5.11, new

FIGURE 5.11 Wearable Technology

© Sony

FIGURE 5.12 Wearable Technology

technology is allowing you to track your health, for example, your blood pressure. What if you didn't want anyone to know you had a heart condition? High blood pressure? Well, you're recording this information in a tracking device that, if it got into the wrong hands, could be used against you.

The answer to this dilemma is to encrypt the data. In order to protect against data breaches outside of tracking your location, you need to ensure that all the data collected is secure. The threat is at the network layer, wherein in few instances, these devices use Bluetooth that could connect and emit data to other Bluetooth-enabled devices (or emitters) and send and receive data. As shown in Figure 5.12, the devices you wear could transmit data to unauthorized devices and your protected data can be stolen in real time before it can be secured without your knowledge.

It is also possible to gather location information in this fashion. That being said, these devices (such as smartwatches) could also be used for spying. For example, someone may be checking their time and, unbeknown to you, taking your picture or recording video or audio.

Other devices, such as the ones shown in Figure 5.13, can be used to track your luggage, which, if in the wrong hands, can show your vacation patterns; this becomes good for those who are looking to commit crimes against your home and personal belongings when you are away. What is worse than leaving your light on a timer to show that you are at home when in fact your wearable technology tells an attacker a different story! That is, if you didn't post pictures of you on vacation on Facebook while you are out of town.

These threats are still under review and security systems will be built to ensure safety, but But this does not mean we are there yet nor does it mean you should

FIGURE 5.13 Wearable Technology

bypass protecting yourself until it is. To mitigate against wearable technology threats, you should consider protecting yourself.

- Make sure you are careful of unauthorized Bluetooth pairing of and for your device.
- Make sure that malicious software is not installed on any device you own.
- Consider your surroundings.
- Limit your exposure (limit the use of wearable technology).

Location Tracking and Wearable Technology

Embedded within the mobile phones technology is a service called LBS; it is growing in popularity with wearable technology, specifically Google Glass and smartwatches. This allows location data to assist with providing enhanced functionality. The applications are developed so that you do not have to input information; the information required is simply queried from your device. As we discussed, in Apple's iPhone, the operation system (iOS) is deployed with a standard LBS functionality that allows applications to be able to track where you are and report it to the querying application. Maps can use LBS to track your current location on a map for the purpose of making your life easier.

As shown in Figure 5.14, the growth of smartwatches has begun and they will soon be mobile computing devices with the same baked-in technology of most

FIGURE 5.14 Using Smartwatches (Casio)

FIGURE 5.15 Using Smartwatches (FiLIP)

tablets or smartphones. That being said, LBS will need to be disabled or refined within them as well. Yes, you still need to consider and mitigate threat with Bluetooth; however, location tracking of your smartwatch is also a concern today.

Today, we are watching smartwatches evolving quickly. Google Android is currently leading the effort with their smartwatch offerings. As with mobile devices (phones and tablets), they are still vulnerable to penetration and could be hijacked and manipulated by an attacker. They can also track your location. As shown in Figure 5.15, the smartwatch does not look like a mobile device; however, it is a computer-based mobile device that you wear as a watch.

As a final example, the FiLIP smartwatch is used by parents to help track a child's location. You can program this limited use phone for a child so that it contains a few numbers and can be dialed easily, especially in an emergency; however, what it does do well is help you track the location of your child. This technology is continuing to grow and you should not only be prepared for it, but you should embrace it because it is not going away. You can limit your exposure to it by awareness that is what we intend to show you in this chapter. You can secure your privacy but you need to know the difference between how technology can be misused, what the threats are, and mitigate them if possible.

LEGAL AND ETHICAL CONCERNS

As explained in this chapter, tracking is done with ease and we, as consumers, can make it even easier. Although we await more cyberlaw-related crime in this arena, we can review some of the other cases that are brought to light where even companies such as Microsoft are involved in a civil action. In this case, Microsoft was accused of cybertracking. Although this case seems baseless, it shows that more case law will be coming in the future based on wearable technology, especially Google Glass.

The following memorandum from the US District Court, Eastern District of Pennsylvania, involves the plaintiff Antonio A. Ransom who brought a civil action against Microsoft (Bill Gates), William Clark, Diondre King, Beyock Williams, and Neicy Clerk alleging that the defendants could run electricity through his heart to produce a heart attack, and that the defendants "put him on the Internet and kept track of him." Ransom asks to the court to order the defendants to stand trial for cyber stalking, electronic harassment, body electronic surveillance, and torture interference.

The court dismissed the complaint as factually and legally frivolous. Ransom will not be given leave to amend because amendment would be futile.

IN THE UNITED STATES DISTRICT COURT

FOR THE EASTERN DISTRICT OF PENNSYLVANIA

ANTONIO A. RANSOM CIVIL ACTION

v.

MICROSOFT, et al. NO. 12-3575

MEMORANDUM

BAYLSON, J. JUNE 2012 J1,

Plaintiff Antonio A. Ransom brought this civil action against Microsoft (Bill Gates), William Clark, Diondre King, Beyock Williams, and Neicy Clerk. The complaint alleges that the defendants "can run electricity through [plaintiff's] heart to produce [a] heart attack." (Compl. III.C.) Plaintiff also alleges that the defendants "[p]ut [him] on the internet and [kept] track of [him]." (Id.) He asks to the court to "order [the defendants] to stand trial for cyber stalking (online tracking) electronic harassment body electronic surveillance and torture interference." (Id. V.)

Plaintiff's motion to proceed in forma pauperis is granted because he has satisfied the requirements set forth in 28 U.S.C. § 1915. Accordingly, 28 U.S.C. § 1915(e) (2) (B) applies. That provision requires the Court to dismiss the complaint if it is frivolous or malicious, fails to state a claim, or seeks monetary relief from a defendant who is immune. A complaint is frivolous if it "lacks an arguable basis either in law or in fact." Neitzke v. Williams, 490 U.S. 319, 325 (1989). A complaint is legally baseless if it is "based on an indisputably 'lleritless legal theory, fl Deutsch v. United States, 67 F.3d 1080, 1085 (3d Cir. 1995), and factually baseless \\when the facts alleged rise to the level of the irrational or the wholly incredible. fl Denton v. Hernandez, 504 U.S. 25, 33 (1992).

This Court will dismiss the complaint as factually and legally frivolous. Plaintiff's allegation that the defendants, including Bill Gates, are using the internet to run electricity through him to produce a heart attack lack a basis in reality. Furthermore, his complaint lacks a basis in law because he may not pursue criminal charges by filing a civil action. Plaintiff will not be given leave to amend because amendment would be futile. See Grayson v. Mayyiew State Hosp., 293 F.3d 103, 112-13 (3d Cir. 2002). An appropriate order follows.

Retrieved from: http://law.justia.com/cases/federal/district-courts/pennsylvania/paedce/2:2012 cv03575/464496/2

SUMMARY

In this chapter, we discussed the threats associated with tracking, wearable technology, and why you should be concerned. In previous chapters, we covered the fundamentals of tracking and focused on the mobile device that is likely to be your cell phone, although we find ourselves carrying it or within devices that can also be tracked, such as your car. We carry our cell phones everywhere we go that basically gives those with access a clear line of sight into your movement, activities, communications, and more. However, beyond the cell phone, there are many other products, services, devices, and applications we use that also track our behavior. In this chapter, we looked at not only the mobile phone but also other mobile devices that can be tracked. We also looked at other devices that you may not know can be tracked, such as your vehicle.

Another interesting trend emerging in today's technology is the "physical tracking" of items with devices. Other devices exist that help those who are forgetful. New devices are coming to market that allow you to place trackers on items you would normally misplace, for example, a set of keys. More commonly, tools are being sold to "track your pets" with sensors that only operate with Bluetooth and can only be tracked so far; some offerings can track you within larger radiuses. Another growing trend is with wearable technology where a new market has opened. This technology will allow tracking and the data collected is used with an application so you can track your health, diet, and medical condition. In sum, you should attempt to limit your digital footprint, always be concerned about how much information you share, and be cautious of how much you expose yourself and your data to those not privy.

CHAPTER 6

Web Camera and Video Tracking

CAMERA TRACKING

The increased use of mobile devices with cameras, personal computers (PCs) with webcams, and camera systems installed at homes, businesses, and out in the general public are growing at an alarming rate; the threats are also growing to expose security issues with them that violate your privacy. In this chapter, we will look at the growing use of this technology, what the technology is capable of, what purposes are served for good and evil, and why we should be concerned.

As we discuss these topics and how they relate to reconnaissance and surveillance, it will become evident that you are now always on camera. We carry one with us everywhere we go. There tends to be a camera located everywhere. Let's consider this example: You wake up and get ready for work, while in your home you are on camera as your home has an active internal security surveillance system. You check your e-mail before you leave the house on your laptop configured with a webcam. You pack up to leave and grab your mobile phone and tablet and get into your car. Your drive to work passing roughly 10 traffic lights before pulling in and parking in the parking garage. There is video surveillance feeds in the garage. You enter work and each entrance/exit and floor contains surveillance equipment. You dock your work laptop (with integrated webcam) and get to work briefly checking your mobile devices that are directly sitting next to you. Each time you leave your desk to move within the office, you take your phone with you. You leave for lunch and go to mall to eat in the food court with a few friends. The mall has video surveillance feeds. After work, you drive back home (10 traffic lights) and settle in for the evening. After dinner, you decide to load a game on your Microsoft Xbox and join a few friends online to play games. Later, you check your social media sites online and Skype with a friend.

We can go on and on but I think you get the picture. You are on camera 24 hours a day and this does not include the government's ability to pinpoint and track your whereabouts via satellite. This does not include military or law enforcement being able to use satellite tracking. In this chapter, we will discuss all of the ways you may or may not know you are being captured on camera and how you protect yourself. Digital surveillance is here to stay and will probably become more invasive over time, so learning how to mitigate threats and being aware of new threats is the key to regaining your privacy.

Tracking Examples

In the example given, we covered quite a few things that you may or may not be aware of. Let's recapitulate.

In the example: You wake up and get ready for work, while in your home you are on camera as your home has an active internal security surveillance system.

The reality of this is, although deemed secure, you are on camera in your own home. If you have a provider watching, they obviously have policies in place to protect your privacy; however, what if they are hacked? What if stored information is exposed? Although not likely, it is possible. What if those same cameras had a flaw and can be hacked by a neighbor or someone passing by?

You check your e-mail before you leave the house on your laptop configured with a webcam. You pack up to leave and grab your mobile phone and tablet and get into your car.

As we will discover while exploring this chapter, there are new forms of malware and hacking applications that allow an intruder to take over your device completely and view your surroundings from your webcam. Mobile devices are also exploitable via apps that also perform this behavior.

Your drive to work roughly passing 10 traffic lights before pulling in and parking in the parking garage. There is video surveillance feeds in the garage. You enter work and each entrance/exit and floor contains surveillance equipment.

As we have learned in earlier chapters, traffic lights (as well as bridges and other infrastructures) are protected with cameras that track your location. Surveillance systems are normally installed in public places such as parking garages and at the entrance of company locations. These same systems are also located within company work spaces.

You dock your work laptop (with integrated webcam) and get to work briefly checking your mobile devices that are directly sitting next to you. Each time you leave your desk to move within the office, you take your phone with you.

The same risks at home have now transferred with you to work. You are working on a system with a webcam (usually, directly integrated into your laptop or workstation) and your mobile devices are always close by.

You leave for lunch and go to mall to eat in the food court with a few friends. The mall has video surveillance feeds. After work, you drive back home (10 traffic lights) and settle in for the evening.

When you leave work, you pass all of the same surveillance gear you encountered on your journey into work and, similarly, where you go there will be more.

After dinner, you decide to load a game on your Microsoft Xbox and join a few friends online to play games. Later, you check your social media sites online and Skype with a friend.

You are back at home with the same possible threats but now you have opened even more by using other cameras located in your home.

Although this evidence may seem overwhelming, nothing can be further from the truth – it is possible that you are always on camera. In this chapter, we will look into each of these threats, how they have been exploited in the past, and, if possible, why it is important to be vigilant in securing against them.

Security Surveillance Systems (Private Home)

Systems put in place at home to protect your belongings, from intrusion and otherwise, can be helpful. There are actual cases where these systems have been helpful in not only preventing crime but also solving cases of crimes that have been committed. There are two classes of these types of surveillance systems. One you set up and monitor yourself or a professional system that is monitored by a third party. These systems can be internally and externally located at your home. Obviously, you would want these systems to be located.

In the summer of 2013, an arrest was made on a man who conducted a home intrusion in New Jersey and assaulted a woman in front of two small children. Jewelry was stolen and the suspect fled. A "nanny cam" had been installed in the woman's home used to keep an eye on the sitting services while away from the home. These webcams are common so that those who put their kids in the hands of others can be watched, so they can monitor how their children were handled that day. The suspect wanted in this home invasion had been captured on camera, and during investigation by the local law enforcement as well as the Federal Bureau of Investigation (FBI), an arrest was made to take the man into custody. As we can see, security systems do in fact provide a wealth of value when they are used for good. As seen in Figure 6.1, the camera caught the invasion and provided all of the evidence required to prosecute this attacker.

So, what about the privacy of the nanny? Was it disclosed that there was a nanny cam installed? Although this question may not even come up because of the nature of how successful this cam had been in capturing a criminal; however, this is also a concern because if not disclosed, this camera would be watching those entering the home and recording their actions without their knowledge or consent. This is where the argument comes in – where does privacy end and security begin? On one hand, a criminal was caught and taken off the streets. If the hired daycare or sitter watching children did something heinous, it would

FIGURE 6.1 Home Invasion Caught on Nanny Cam

be caught. These are positives and gain the support of many, but what about privacy of those who do not know they are being recorded such as a good babysitter who cares for the children and never know that their private conversations on their cell phone are overheard and so on.

Another concern with personal home security systems is that they can be hacked. Most systems work off of wireless networking and TCP/IP, therefore, if not secured correctly, can be easily penetrated and remotely used. Your living room has now become a prime time television for a stalker.

If you are not using a personal security system and have installed camera systems for a third party vendor or company to monitor for you, you should be aware that this means that a third party has the ability to see what you do in the name of "security." If these personal security systems monitored by a third party are exploited by someone attacking the vendor, then you could also be at risk.

Security Surveillance Systems (Businesses)

Systems put in place at businesses mirror those previously discussed when we did an overview on home-based security systems. Businesses need to protect their interests and assets the same way that a personal home owner would, and more so, because they are responsible for activities of their workforce. For example, what if someone in the office stole a piece of equipment and/or stole something from another co-worker? What if a crime is committed? There are legal implications that need to be considered.

Besides basic security, these cameras also provide a deterrent feature. Those who believe they will be caught are less likely to commit a crime. When you work for a company, go through on-boarding, and use the company's resources, it should not come as a surprise to you that you will be monitored.

Where this seems to cross borders is, what type of business are we talking about? For example, if this is a fortune 500 company where workers come in to do business everyday, it may not seem inappropriate to have security cameras placed in common areas; however, what if the business we are talking about is a school? What if it was a church? What if your right to privacy was invaded based on the business that was under surveillance?

Another concern is what if business systems then invaded your personal privacy at home? A great example of this can be seen when a school district in Pennsylvania during 2010 activated student webcams on school-loaned laptops used by the students. Parents were not informed and student privacy (and safety) was put at risk.

It can be said that in some instances, these cameras provide protection, can be used as a deterrent, and, in some cases, prevent or solve crimes, whereas in some instances, it can be used to commit crimes and evade your privacy. In such situations, understanding your surroundings and doing due diligence (covered in Chapter 8) will help you mitigate risks as much as possible.

Privacy or Security?

"Those who give up liberty for safety deserve neither" – Benjamin Franklin.

Those words ring true today more than ever. There is a large debate taking place and has been growing each day over the amount of "security" we need to be "safe." What is more concerning is the amount of privacy we wipe away as citizens under the guise of false security. Yes, it can be argued that cameras can be used for good, but in the wrong hands they are extremely dangerous. Civil rights are invaded, privacy is slowly eliminated ... what more will it take to show those who believe in being a free society that we are moving closer to George Orwell's 1984 each and every day we allow cameras to become a part of our lives? We carry a phone that tracks our every location. We drive in cars that can be tracked. We do things online that can be tracked. We make transactions that are tracked. Now, we do it all in front of cameras.

The question of privacy or security is one that cannot be answered easily. As long as there are those who live in fear and believe that the security offered is worth the rights they give up are worth it outweighs those who do not, we will continue to head down a path of giving up those rights. This question I believe is one that will be answered over time and through experience. We will have to take the ride and see where we get off. Hopefully, we do not live in an over-secure world and have given up all of our rights.

Security Surveillance Systems (Public)

If you are a fan of popular television drama, there are many shows available where crime is investigated by pulling camera footage to establish a timeline, to show specifics on "who was at the location" and otherwise. Although this is exciting on drama TV, it should be considered that these activities really do take place. As a matter of fact, many crimes are investigated in this manner.

FIGURE 6.2 Boston Marathon Video Surveillance

Part of doing Digital Forensics is recovering data stored on systems to re-enact a crime or offer evidence of a crime taking place.

Traffic lights, bridges, traffic cams for news outlets, and many other areas where we publically congregate are increasingly being put under video surveillance. Are we at risk or will this offer protection? There is much debate in this area; however, we can highlight examples where this type of surveillance was deemed to be helpful. The Boston Marathon example is one that sheds light on the helpfulness of video surveillance in public areas. As seen in Figure 6.2, the two suspects caught performing this heinous act were caught because law enforcement officials sifted through all available public video surveillance to put together the timeline and acts of terrorists performing an attack.

As mentioned, this is a good thing. The wrongdoers were captured because of the fact that they were caught in the act by the video footage. This advocates for more video surveillance to be placed in public places in order to stop these types of activities all together or to deter those from doing them. What the public may not know is, in order to provide this level of security video must be recorded at all times.

What the public may not know as well is, advanced computing systems are in place to scan video surveillance footage stored in databases that perform facial recognition as an example. Software is being developed to do advanced mining of data to create maps, pinpoint location, and other highly questionable tasks that if in the wrong hands could spell trouble for anyone's privacy.

Regardless, you should be made aware that you are under surveillance. This can be done by anyone who is using this technology by posting a sign to let those in the vicinity know that it is taking place. As seen in Figure 6.3, the signs can alert the public that the area that they are in is under surveillance.

This technology is also considered closed-circuit television (CCTV). CCTV is the technical name for a "network" of video cameras, viewing stations, and a digital video recorder (DVR) system that records, stores, and allows you to

FIGURE 6.3 Video Surveillance Warning Signs

retrieve video data. DVR systems that store data generally have hard disks that store the data they record. Since video is generally large in size when stored, the disk drives used to store them need to be large in size. Generally, the quality of the video can be lessened to decrease the amount of size it can be when stored. This will create a problem when forensics is done in a criminal case. It can be argued that the picture is not "clear" so it cannot accurately show the identity of someone accused.

Other types of public surveillance you should be concerned about are with law enforcement. Generally, police officers have recording equipment as part of standard issue on all police cruisers and other transportation equipment. Some enforcement agents also use body worn video cameras to show all actions taken while doing their work. Although this can help the enforcement agent, it can also create issues with privacy on routine stops or if you were suspected but innocent of a crime. The material is still recorded regardless.

According to the American Civil Liberties Union (ACLU), there are major problems with public video surveillance. The opinion is that video cameras and CCTVs are being made more and more of a necessity based on the fear brought on by the media, the government, and the voice of terrorism. Obviously, some form of this security is needed, specifically around high target areas or national landmarks but the proliferation of it to every corner of our lives is deemed ineffective.

As an example, when criminologists and other experts have reviewed cases based on terrorism, video cameras did not deter their consideration or ability to attack at all.

Another concern by the ACLU is that CCTV is prone to serious abuse. For example, in 1997, a police official used information captured by a police database to blackmail patrons of a gay club. Other forms of abuse such as institutional abuse and personal abuse are also possible. Targeting, discrimination, and other concerns also top the list.

The ACLU is also concerned about the lack of limits of controls on camera use, for example, public CCTV systems that can do facial recognition. The US Supreme Court since the late 1960s has used the verbiage "reasonable expectation of privacy" to assist with adding a level of privacy to police searches. The Fourth Amendment to the US Constitution allows for protection against police-based video searches; however, today no rules stop the abuse of CCTV. Some protection against video searches conducted by the police exists, but there are currently no general, legally enforceable rules to limit privacy invasions and protect against abuse of CCTV systems.

Another concern is that growing and uncontrolled use of video surveillance systems will change the face of society as we know it, as public citizens will begin to act differently when they know they are being watched and monitored at all times.

Satellite Surveillance Systems

Government/military agencies use satellite-based surveillance systems to perform reconnaissance operations domestically and globally. One may argue that these systems invade privacy; however, they have also proven to establish and maintain global security. Again, in the wrong hands this information could be problematic for anyone who deem privacy important, but what about security? Let's discuss an example where these satellite systems have proven to be helpful.

Reconnaissance satellites are generally ones that observe the Earth and can zoom in to view everything and anything from space to Earth's surface. Generally, used for military operations or law enforcement intelligence, these systems allow for high-resolution viewing, eavesdropping visually, and, at times, with audio and recognition.

As seen in Figure 6.4, the capture of Osama Bin Laden was largely done by observing the compound in which he was suspected (and later found to be inhabiting) via satellite. These same techniques were used in the second Iraq war to find Saddam Hussein.

Again, we can see where it is helpful, but this same technology can be used to track anyone, anything, and at any time globally and that when used by a malicious entity could prove to be considerably damaging. On a smaller scale, Google Earth and other tools allow for this level of pinpointing (nonmilitary grade) via latitude and also longitude.

PC Devices and Webcams

Now that we have reviewed video surveillance and its many applications, we should look at video at the PC level. Web cameras (or webcams for short) are not new and have been around for years. They allow a user of a PC to incorporate

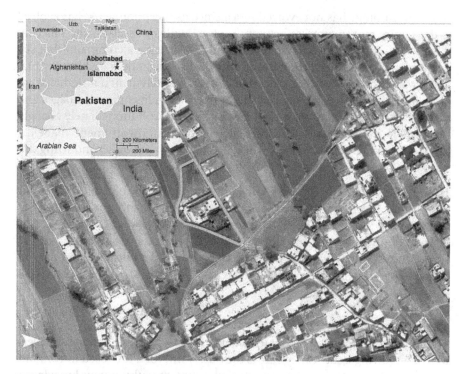

FIGURE 6.4 Using Satellite for Military Operations

video into software on their PC such as Webex, chatting software (such as Apples iChat), and Skype. Although this technology has been in use for years, it has grown to become more of a threat over recent years. As seen in Figure 6.5, the webcam can be a device either mounted on a PC or integrated directly into it.

FIGURE 6.5 PC Webcams

As this technology has not evolved much since its inception, what has evolved is the nature of the attacks that can be done with it. In 2013, the FBI conducted a probe after Miss Teen USA Cassidy Wolf made a complaint that she had been a victim of sextortion. Later, after the investigation, Jared James Abrahams was arrested for using Blackshades and remotely penetrating her computer and viewing her through her webcam. He made copies of images and sent them to her demanding sexual favors. Cassidy Wolf immediately brought this issue to the authorities and after law enforcement involvement, made the arrest of Abrahams. Abrahams had also pled guilty to not only conducting this operation but also against 100–150 other women.

This highlights the use of creepware, and through this probe and others like it, 90 other people were arrested in a hacker sting of other using this software. During this sweep, the co-creator of Blackshades was also arrested. The remote administration tool (RAT) was used to access the webcams of unsuspecting victims and spy on them. This arrest led to the development of counter-spy software (SnoopWall) that can be used to thwart these types of attacks.

Creepware

According to a report by Symantec (maker of anti-malware software), creepware is a growing issue. Creepware is the buzz word for a RAT used in conjunction with a Trojan to access and control your system without your knowledge. Essentially, it needs to be installed on your system; however, with spoofing e-mail and other common methods, getting it installed is generally not an issue for someone not savvy with keeping their systems clean, those not using anti-malware software, or those just tricked into installing it. Someone could also locally install it without your knowledge.

There are many flavors of the software to include but not limited to Blackshades (W32.Shadesrat), Poison Ivy (Backdoor.Darkmoon), and DarkComet (Backdoor.Krademok). Symantec and other malware fighters have said that you should be aware that the software running can remain undetectable to the common eye and you will need to scan for it to ensure that it gets cleaned off. Obviously, due diligence helps as well – never install something on your system from an untrusted source.

Mobile Devices

Mobile devices pose the same exact threat as PC systems do. Your video camera can be used against you no matter what device you use or what vendor you select. If the device has a camera, software can be installed to use it for malicious reasons. As we covered in Chapter 4, mobile devices can be tracked everywhere they go. Now, you can also install an app on it (hidden of course) and the video can be remotely accessed by an attacker.

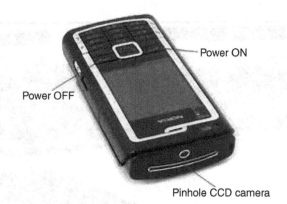

Power ON

Power OFF

Pinhole CCD camera

FIGURE 6.6 A Fake Surveillance Device

Another concept to wrap your head around is just how in depth that spying can go. According to a new research, a form of visual malware (also called PlaceRaider) can be used to create 3D models using your camera to build models of your environment in order to create a map. This highly advanced surveillance tool can be used to reconstruct a physical environment. Because this technology is new and has been created by the US Naval Surface Warfare Center, it is being claimed to be out of reach of the general hacker. This does bring to light that the government, however, can pull off such surveillance should be a concern.

Another concern may be false devices. This may seem very "James Bond" to you, but … dummy devices are used to spy on you as well, such as a fake mobile device that is really a recording device. As seen in Figure 6.6, the wireless charge-coupled device (CCD) spy camera/cell phone CN-SPY008 is a device that contains a color CCD camera and wireless video and audio used to capture data inconspicuously.

All of these devices should concern you. James Bond just became more advanced and anyone with a credit card can find, purchase, and use these stealth devices. Hackers can penetrate your legitimate devices or government agencies can access your devices for information.

Gaming Consoles

One of the biggest and growing threats today is with gaming consoles. Sony Playstation, Nintendo Wii, and Microsoft Xbox are few of the providers of devices that essentially do it all; however, they fly under the radar because they are not generally seen as a mobile device, a PC, or an entertainment system. What is interesting is, they are all three and much more. These gaming consoles have network connectivity, the ability to integrate into your systems and TV, and allow for the same as well as more application usage than all of these

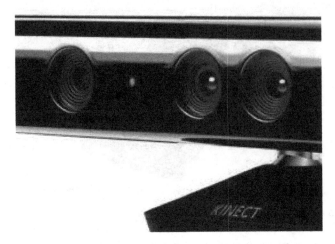

FIGURE 6.7 Microsoft's Xbox Kinect System

devices put together. They fly under the radar because they are generally not viewed as more than just being game consoles.

These devices also ask for your personal information, your financial information, and other data in order to allow you to interact with the vendor to get software, team up with other players, and interact with both vendor and gamers. Having read about all of the threats associated with surveillance thus far, this one should worry you the most. Consider your children use this system in their bedrooms, or perhaps you do. You may be under surveillance.

Microsoft's Xbox (360 and now Xbox One) uses a motion detection system that functions off of a video camera called the Kinect. As seen in Figure 6.7, the Kinect can capture motion, allow players to view each other, and much more.

According to researchers, this platform is considered highly sensitive to causing privacy issues. Children use it, it's located in private locations in the home, it's not secure by default ... these are but a few of the high-level concerns many have about the system.

The system has also been found to be crawling with child predators and has even been considered to be a channel in which terrorists communicate. Because of this issue, earlier this year, Edward Snowden released that the UK version of the NSA (GCHQ) had considered using the Kinect for mass surveillance. The program called "Optic Nerve" was said to have targeted over a million users for facial recognition database collection. Because of this release of information, Microsoft responded that they did not authorize this and that they were concerned. Their response would be to expand their use of encryption and bolster security. It should be considered that the Xbox One now ships with the Kinect by default and has already sold millions of units. This means that these systems are everywhere and could potentially be used as a surveillance tool. The Xbox One has additional privacy controls that can be used; however, the question of how safe it really is still remains.

This can be said for any game console that allows for video interaction. As more and more consoles are shipped with interactive gear, this threat only grows. To mitigate these threats beyond applying controls to them, simply not using them is advised and/or if your children use them ensure that they only use them under supervision, with privacy controls enabled, and in a common area in the home.

LEGAL AND ETHICAL CONCERNS

In this section, we will review case law in regard to how webcams can be used to spy against individuals and how they are brought forth in a court of law. In the following case, we will read about the Plaintiff Mr. Lammle who filed a claim against his then employer, the defendant, Ball Aerospace & Technologies Corporation, when Mr. Lammle was informed that his position had been filled after taking two separate leaves of absence.

Among other claims, Mr. Lammle also alleged that he was "falsely accused" of sleeping on the job and a webcam allegedly was used to spy on him. Mr. Lammle did not come forth with any evidence to establish the truth of each of these allegations.

In conclusion, the Defendant's Motion for Summary Judgment is granted. "Judgment shall enter in favor of the Defendant on all of the Plaintiff's claims, and the Clerk of the Court shall close this case."

IN THE UNITED STATES DISTRICT COURT

FOR THE DISTRICT OF COLORADO

Honorable Marcia S. Krieger

Civil Action No. 11-cv-03248-MSK-MJW

ALAN C. LAMMLE,

Plaintiff,

v.

BALL AEROSPACE & TECHNOLOGIES CORPORATION,

Defendant.

OPINION AND ORDER GRANTING

DEFENDANT'S MOTION FOR SUMMARY JUDGMENT

This matter comes before the Court on the Defendant Ball Aerospace & Technologies Corporation's Motion for Summary Judgment (#116). The pro se Plaintiff Alan C. Lammle has not responded to the motion.[1]

I. Material Facts

Where a party fails to respond to a motion for summary judgment, the Court does not reflexively grant relief to the movant. Rather, it must examine the movant's submissions to determine whether the movant has met its burden of demonstrating that no material issues of fact remain for trial. Reed v. Bennett, 312 F.3d 1190, 1194-95 (10th Cir. 2002); Fed. R. Civ. P.

Lammle v. Ball Aerospace & Technologies Corporation Doc. 156

Dockets.Justia.com

56(e)(3). In doing so, however, the Court deems Mr. Lammle to have conceded the truth of any properly-supported facts alleged by the Defendant. Fed. R. Civ. P. 56(e)(2). With that standard in mind, the Court turns to the facts as asserted in the Defendant's motion. In 2005, Mr. Lammle was hired by Ball Aerospace & Technologies Corporation (Ball), an information technology company, as a computer technician in the Information Management (IM) Department. In that position, Mr. Lammle served as the dedicated technician for engineers working at Ball. He was responsible for servicing and repairing their computers, troubleshooting software problems, and performing service calls to the engineers.

In June 2008, Mr. Lammle was hospitalized with pancreatitis. Due to his health problems, Mr. Lammle took a leave of absence from work until March 3, 2009. Upon returning to work, Mr. Lammle discovered that in his absence, the IM Department had been reorganized. Mr. Lammle was told that he would no longer be providing field support to the engineers. Instead, he was assigned to a service desk position. At the service desk, Mr. Lammle was responsible for providing remote computer service to all customers. Mr. Lammle continued to receive the same salary and benefits as he did before his leave of absence. Shortly after returning to work, Mr. Lammle complained to his supervisors that he had been demoted. He also complained that he was not being provided with sufficient training for his new position. In an e-mail sent to the Human Resources manager, Toya Specman, Mr. Lammle stated that he thought he would eventually be laid off because of his age and his "perceived disability." About a week later, Mr. Lammle's wife and former attorney, Amy Jane Simmons, sent a letter to Ball's legal department, alleging that Mr. Lammle had been falsely accused of sleeping on the job and that the accusation was part of a scheme intended to bring about Mr. Lammle's termination. On March 27, 2009, Ms. Simmons sent another letter to Ball's legal department. Ms. Simmons alleged that Mr. Lammle was suffering "harassment" because his pay was not directly deposited into his bank account that afternoon. On March 31, 2009, Mr. Lammle filed a Charge of Discrimination with the Equal Employment Opportunity Commission. In his Charge, Mr. Lammle alleged that he had been "discriminated against based

---

[1]*Mr. Lammle was given numerous opportunities to file a response. The motion for summary judgment was filed on December 17, 2012. On February 12, 2013, the Court granted (#133) Mr. Lammle's first request for more time to respond. The Court specified that no further extensions would be granted. On February 21, 2013, Mr. Lammle filed a second motion for extension of time (#138), and on March 21, 2013, he filed a third motion for an extension of time to "respond to existing motions" (#145). By text order on April 2, 2013, the Court granted in part (#146) Mr. Lammle's requests for more time. The Court ordered that Mr. Lammle had 14 days in which to comply with any pending deadline. Still, no response was filed. Despite having nearly four months to respond to the motion, Mr. Lammle has failed to do so. The Court therefore considers the motion without a response.*

on [his] age, 47, in violation of the [ADEA] and based on a perceived disability... in violation of the ADA." Specifically, he alleged that after his "demotion," he was "subjected to harassment and adverse terms and conditions of employment when [Ball] failed to give [him] appropriate training, and access to tools needed to perform the duties of [his] reassigned position." He further alleged that he was "issued a fabricated verbal warning [for sleeping on the job] under threat of termination on March 20, 2009."

In April, Mr. Lammle sent another e-mail to Ms. Speckman, raising additional allegations of harassment. In addition his allegations of being denied training and not being paid properly, Mr. Lammle alleged that another service desk employee appeared to have a web camera directed at him, so that "[he] could be fired for sleeping on the job" if he even "blinks or closes his eyes." Finally, in May, Ms. Simmons wrote another letter to Ball's legal department. She alleged that not only was Mr. Lammle being monitored by web cam and remote access of his desktop, but that someone was going through his personal lunchbox. She alleged that someone had stolen a used insulin syringe out of his lunchbox. Ms. Simmons suggested that perhaps the syringe was taken so that it could be tested for other substances and used "to fabricate another reason to terminate [Mr. Lammle]."

In June 2009, Mr. Lammle was hospitalized again. After he was discharged, Mr. Lammle did not report back to work. Instead, he began a second leave of absence. When he returned to work on December 1, 2010, he was informed that his position had been filled. Mr. Lammle received a right to sue letter from the EEOC in September 2011. He then commenced this action. As narrowed by earlier proceedings, Mr. Lammle has three remaining claims in this case: (1) disability discrimination under the Americans with Disabilities Act (ADA), (2) age discrimination under the Age Discrimination in Employment Act (ADEA), and (3) common law intentional infliction of emotional distress. Ball seeks summary judgment on each claim.

II. Summary Judgment Standard

Rule 56 of the Federal Rules of Civil Procedure facilitates the entry of a judgment only if no trial is necessary. See White v. York Intern. Corp., 45 F.3d 357, 360 (10th Cir. 1995). Summary adjudication is authorized when there is no genuine dispute as to any material fact and a party is entitled to judgment as a matter of law. Fed. R. Civ. P. 56(a). Substantive law governs what facts are material and what issues must be determined. It also specifies the elements that must be proved for a given claim or defense, sets the standard of proof, and identifies the party with the burden of proof. See Anderson v. Liberty Lobby, Inc., 477 U.S. 242, 248 (1986); Kaiser-Francis Oil Co. v. Producer's Gas Co., 870 F.2d 563, 565 (10th Cir. 1989). A factual dispute is "genuine" and summary judgment is precluded if the evidence presented in support of and opposition to the motion is so contradictory that, if presented at trial, a judgment could enter for either party. See Anderson, 477 U.S. at 248. When considering a summary judgment motion, a court views all evidence in the light most favorable to the non-moving party, thereby favoring the right to a trial. See Garrett v. Hewlett Packard Co., 305 F.3d 1210, 1213 (10th Cir. 2002).

If the movant has the burden of proof on a claim or defense, the movant must establish every element of its claim or defense by sufficient, competent evidence. See Fed. R. Civ. P. 56(c)(1)(A). Once the moving party has met its burden, to avoid summary judgment the responding party must present sufficient, competent, contradictory evidence to establish a genuine factual dispute. See Bacchus Indus., Inc. v. Arvin Indus., Inc., 939 F.2d 887, 891 (10th Cir. 1991); Perry v. Woodward, 199 F.3d 1126, 1131 (10th Cir. 1999). If there is a genuine dispute as to a material fact, a trial is required. If there is no genuine dispute as to any material fact, no trial is required. The court then applies the law to the undisputed facts and enters judgment.

If the moving party does not have the burden of proof at trial, it must point to an absence of sufficient evidence to establish the claim or defense that the non-movant is obligated to prove. If the respondent comes forward with sufficient competent evidence to establish a prima facie claim or defense, a trial is required. If the respondent fails to produce sufficient competent evidence to establish its claim or defense, then the movant is entitled to judgment as a matter of law. See Celotex Corp. v. Catrett, 477 U.S. 317, 322-23 (1986).

III. Analysis
A. Claims under the ADA and ADEA

Mr. Lammle presents two theories of recovery for each of his statutory claims. First, he claims that he was subjected to disparate treatment because of his age and/or perceived disability when he was reassigned to a service desk position and was not provided training related to his new position.[2] Second, Mr. Lammle claims that since he returned to work, he was repeatedly harassed and subjected to a hostile work environment because of his age and/or perceived disability, in violation of the statutes.

1. Disparate Treatment

Mr. Lammle claims that when he returned to work in March 2009, he was "demoted" to an office position and was denied training on certain software systems.

The ADA provides that "[n]o covered entity shall discrimination against a qualified individual on the basis of the disability in regard to job application procedures, the hiring, advancement, or discharge of employees, employee compensation, job training, and other terms, conditions, and privileges of employment." 42 U.S.C. § 12112(a). To prevail on a disparate treatment or discrimination claim under the ADA, Mr. Lammle must show that Ball intentionally discriminated against him for a reason prohibited by the statute. Jaramillo, 427 F.3d at 1306. In so doing, Mr. Lammle must make out a prima facie case, showing that (1) he is a disabled person as defined by the Act; (2) he was qualified, with or without reasonable accommodation, to perform the essential functions of the job held or desired; and (3) his employer discriminated against him because of his disability. See Mackenzie v. City & Cnty. of Denver, 414 F.3d 1266, 1274 (10th Cir. 2005). To demonstrate "discrimination' under the third element, Mr. Lammle must show that he suffered an "adverse employment action because of the disability." EEOC v. C.R. England, Inc., 644 F.3d 1028, 1037-38 (10th Cir. 2011). Similarly, to establish a prima facie case under the ADEA, Mr. Lammle must prove that (1) he is a member of the class protected by the ADEA; (2) he was qualified for the position at issue; (3) he suffered an adverse employment action; and (4) he was treated less favorable than others not in the protected class.

Jones, 617 F.3d at 1279.

When, as here, there is no direct evidence of discrimination, the Court applies the burden-shifting framework outlined in McDonnell Douglas Corp. v. Green, 411 U.S. 792, 802-02 (1973). The McDonnell Douglas framework applies to Mr. Lammle's discrimination claims under both the ADA and the ADEA. See Jaramillo v. Colo. Judicial Dep't, 427 F.3d 1303, 1306 (10th Cir. 2005); Jones v. Oklahoma City Public Schools, 617 F.3d 1273, 1278 (10th Cir. 2010). Under this framework, Mr. Lammle must first make out a prima facie case of discrimination, as described above. If he is successful, the burden shifts to Ball to articulate a legitimate, nondiscriminatory

[2]Mr. Lammle's statutory claims are limited by the scope of his allegations in the charge of discrimination submitted to the EEOC. See MacKenzie v. City & County of Denver, 414 F.3d 1266, 1274 (10th Cir. 2005); see also Jones v. U.P.S., Inc., 502 F.3d 1176, 1186 (10th Cir. 2007).

reason for its employment actions. If Ball proffers such a reason, the burden shifts back to Mr. Lammle to ultimately show that the stated reasons are merely "pretextual."

McDonnell Douglas, 411 U.S. at 804-05.

Assuming, without necessarily finding, that Mr. Lammle could establish a prima facie case on the undisputed facts here, Ball has carried its burden by proffering a legitimate, nondiscriminatory reason for Mr. Lammle's change in employment conditions in March 2009 – namely, that Mr. Lammle's reassignment was necessary due to the reorganization of the IM Department. Ball proffers that the reorganization was due to budgetary concerns and the need to create more efficiency. It also proffers that Mr. Lammle was not provided training on certain computer systems because other service desk employees were already providing support on those systems. Thus, to survive summary judgment, Mr. Lammle must show a genuine dispute as to whether Ball's proffered reasons for its employment decisions are pretextual. In other words, Mr. Lammle must show that the stated reasons are untrue, and that age and/or disability discrimination was the real reason.

An employee produces sufficient evidence of pretext when he shows "such weaknesses, implausibilities, inconsistencies, incoherencies, or contradictions in the employer's proffered legitimate reasons" for its actions that a reasonable fact finder could rationally find them unworthy of belief and therefore infer that the employer did not act for the asserted nondiscriminatory reasons. Jaramillo, 427 F.3d at 1308. The Court is mindful that when evaluating pretext, the pertinent question is not whether the employer's proffered reasons were right, wise, or fair, but whether the employer honestly believed those reasons and acted in good faith upon those beliefs. Stover v. Martinez, 382 F.3d 1064, 1076 (10th Cir. 2004).

In support of their position, Ball proffered the affidavit of Toya Speckman, its Senior Human Resources Manager. Ms. Speckman testified that in 2008, budgetary constraints required that IM Department improve its efficiency and lay off several employees. The evidence shows that the reorganization of the IM Department resulted in greater use of outside contractors, thereby reducing the need for Ball's technicians to work in the field. Further, the IM Department began delegating a higher volume of service calls to the service desk, where computer technicians could resolve problems remotely. Ms. Speckman testified that to implement the necessary layoffs, the IM Department manager, John LaFalce, conferred with the Human Resources and together they compared each employee's skills and performance level to those possessed by other layoff candidates and Ball's operational requirements. Ms. Speckman testified that the review identified three candidates for layoff – Mr. Lammle was one of them. She testified that although Ball laid off the other two candidates, it did not lay off Mr. Lammle. Ball opted instead to reassess its needs when Mr. Lammle returned from his leave of absence. Ms. Speckman stated that the individuals who were laid off were 28 and 30 years old, and neither was disabled. The evidence shows that although Mr. Lammle previously provided dedicated support to Ball's engineers, after the reorganization, Ball employees no longer served in that capacity. Ms. Speckman testified that when Mr. Lammle returned to work in March 2009, no technician positions involving field work were available. She stated that because Ball needed a service desk position filled when Mr. Lammle returned, he was assigned to that position. Ms. Speckman testified that there were at least two other individuals who were formerly computer technicians who were assigned to the service desk during the reorganization. One of those individuals was 54 years old, and the other was 36 years old; neither of them was disabled.

The evidence also shows that Ms. Speckman explained to Mr. Lammle that he had not received training on the "IFS" computer system because another service desk employee was already providing assistance on that system. During Mr. Lammle's performance review in June 2009, he was informed on how to access free online training and given suggestions for ways that he could increase his knowledge base and advance his career. Indeed, Mr. Lammle admits that he eventually did receive extensive training related to his position at the service desk.

Having reviewed the record, the Court finds that there is nothing to support an inference that Ball's proffered reasons for Mr. Lammle's reassignment and any denial of training are unworthy of belief. There is nothing implausible, inconsistent, or contradictory about Ball's reasons for its employment decisions. Rather, it appears that the decision-makers at Ball made choices that they determined were in the best interest of the company. Accordingly, the Court finds that nothing in the record that creates a genuine dispute of fact as to whether Ball's proffered reasons for changes in his employment were pretextual. Thus, Ball is entitled to summary judgment on Mr. Lammle's claims.

2. Hostile Work Environment

Mr. Lammle claims that, beginning in March 2009 when he returned to work, he was subjected to harassment. Ball moves for judgment in its favor on this claim, arguing that Mr. Lammle cannot prove that he was subjected to severe or pervasive harassment that altered the conditions of his employment, nor can he prove that the alleged harassment occurred because of his age or disability.

For a hostile environment claim to survive summary judgment, the plaintiff must show that a rational jury could find that the workplace was permeated with discriminatory intimidation, ridicule, and insult that were sufficiently severe or pervasive to alter the terms, conditions, or privileges of employment, and the harassment stemmed from age- or disabilityrelated animus. See Mackenzie, 414 F.3d at 1280; Lanman v. Johnson Cnty., Kansas, 393 F.3d 1151, 1155 (10th Cir. 2004). To evaluate whether a working environment is sufficiently hostile or abusive, the Court examines the totality of the circumstances, including the frequency of the conduct, the severity of the conduct, whether the conduct was physically threatening or humiliating or a mere offensive utterance, and whether the conduct unreasonably interfered with the employee's work performance. Harris v. Forklift Sys., Inc., 510 U.S. 17, 23 (1993).

Additionally, the environment must be both subjectively and objectively hostile. Id. Applying these principles, the Court concludes that the record falls far short of showing age- or disability-related harassment. Several of Mr. Lammle claims of harassment relate to the employment decisions made by Ball, such as the reassignment and denial of training. These decisions cannot be considered "harassment" because they were not undertaken for the purpose of intimidation, ridicule, or insult. Mr. Lammle also alleges that (1) he was "falsely accused" of sleeping on the job, (2) a webcam allegedly was used to spy on him, (3) he was allegedly yelled at on two occasions by his manager, (3) he did not receive his direct deposit on time, and (4) someone allegedly stole a used syringe from his lunchbox. Mr. Lammle has not come forth with any evidence to establish the truth of each of these allegations. Assuming he could do so, and assuming that these incidents could be considered forms of harassment, there is simply nothing in the record to support an inference that what happened to Mr. Lammle was because of his age or a perceived disability. Accordingly, the Court finds that there is no genuine dispute of fact with regard to Mr. Lammle's hostile work environment claims under the ADA and ADEA, and Ball is entitled to judgment on these claims.

B. Intentional Infliction of Emotional Distress

Finally, Mr. Lammle claims that he suffered severe emotional distress as a result of the "comments, actions, and inactions of [Ball]." He alleges that Ball failed to "provide any relief or assistance to [him,] severely altered [his] employment circumstances and created a hostile employment environment."

Under Colorado law, a plaintiff may recover for the tort of intentional infliction of emotional distress (otherwise known as "outrageous conduct") if the plaintiff proves that (1) the defendant engaged in extreme and outrageous conduct, (2) recklessly or with the intent of causing the plaintiff severe emotional distress, and (3) causing the plaintiff to suffer severe emotional distress. Han Ye Lee v. Colo. Times, Inc., 222 P.3d 957, 966-67 (Colo. App. 2009).

Ball argues that Mr. Lammle cannot prove any of these elements.

Before permitting a plaintiff to present a claim for outrageous conduct to a jury, however, the Court must rule on the threshold issue of whether the plaintiff has alleged conduct that is outrageous as a matter of law. Coors Brewing Co. v. Floyd, 978 P.2d 663 (Colo. 1999). A claim for outrageous conduct contemplates only acts that are "so outrageous in character, and so extreme in degree, as to go beyond all possible bounds of decency, and to be regarded as atrocious, and utterly intolerable in a civilized community." Destefano v. Grabrian, 762 P.2d 275, 286 (Colo. 1988).

Here, it appears Mr. Lammle alleges that Ball engaged in outrageous conduct when it took certain employment actions against him, and when it failed to prevent the "discrimination" from occurring. To the extent Mr. Lammle relies on the same conduct that formed the basis of his statutory claims, that conduct cannot be used as the basis of his claim for intentional infliction of emotional distress. See Emerson c. Wembley USA Inc., 433 F.Supp.2d 1200, 1228 (D.Colo. 2006); see also Katz v. City of Aurora, 85 F.Supp.2d 1012, 1021 (D.Colo. 2000) (noting under Colorado law, where the allegations forming the basis of a claim for outrageous conduct are the same as those forming the basis for a claim of discrimination, and nothing more, they fail to state an independently cognizable claim). Disregarding Mr. Lammle's allegations that form the basis of his statutory claims, his only allegations as to his outrageous conduct claim are that Ball failed to "assist and/or attempt to rectify the discrimination." As to those allegations, the Court finds that they are not sufficiently outrageous to support a claim for outrageous conduct. Indeed, as noted above, Mr. Lammle has failed to establish that he was subjected to discrimination. Accordingly, the Court finds that Ball is entitled to judgment on this claim.

IV. Conclusion

For the forgoing reasons, the Defendant's Motion for Summary Judgment (#116) is GRANTED. Judgment shall enter in favor of the Defendant on all of the Plaintiff's claims, and the Clerk of the Court shall close this case.

Dated this 1st day of September, 2013.

BY THE COURT:

Marcia S.Krieger

Chief United States District Judge

Retrieved from:

http://law.justia.com/cases/federal/district-courts/colorado/codce/1:2011cv03248/130043/156

A Right to Know

Public venues that use surveillance cameras generally post signs that inform people that they are being watched and recorded. This is considered a fair-minded approach to informing the public that any activity that is illegal or otherwise not allowed will be captured on a recording. This practice of giving notice of such use of surveillance cameras is followed voluntarily by most public and private security entities, and in many countries is mandated by law. Canada is one nation that has passed such legislation, which is part of the Personal Information Protection and Electronic Documents Act.

Proprietor's Duty to Protect

One of the legal issues regarding surveillance cameras concerns the duty of a business owner to provide an adequate level of security to his customers and clients. Property management companies that oversee residential complexes are expected to ensure the safety of their tenants against illegal activity and personal injury. Regardless of any tenant's personal opinion about her right to privacy, surveillance cameras are seen by most people as a necessary and reasonable method of ensuring the security of all tenants of the property.

Surveillance in Schools

Perhaps, one of the most controversial legal issues has been the use of surveillance cameras in schools. This use of security cameras was a result of an increased level of illegal and sometimes violent activities that has affected many schools, especially in larger cities. A case in Tennessee involving a middle school installing surveillance cameras in locker rooms raised legal issues when the stored tapes were made accessible on the Internet. The state Supreme Court ruled that this use of surveillance cameras inherently violated students' right to privacy under the Fourth Amendment to the US Constitution.

Silent Video Surveillance

Title I of 18 US Code Section 2510 of the Electronic Communications Privacy Act of 1986 states that video surveillance cameras are allowed to be used for watching and recording citizens without their knowledge or consent as long as no sound is recorded. Although proponents of the Fourth Amendment have contended that this violates the right to privacy, the code has been used by many government entities in this capacity without legal redress. This function is widely applied as of 2010 for watching and taping public highways and streets.

Protecting Potentially Dangerous Venues

Surveillance cameras are used to prevent access to certain especially important areas that present a potential danger to the public. Hospitals and scientific laboratories often contain chemicals and substances that could be lethal if exposed to the public. In these instances, the use of surveillance is not considered to be an invasion of privacy, due to the understood need to watch workers as they access these sensitive areas.

Retrieved from:

http://www.ehow.com/about_6049703_legal-issues-concerning-surveillance-cameras.html

SUMMARY

The increased use of mobile devices with cameras, PCs with webcams, and camera systems installed at homes, businesses, and out in the general public are growing at an alarming rate, and the threats are growing to expose security issues with them that violate your privacy. In this chapter, we have looked at the growing use of this technology, what the technology is capable of, what purposes are served for good and evil, and why we should be concerned.

As we discussed these topics and how they relate to reconnaissance and surveillance, it will become evident that you are now always on camera. We carry one with us everywhere we go. There tends to be a camera located everywhere. Let's consider this example: You wake up and get ready for work, while in your home you are on camera as your home has an active internal security surveillance system. You check your e-mail before you leave the house on your laptop configured with a webcam. You pack up to leave and grab your mobile phone and tablet and get into your car. Your drive to work roughly passing 10 traffic lights before pulling in and parking in the parking garage. There is video surveillance feeds in the garage. You enter work and each entrance/exit and floor contains surveillance equipment. You dock your work laptop (with integrated webcam) and get to work briefly checking your mobile devices that are sitting directly next to you. Each time you leave your desk to move within the office, you take your phone with you. You leave for lunch and go to mall to eat in the food court with a few friends. The mall has video surveillance feeds. After work, you drive back home (10 traffic lights) and settle in for the evening. After dinner, you decide to load a game on your Microsoft Xbox and join a few friends online to play games. Later, you check your social media sites online and Skype with a friend.

We can go on and on but I think you get the picture. You are on camera 24 hours a day and this does not include the government's ability to pinpoint and track your whereabouts via satellite. This does not include military or law enforcement being able to use satellite tracking. In this chapter, we discussed all of the ways you may or may not know you are being captured on the camera and how you protect yourself. Digital surveillance is here to stay and will probably become more invasive over time, so learning how to mitigate threats and being aware of new threats is the key to regaining your privacy.

CHAPTER 7

Data Capture and Exploitation

DATA THREAT

Data is everywhere. We leave digital footprints or impressions everywhere we go and by doing anything online or on a computer system, we leave our mark. Most, if not all, of this activity is traceable and can be tracked, and it is also available for data theft. We can attempt to protect ourselves or operate in a stealth manner; however, it is possible that your actions will be logged, tracked, and proven based on many factors. Digital forensic teams are called in to review systems that have been tampered with and/or when data theft has taken place, and there are many tools that can be used to prove certain activity has taken place. Lest we forget, there may also be cameras showing you were in the vicinity of a target system proving you were involved. You can remotely access these systems and it can be proven that by a source Internet protocol (IP) address, you may be involved. Even if it's spoofed, there are other ways to track this activity.

As we see, data tracking and doing forensic work in the digital domain can prove to be helpful; however, it is not always a guarantee that data can be kept secure. As many security analysts learned in the past decade, all of the security measures in the world did not stop a perpetrator from removing classified information about the US nuclear weaponry with a thumb drive.

In this chapter, we will discuss data at rest and data in motion, how it can be stolen, and what is at risk. We will discuss other methods of data exploitation and theft as well as cover how digital forensics can be used to reconstruct a crime scene and provide evidence. Other topics will include how to mitigate this threat specifically with encryption and how we can safeguard our data and identities.

Data Theft and Surveillance

While working as a security analyst, you may be asked to investigate data loss or theft. Data loss prevention (DLP) is the activity where you or your business entity does whatever possible to safeguard from data leakage or theft. With data everywhere, safeguarding it is a considerable challenge. Data leakage, loss, or theft causes one major problem – it is no longer secure or secret.

Data theft is also a problem that is getting considerably worse. As mobile devices are stolen, data is taken on thumb drives or websites are hacked and credentials are leaked; more and more attackers are able to spy on those they target or find targets through the data they acquire. This data can have confidential information such as passwords to financial accounts, pictures of loved ones that can also become targets, and/or medical information you wish to keep secret.

Just recently, it is alleged that Apple's iCloud has been hacked and hackers got their hands on 100's of nude celebrity photo's to include Kaley Cuoco, Avril Lavigne and Hayden Panettiere, Kim Kardashian, Hope Solo and Vanessa Hudgens. The claim is, although these women thought their private cloud backup was secure, it was hacked into and their private data was stolen.

Data theft can happen many ways. Physically, a pocketbook or a wallet can be stolen. Your phone or mobile device can be taken. Your laptop can be stolen. The data could be with a service provider and they could potentially become a target inadvertently making you the next target. A great example is with Target, where a security breach caused the loss of as many as 70 million customer credit cards to the hands of hackers. This is only one of many such examples; however, this one gained national attention because of the fact that many people shop at this chain of stores and use credit cards to pay for purchases.

So why is this such an issue when it comes to protecting your assets from surveillance, becoming a target and/or victim? Your data if not protected can be used against you. As an example, if your mobile device is lost or stolen and the attacker gains access, they can pose as you that is identify theft. They have access to your private information that can be used to launch a series of attacks against you and those you know.

Due diligence should be done in an effort to protect against becoming a target such as using encryption on your data so that if it is accessed, it cannot be used. Password protection allows those who gain access to a device to be challenged that may dissuade them from attempting to steal your data; however, if your password protection is not strong, it can easily be hacked. When considering surveillance, never store data that can be used against you without protecting it. It is up to you to protect against a data breach to ensure that your data is safe and secure.

Basic Data Capture Techniques

Data theft can be classified as being a physical theft or a logical theft. Physical theft is most likely to occur because it's the easiest way to steal data. If I can steal an entire computer and access the hard disks, memory, and so on, I stand a better chance of getting the data instead of coming over the network in an elaborate hack to penetrate firewalls and other protection methods in place.

Stealing print jobs off a printer is much easier than accessing a protected database logically to take data. If I can get your wallet or pocketbook and find paystubs, ATM receipts, and credit cards, I have a better chance at launching an attack then attempting to gather this information online.

Physical theft is not easy to limit if you are at risk or threatened; however, if you are not directly threatened, there are many ways to protect yourself and your data. For example, any form of physical security will limit your exposure. Something as simple as putting your wallet in your front pocket instead of your back pocket or removing items from your wallet that you do not need may help. Inventory of assets and evaluating risk are keys to mitigating the threat of physical theft. Limiting your footprint, being aware of your surroundings, doing due diligence, and assessing threats in real time can help.

Logical theft can be classified as a cyber attack. The first and most obvious way to steal data is to conduct surveillance on what is freely accessible. As we learned earlier in this book, we put a lot of information online that probably does not need to be there. Our friends and family add to it by using social media sites that increases the attacker's ability to gather information. When entering the digital domain, there are many ways that data theft can take place, which we will discuss in depth in this chapter. Considerations to take would be how to protect data at rest or data in motion as well as physical versus logical security concerns.

Data at Rest

Data at rest simply means that you have data saved somewhere and it is not currently being transferred digitally from one location to another. The best way to view this is with an example. Consider you have joined a new social media website and it has asked you to set up a username and a password. Once you do, your information is saved in a database used to validate your request to login. When you attempt to login, your information is sent to the database for validation (data in motion), where it's checked against your stored credentials in the database (data at rest). This example can be transferred to the using of file. If you create a word processor document and save it locally on your hard drive, it is data at rest. When you send that file via e-mail to a friend, it is in motion.

As seen in Figure 7.1, we can visualize how data can be stolen. Here, we can see that the computer in use can be stolen with the data on it or the server as well although it's likely to be kept in a secure location. Data can be remotely taken from the systems via a remote attack such as a penetration. They can be stolen locally with a thumb drive.

When considering an attack where data is in motion, it's important to understand that this will take place while the data is in transit. This means, if the data is sent from the client computer to the server, or downloaded from the server, while it is traversing the network, it can be taken. There are many forms of this type of theft that we will discuss in this chapter.

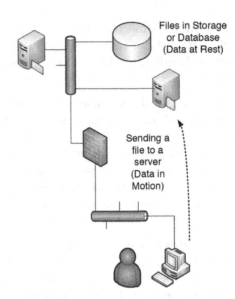

Files in Storage
or Database
(Data at Rest)

Sending a
file to a
server
(Data in
Motion)

FIGURE 7.1 Types of data theft.

Malware Protection

Malware protection can be used to protect both data at rest and data in motion. However, it is more likely it will be protecting data at rest. When you install antivirus or anti-spyware software on your computer systems, you are attempting to protect your data from malicious attack. If a malware gets on your system, it may attempt to corrupt your data, destroy it, or allow it to be sent to an attacker. If data is infected with malware and your antivirus software is active, updated, and not corrupted itself, the software will alert you and attempt to quarantine the malware as per design.

As seen in Figure 7.2, the antivirus software can protect your system (and the data) from virus and spyware threats as well as provide other safeguards such as network threat protection to protect against incoming attacks.

INTRUSION DETECTION, PROTECTION, AND PREVENTION

There are other forms of threat protection such as host"-based intrusion detection (HIDS) software that will alert you to the fact that an "attempt" to access your data was made. It operates off of a threat database that uses heuristics to look for trends in traffic that seem malicious. There are network-based forms of this protection such as network-based intrusion detection system (IDS) or intrusion prevention system (IPS), where it will attempt to prevent intrusions or detect that they have occurred.

When you think about surveillance activities, data gathering is a key to learning about your target and preparing for more advanced attacks. When attackers probe systems to gather data, data is logged in systems, firewalls, and sometimes can be flagged by IDS and IPS units. While, typically, IPS and other intrusion softwares are meant to block attacks such as IP fragmentation attacks, SYN attacks, and other types of network-based attacks, they can be referenced when scans are done to learn about a network architecture; so this may be a clue that someone is trying to gather information to learn a way to map or penetrate the network in order to obtain data.

DLP Software

DLP software is a suite of applications that allow you to safeguard data from theft from file servers, e-mail servers, local systems, the cloud, and other locations where data is kept. It is used to consider data in motion and at rest and allows for the safeguarding of key data when used. It works by first making sure that an inventory of your data is recorded and will flag key data leaving your systems or network based on its sensitivity.

As seen in Figure 7.3, confidential sensitive data is selected to be secured and if it attempts to move beyond its policy points, it will be flagged as a violation. A good example of this is when considering health records. If sensitive patient information is added as a marker for DLP and someone attempts to e-mail patient information, DLP can be used to ensure that it is not sent thus safeguarding it.

Databases, file shares, e-mail, local computers, and servers can all be configured as "endpoints." Network DLP can be configured to safeguard sensitive data leaving your network moving from private network to public network

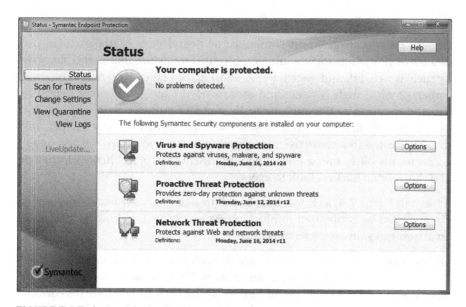

FIGURE 7.2 Typical antivirus software.

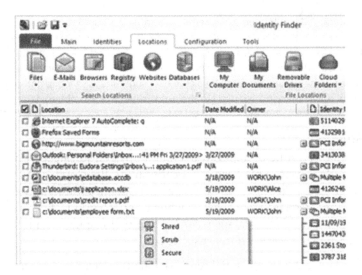

FIGURE 7.3 Using identify finder for data loss prevention.

segments. An example would be to ensure that endpoints are configured to monitor and control active threats and use network DLP at your exit (or egress) points on your network. If an attacker is able to penetrate or an internal threat such as a malicious employee decides to send sensitive data, DLP will ensure that it is kept secret.

Firewall Systems

Firewall systems are generally configured on host devices or in particular parts of a network such as ingress and egress points to ensure that malicious activity such as network and system penetration do not take place. As we discussed earlier, physical theft is easier and more likely to succeed because logical security in the form of IPS units, firewalls, and DLP software make stealing data extremely difficult to do. Since most firewalls (and other security devices) ship to the customer in a restrictive configuration making you open what you need access to, it's likely that a misconfiguration will take place; however, they do and this is what hackers look to expose.

As seen in Figure 7.4, a typical host-based firewall (such as Microsoft Windows Firewall) can be configured to block access to a system making it difficult for an attacker to gain access to steal data.

Online attacks and remote attacks are difficult because the firewall will block or restrict access and alert you to an attempt. By doing so, this prevents many attempts to penetrate the system as long as the firewall is active; it's correctly configured and set to update you when a breach may have taken place.

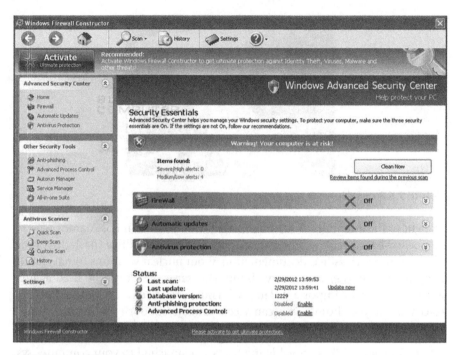

FIGURE 7.4 Typical host-based firewall.

Removable Media

As we have learned, remotely attacking a system has grown difficult. There was a time where you could potentially run a quick identification scan, find an open system, enter it, and have access to the data on the system. As computer system evolved, so did the many ways in which is can be secured. While we as security analysts and engineers learn of holes in our security design, we make attempts to close them with tools, software, and other methods. As we close them, attackers learn of new ways to penetrate systems around the protection methods put in place. One of the key ways data theft grew based on the period of time where firewalls and other security tools were put in place was by stealing the data locally directly from the system. For example, removable media such as DVD-ROMS, external and thumb drives, and other forms of media were used to access a system locally, dump the data directly on to them, and then walk away without being caught. Note that if there are cameras or other forms of security in place, you will still be seen touching the system; however, not all systems are protected with video surveillance.

Thumb drives are the most common because they fit in your pocket avoiding detection and allowing you to quietly and covertly take data from a system without anyone's knowledge. One of the best examples of a major data theft that was

FIGURE 7.5 Removable media threat.

brought to the attention of national news headlines was in Los Alamos when a US nuclear-based vault was penetrated and a USB thumb drive (flash drive) was used to remove classified documentation about nuclear weapons. What should a common computer user worry about? This same attack can be used against you to gather your important data. A friend or relative can conduct the same exact attack at your home. They can access your system during Christmas dinner by downloading all of your important documents and data in seconds.

As seen in Figure 7.5, removable media can be attached to your computer system and data can be taken without your knowledge. In this example, a simple flash drive was inserted in an open USB slot that allowed the drive to be populated with data and was quickly removed and taken with the attacker.

Removable media attacks are a convenient way for an attacker to quickly access and remove your data from your machine. We see this being done in movies all of the time. This type of attack is called thumbsucking. What makes this attack so concerning is that as devices evolved, their capacity has also increased exponentially that gives the attacker the ability to potentially take all of the data on your drive without being caught.

DATA EXPLOITATION CONCERNS

Data exploitation concerns are many. Any data saved on your local computer can be used against you and this data may contain financial records, medical records, personal information, work-related information, family information, pictures, and more. Just consider that the perfect mitigation strategy for this type of attack would be to ensure that any local devices are secure, and mobile devices are not left in a place where they can be stolen. Always set up a lock code on your device for a little extra protection and as a deterrent.

If devices are left out, it should be noted that any open ports that are unneeded are disabled. Logging can be turned on to validate when access has taken place. Encryption can be used to safeguard any and all data saved locally or sent in transit.

Encryption Protection

With the concerns of removable media attacks, data in motion, and data theft, in general, a method to protect against each form was invoked to ensure that if data was in fact stolen, it would be unusable to those who may have gathered it. Encryption is the process of applying a cipher to make data unreadable to those without the ability to decrypt it. Encryption can be applied to data at rest and in motion. It should be noted that encryption protection can in fact be thwarted. There are tools out there that can be used to break encryption to decipher and gain access to your protected data. Thus being said, make sure that you use a "strong" encryption method allowing for data to be secure if stolen.

As seen in Figure 7.6, encryption through a software tool can apply encryption to folders of data, to drives, and even protect access against USB drives where if used for malicious purposes will only allow those who may have stolen data to read it if they have the key or passphrase.

Other methods such as encrypting an entire disk drive is recommended for those who want to ensure that if their system is stolen, the data cannot be accessed without unlocking it first. This is very handy for those who want to safeguard their mobile systems such as laptops.

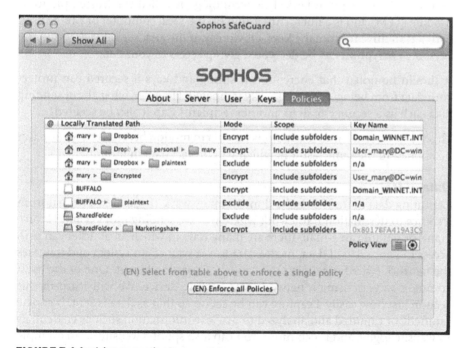

FIGURE 7.6 Applying encryption to your system.

FIGURE 7.7 Using Windows BitLocker encryption.

Windows BitLocker drive encryption is a Microsoft-based encryption method where data protection can be applied through encrypting all of the data stored on your drive. It will encrypt volumes on your drive (the logical location where your data is stored) such as Drive C. As seen in Figure 7.7, if you apply Bit-Locker on your local drive, you can protect the data if the device is stolen.

To use this technology, it should be noted that specialized hardware can be used to store encryption keys. This technology is called the trusted platform module (TPM) and is a microchip found on the local computer or can be used with a USB drive to store the keys. Obviously, if the attacker gains access to the keys, the encryption can be decrypted giving access to your data.

It should be noted that encryption if strong and keys if secured can protect your data from being stolen or locally tampered. However, what about sending data such as a secure e-mail to another recipient? Can it also be secured?

This is a good segue into discussions on data in motion because encryption can be applied in the same fashion, which will protect data in motion.

Data in Motion

Capturing data in transit can be done in many ways. If you are viewing it from a source to destination framework where you are sending files via an FTP program, or sending an e-mail, there are many ways in which an attacker can gain access to your secured data. As the data leaves your client system and traverses the network (wired or wireless), it can be captured in transit. One of the most common ways is using a network data capture device. We will learn in this section just how easily a capture can be set up so that as data is sent, it can be "sniffed" or captured and analyzed to disclose information such as credentials to website logins and much more. You can also spoof a website as an example and capture data such as credentials as it flows from source to destination. This way, a victim will send data from source to destination and it can be captured in transit by a collection device.

You can also skim data from a credit or a debit card through a hardware device as it sits as a shim in between the card and the actual reader. Attackers are getting good at stealing data and one of the key ways they are able to steal financial data is with card skimmers.

DLP software can protect egress points as well as firewalls; however, they cannot capture anything. Lower exposure by educating yourself and others on what should be sent and how it would limit risk; however, DLP can be used to capture and analyze data in motion that goes against security policies in place.

There are also ways that data can be secured in transit. Endpoints can be encrypted from point to point, such as via VPN tunnel that can prevent eavesdropping attacks from taking place. Mail can be sent with encryption and can be decrypted by the recipient. Although most of these tasks require effort, they can help prevent exposure and data theft.

Sniffers

A protocol analyzer (also known as a sniffer, packet analyzer, network analyzer, or traffic analyzer) can capture data in transit for the purpose of analysis and review. Sniffers allow an attacker to inject themselves between a conversation between a digital source and destination in hopes of capturing useful data. Some data if unencrypted can be opened and viewed. Credentials can be sent in cleartext exposing your secured logins to risk. As seen in Figure 7.8, unless encrypted in a way that cannot be decrypted easily, any and all data sent to and from can be viewed and used for wrongdoing.

Sniffers are used for good reasons and mostly to troubleshoot problems on networks and systems. It is when they are used for the wrong reason that threats can take place, for example, if an attacker was able to set up a sniffer to capture the traffic you send and is able to capture unencrypted e-mail, passwords to websites, and so on, in order to use this data against you. As you can see, this data can be deciphered to show you source IP addresses as well, which may show the attacker where they need to focus a penetration attack. As seen in Figure 7.9, an attacker could capture a source IP address (which is where you may be originating from) in order to launch a logical attack to gather data, conduct other reconnaissance missions, or penetrate to gain data access.

If this can only be protected against with encryption, how can you thwart these attacks? For one, a sniffer needs to be loaded on a machine for it to be used. There are cases where it can be loaded elsewhere and have data sent to

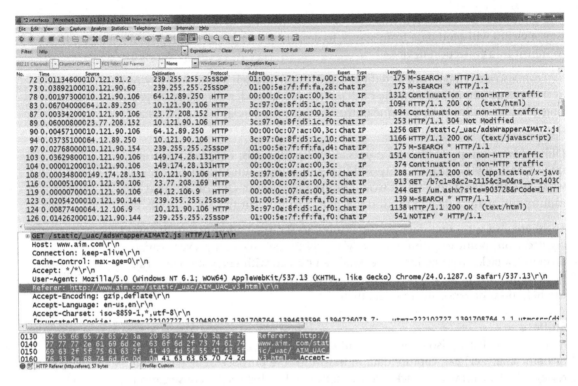

FIGURE 7.8 Using a sniffer to capture data.

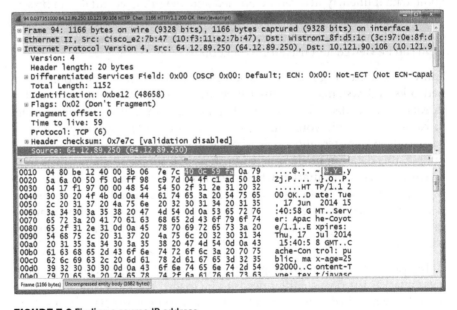

FIGURE 7.9 Finding a source IP address.

it; however, most times the capture will be directly conducted on the source system. Again, you have to be conscious of what is loaded on your systems in order to make sure it's not loading and collecting data. This was the same practice we implemented when we discussed mobile phones and knowing what is loaded on it in order to protect against malware.

SNIFFING AND OTHER ATTACKS

Eavesdropping is a form of attack where an attacker uses a program, device, or tool such as a sniffer to capture data in transit. It can give the attacker information to conduct other attacks, or to steal your data. Man in the middle (MITM) attacks are similar, where an attacker is able to inject themselves into a conversation between source and destination and act as one of the participants in hopes of gaining information from a trusted source. Replays take place by capturing data and replaying it in a way to gain access to systems, reconstruct phone calls, and so on. As seen in Figure 7.10, a voice over IP (VOIP) conversation can be captured and replayed with a sniffing program.

Skimmers

As ATM cash machines and other card swipe systems grow to expand financial institutions reach, make cash ready and easy to access, and allow ease of use for consumers to use credit cards, more and more attackers are deploying card skimmers to capture your credit or debit card information as you enter it into a legitimate machine to access your banking information.

Data skimmers, generally used to obtain financial gain, make duplicate cards or sell your information to others for identity theft exploitation. Data exploitation causes those who pull off these attacks to experience financial gain and access to your data. This form of data theft can occur anywhere worldwide, anywhere an ATM or a card swipe technology is available.

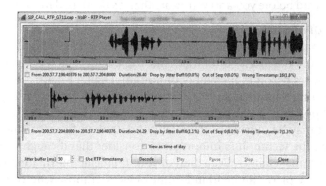

FIGURE 7.10 Replaying a captured VOIP call

FIGURE 7.11 Data theft via card skimmer.

What makes this attack incredibly frustrating to those who are victimized is that it is so hard to detect. Most times, attackers are able to put a skimmer on a legitimate ATM machine and unbeknownst to those who use it, it collects the data from the card without the victim's knowledge. As seen in Figure 7.11, card skimmers can be installed quickly and easily as they cover the face of the real card reader allowing the attacker to collect this data while you are able to still conduct your original transaction.

Once the card information is collected, it can be used as it will collect all information on the card including the track information. Once this is collected, the card can be duplicated and used. To mitigate this threat, attempt to only use ATM systems and other card swipe technology that is under video surveillance, which will limit an attacker's ability to install a skimmer. Generally, those who are able to view a skimmer by eye will see that at times it protrudes from the original reader slightly; however, you may not always be able to see them. If you feel that your card information has been stolen, immediately call your financial institution. Today, most financial institutions track fraud in real time and will shut down your card before you are even aware that it's been used in a fraudulent way.

Digital Forensics

Once data has been stolen, it may wind up in the court of law as evidence if in fact a crime has been committed and the evidence is recoverable. This is where forensics becomes incredibly important. Digital forensics is the process of investigating data theft so that it can be analyzed for artifacts, proof, evidence and possibly to reconstruct a crime scene. We explain this here because although it may be outside of the realm of data theft from an attacker where you may be the victim, it is important to consider that if caught, the attacker may face criminal charges. Data theft of your financial information that causes a crime to take place can be found in the devices of those who conducted the crime and if this evidence is captured, could be used against the attacker.

What is also important to consider is, from a surveillance point of view, any data even data you think you may have erased could possibly be resurrected with digital forensic tools and software. As an example, if you are using a mobile device and a crime has been committed, it's recommended to plug the phone in and keep it powered on until it can be investigated so that everything that remains in memory can be captured whereas if you power it off, data may be lost. It is also important to consider that where you believe that by securing your data, that does not mean that a government agency such as the FBI or NSA cannot recover it.

Devices and Applications

There are many devices and applications that can be used to capture data on a system or in memory in order to perform forensic work. Once of the most common applications in use today is Encase. This software created by Guidance Software is one of the *de facto* standards used to do digital forensics and e-discovery to reconstruct crime scenes. This tool can be used on computer systems, servers, mobile devices, and more. As seen in Figure 7.12, performing forensic work can also take place with hardware devices that can be plugged into and used to capture data from devices such as a mobile phone. In this example, a UFED device from Cellebrite is used to capture mobile data.

Mobile forensics will allow an analyst to view call logs, text logs, data on the phone, in memory, and much more. There are other devices as well such as a Tableau analyzer as seen in Figure 7.13, which allows data to be captured and advanced analytics to be performed. Although this focuses on business intelligence analytics, data is still being captured, read from a device, and used to reconstruct evidence.

In sum, it should be noted that digital forensics is done for the purpose of good, to reconstruct a crime and provide evidence. As we have learned throughout this book, that does not mean these devices will always be used by those with good intentions. It also does not mean that those entrusted with using them will not alter the data they find or delete it completely.

FIGURE 7.12 Mobile device forensics.

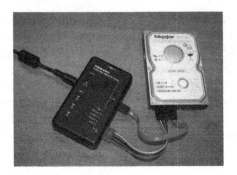

FIGURE 7.13 Advanced data capture and analysis.

This is what is so concerning about these tools and how most if not much of what we do resides in the digital domain. Your data is not secure; there is a way to get it either from attackers or working professionals. As we move into our last chapter, we will solely focus on how to mitigate most if not all of the risks brought to light in this book in hopes that by now you understand that you need to consider the risks of using anything digitally. That mobile devices are a threat if stolen, you can be tracked … you can be spied on easily.

STOCHASTIC FORENSICS

Technically, digital forensics is performed by reviewing artifacts left behind, such as entry into a file where that entry can be found digitally within the system, logs, or memory. Unfortunately, crimes can be committed by those who are allowed to have access to the system and these trusted individuals were for some time able to get away with crimes because of the inability of being able to track it. Therefore, a new form of forensics has taken hold called stochastic. This form of forensics is able to assist in reconstructing a crime without the need to review artifacts, technically because they may not be able to be reviewed. Data theft can still be identified with this form of forensics by viewing other important remnants outside the realm of artifacts such as metadata.

LEGAL AND ETHICAL CONCERNS

In this section, we will discuss another case where legal issues and concerns were brought to light. In this murder charge where cybercrime was involved, data exploitation and other tactics were involved by the attacker.

In early 2000, Defendant Michelle Catherine Theer met United States Army Sergeant John Diamond, a Special Forces soldier stationed in Fayetteville at Fort Bragg, via the Internet and began an extramarital affair with him. Months later Sergeant Diamond sent e-mails to Theer indicating he was unhappy about the possibility of their relationship ending and her remaining with her husband.

At sentencing in December 2004, a jury trial found Theer guilty of first-degree murder by aiding and abetting, and of conspiracy to commit first-degree murder in the death of her husband, United States Air Force Captain Frank Martin Theer.

Some of the evidence used to convict her consisted of documents and computer records. The jury was also presented with evidence as to Theer's Internet posting and alternative lifestyle for the limited purpose of evaluating of the marital status of the defendant and her husband, as well as Theer's mental status, Theer argues that this testimony about the computer documents and e-mails should have been excluded as bad character evidence, as it made her out to be a "moral degenerate' and went beyond simply chronicling her extramarital affairs.

COURT OF APPEALS OF NORTH CAROLINA.

STATE OF NORTH CAROLINA V. MICHELLE CATHERINE THEER.

No. COA05-1640.

Decided: January 16, 2007

Attorney General Roy Cooper, by Assistant Attorney General John G. Barnwell and Assistant Attorney General Kathleen U. Baldwin, for the State. Daniel R. Pollitt, Assistant Appellate Defender, for the defendant-appellant.

On 3 December 2004, Defendant Michelle Catherine Theer was convicted of first-degree murder by aiding and abetting and of conspiracy to commit first-degree murder in the death of her husband, United States Air Force Captain Frank Martin Theer. Defendant appeals to this Court, challenging the sufficiency of the evidence to convict her and arguing that the trial court committed either error or plain error in her trial. Upon our careful review of her appeal, we hold that Defendant received a fair trial that was free of prejudicial error.

At trial, the evidence tended to show that the Theers married in 1991 and subsequently lived in several different states as Captain Theer was stationed at Air Force bases around the country. In 1999, the couple moved to Fayetteville, where Captain Theer was posted on Pope Air Force Base and Defendant was employed by psychologist Thomas Harbin, as she worked toward getting her own permanent license as a psychologist. Throughout this time, Captain Theer was often deployed overseas and away from home for long stretches of time, and the marriage struggled.

In early 2000, Defendant met United States Army Sergeant John Diamond, a Special Forces soldier stationed in Fayetteville at Fort Bragg, via the Internet and began an extramarital affair with him. In June 2000, Defendant rented her own apartment and lived separately from Captain Theer; the two started marital counseling in July while also going through a trial separation. In October, Defendant reconciled with Captain Theer, moving back into their home and telling Dr. Harbin that she planned to end her affair with Sergeant Diamond. In November, Sergeant Diamond sent e-mails to Defendant indicating he was unhappy about the possibility of their relationship ending and Defendant's remaining with her husband. On December 9, 2000, Defendant met and engaged in sexual relations with Sergeant Diamond in Raleigh, after telling Captain Theer she was going there to celebrate her birthday with a graduate school classmate.

On December 17, 2000, Defendant and Captain Theer traveled from Fayetteville to Cary with Dr. Harbin, his wife, and another couple, for a dinner to celebrate the holidays. Around 9:00 or 9:30 p.m., as the group prepared to leave the restaurant, Defendant went to the restroom and made a cell phone call to Sergeant Diamond, who was watching a video with his estranged wife and mother-in-law. After the phone call, Sergeant Diamond put on cold-weather clothing and left the house.

Meanwhile, Defendant and Captain Theer took the other couple back to Dr. Harbin's office in Fayetteville, where they had left their car, arriving around 10:30 p.m. Thereafter, Defendant and her husband left the parking lot but returned approximately 10–15 minutes later after Defendant "remembered that she needed a reference book from her office to prepare for two book reports ... due the next day." Defendant later told the police that Captain Theer waited outside while she went inside Dr. Harbin's office to get the books. Shortly thereafter, she heard gunshots, ran outside, and found Captain Theer, unresponsive, at the bottom of the steps outside of the building. Defendant stated that because she had accidentally locked her keys inside the building when she went outside, she ran to a late-night video store about a block away to get help. Captain Theer died as a result of five gunshot wounds, including one fired at close range just behind his left ear.

Following Captain Theer's death, Defendant continued her relationship with Sergeant Diamond, including taking a trip to Florida together. Police later linked Sergeant Diamond to a semiautomatic pistol that was of the same model used to kill Captain Theer. However, after Sergeant Diamond learned that the police wanted to obtain the pistol for ballistics testing, he reported that his vehicle had been broken into on base and the weapon stolen.

As a result of his statements regarding the pistol, military authorities charged Sergeant Diamond with making a false official statement, false swearing, and obstruction of justice. Around February 20, 2001, he was placed into pre-trial confinement at a military facility. Sergeant Diamond was later charged with and convicted by a General Court-Martial of murder and conspiracy to commit murder in the death of Captain Theer and sentenced to life in prison without parole.

On May 21, 2002, Defendant was indicted for first-degree murder and conspiracy to commit first-degree murder in the death of Captain Theer. However, around the date of the indictment, Defendant, who had moved to New Orleans since the murder, left from there, reportedly to "start a new life." She moved to Florida, where she rented an apartment and had plastic surgery performed under an assumed name. Files and documents found in her Florida apartment indicated Defendant had a long-range plan to create several false identities and essentially to "disappear."

The Police located and arrested Defendant in August 2002, and her trial began on September 27, 2004. At the conclusion of the nearly 3-month trial, the jury returned verdicts of guilty of first-degree murder by aiding and abetting, and of conspiracy to commit first-degree murder. The trial court sentenced Defendant to life in prison without parole.

Before this Court, Defendant appeals from those verdicts, arguing (I) the trial court erred by denying her motion to dismiss the charges of first-degree murder and conspiracy to commit first-degree murder because the State presented insufficient evidence that she was a perpetrator of the crimes charged; (II) the trial court improperly expressed opinions about her guilt and defense witness Angela Forcier's credibility; (III) the trial court erroneously admitted irrelevant evidence and argument about her bad character; (IV) the trial court improperly denied her motion for a mistrial based on inadmissible evidence; (V) the trial court erroneously allowed inadmissible and privileged witness testimony concerning her marital counseling; (VI) the trial court erroneously excluded relevant defense evidence; (VII) the trial court committed plain error by allowing State evidence and argument as to her exercise of her constitutional rights to silence and counsel; (VIII) the trial court improperly belittled her trial counsel and denied her motion for a mistrial based on that conduct; (IX) the prosecutor's closing argument was *ex mero motu* error; (X) the trial court erroneously admitted State evidence about computer documents related to body bags; and (XI) the indictment was insufficient.

I.

Defendant argues that the trial court erred by denying her motion to dismiss the charges of first-degree murder and conspiracy to commit first-degree murder. She contends that the State failed to present sufficient evidence that she was a perpetrator. We disagree.

"When a defendant moves to dismiss a charge against him on the ground of insufficiency of the evidence, the trial court must determine whether there is substantial evidence of each essential element of the offense charged and of the defendant being the perpetrator of the offense." State v. Garcia, 358 N.C. 382, 412, 597 S.E.2d 724, 746 (2004) (citation and quotations omitted), cert. denied, 543 U.S. 1156, 125 S.Ct. 1301, 161 L.Ed.2d 122 (2005); see also State v. Morgan, 359 N.C. 131, 161, 604 S.E.2d 886, 904 (2004), cert. denied, 546 U.S. 830, 126 S.Ct. 47, 163 L.Ed.2d 79 (2005); State v. Butler, 356 N.C. 141, 145, 567 S.E.2d 137, 139 (2002). Our Supreme Court has defined "substantial evidence" as "relevant evidence that a reasonable person might accept as adequate, or would consider necessary to support a particular conclusion." Garcia, 358 N.C. at 412, 597 S.E.2d at 746 (citations omitted).

Additionally, "[i]f there is substantial evidence-whether direct, circumstantial, or both-to support a finding that the offense charged has been committed and that the defendant committed it, the case is for the jury and the motion to dismiss should be denied." Butler, 356 N.C. at 145, 567 S.E.2d at 140 (quoting State v. Locklear, 322 N.C. 349, 358, 368 S.E.2d 377, 383 (1988)). In considering a motion to dismiss by the defense, such evidence "must be taken in the light most favorable to the state , [which] is entitled to all reasonable inferences that may be drawn from the evidence." State v. Sumpter, 318 N.C. 102, 107, 347 S.E.2d 396, 399 (1986).

Nevertheless, if the evidence is "sufficient only to raise a suspicion or conjecture as to either the commission of the offense or the identity of the defendant as the perpetrator, the motion to dismiss must be allowed." State v. Malloy, 309 N.C. 176, 179, 305 S.E.2d 718, 720 (1983) (internal citation omitted). "This is true even though the suspicion aroused by the evidence is strong." Id. (internal citation omitted). However, "[c]ircumstantial evidence may withstand a motion to dismiss and support a conviction even when the evidence does not rule out every hypothesis of innocence." State v. Fritsch, 351 N.C. 373, 379, 526 S.E.2d 451, 455 (citation and quotation omitted), cert. denied, 531 U.S. 890, 121 S.Ct. 213, 148 L.Ed.2d 150 (2000). As our Supreme Court has noted,

There is no logical reason why an inference which naturally arises from a fact proven by circumstantial evidence may not be made. This is the way people often reason in everyday life. In this case, the inferences on inferences dealt with proving the facts constituting the elements of the crime. We hold that the jury could properly do this.

State v. Childress, 321 N.C. 226, 232, 362 S.E.2d 263, 267 (1987).

Here, Defendant contends that there was insufficient evidence that she (1) knowingly advised, instigated, encouraged, procured, or aided Sergeant Diamond to commit first-degree murder, or (2) entered into an agreement with Sergeant Diamond to commit first-degree murder. See State v. Bond, 345 N.C. 1, 24, 478 S.E.2d 163, 175 (1996) (outlining required elements for aiding and abetting a crime), cert. denied, 521 U.S. 1124, 117 S.Ct. 2521, 138 L.Ed.2d 1022 (1997); State v. Merrill, 138 N.C.App. 215, 218, 530 S.E.2d 608, 611 (2000) (outlining required elements for conspiracy to commit murder).

While true that much of the State's evidence as to Defendant's involvement in the murder was circumstantial, and the evidence did "not rule out every hypothesis of innocence" presented by the defense, including that Mr. Diamond acted alone, we find that the State introduced ample and sufficient evidence to allow the jury to make reasonable inferences of Defendant's guilt as to each element of the crimes charged. Indeed, testimony and exhibits offered by the State tended to prove Defendant's affair with Sergeant Diamond, ongoing problems in her marriage to Captain Theer, her financial status and the insurance payout, and her suspicious behavior and flight following the murder-all of which could reasonably give rise to inferences that would "prov[e] the facts constituting the elements of the crime," even if evidence also existed to the contrary. We hold that sufficient evidence was offered to show that Defendant was a perpetrator of the crimes charged. Accordingly, we uphold the trial court's denial of Defendant's motion to dismiss.

II.

Next, we address Defendant's argument that she is entitled to a new trial because the trial court improperly expressed an opinion as to her guilt and as to the credibility of a defense witness. We disagree.

The exchange at issue involved the testimony of Defendant's sister, Angela Forcier, during Defendant's case-in-chief. Before Ms. Forcier's testimony, the trial court excused the jury from the courtroom and appointed a local attorney to advise her about her Fifth Amendment rights regarding the possibility of being an accessory-after-the-fact to first-degree murder. After recessing for the day to allow Ms. Forcier the opportunity to consult with counsel, Ms. Forcier elected to take the stand the following morning. With Ms. Forcier's appointed attorney present during her testimony, the trial judge informed the jury that the attorney "was appointed by this Court to protect any Fifth Amendment rights Ms. Forcier may have in the trial of this matter and he will advise her, if necessary."

On direct examination, defense counsel asked Ms. Forcier if she was being threatened with prosecution in this matter. When Ms. Forcier answered that she was "threatened with prosecution for accessory after the fact of murder," the trial judge stopped the questioning and inquired if defense counsel was referring to what the trial judge had said the day before, to which the defense counsel ultimately replied, "I acknowledge that you had just warned her." Thereafter, the trial court addressed the jury, stating:

THE COURT: Ladies and gentlemen of the jury, on yesterday's date, when I sent you out, I simply advised Ms. Forcier of her potential liability in this case of being an accessory after the fact, that she may have some Fifth Amendment rights. It is not my responsibility to prosecute any action in this case. So that's a mischaracter-misstatement. Do you acknowledge that?

DEFENSE COUNSEL: I acknowledge that you just warned her.

THE COURT: I said she had some Fifth Amendment rights and she stood liable for accessory after the fact.

DEFENSE COUNSEL: To first degree murder.

THE COURT: Correct.

Defendant contends that this exchange was an improper expression by the trial court as to her guilt and the credibility of Ms. Forcier as a witness, since Defendant would have to be guilty of first-degree murder in order for Ms. Forcier to be guilty of accessory after the fact to first-degree murder. See State v. Freeman, 280 N.C. 622, 626, 187 S.E.2d 59, 62-63 (1972) ("[I]t is error for the trial judge to express or imply any opinion as to the guilt of the defendant or as to the credibility of any witness."). Such a statement would be improper if "a juror could reasonably infer therefrom that the judge was intimating an opinion as to the credibility of the witness or as to any fact to be determined by the jury." Id. at 628, 187 S.E.2d at 63.

Our standard of review in considering this exchange is whether it created "a reasonable possibility that, had the error in question not been committed, a different result would have been reached at the trial out of which the appeal arises." N.C. Gen.Stat. § 15A-1443(a) (2005). If Defendant succeeds in showing prejudice from the exchange, "[t]he burden is upon the State to demonstrate, beyond a reasonable doubt, that the error was harmless." N.C. Gen.Stat. § 15A-1443(b) (2005). However, "[a] defendant is not prejudiced by error resulting from his own conduct." N.C. Gen. Stat. § 15A-1443(c) (2005); see also State v. Payne, 280 N.C. 170, 171, 185 S.E.2d 101, 102 (1971) ("Ordinarily one who causes or joins in causing the court to commit error is not in a position to repudiate his action and assign it as ground for a new trial.").

Here, Defendant's counsel "join[ed] in causing the court to commit error," such that we conclude there was no prejudice to Defendant stemming from the objected-to exchange. In his statements while the jury was present, the trial judge referred to Ms. Forcier's "potential liability" and that she "may have some Fifth Amendment rights," while also stating that he had no prosecutorial responsibilities in the matter. Defense counsel, however, was the first to elicit from Ms. Forcier the possible charge of accessory after the fact to first-degree murder, which he subsequently reiterated in front of the jury during his exchange with the trial judge.

Rather than expressing an impermissible opinion as to Defendant's guilt or Ms. Forcier's credibility, we find that the trial judge was instead seeking to remedy the situation by clarifying that he had not threatened prosecution, as suggested by defense counsel, and to thereby avoid prejudice, not cause it. We recognize that the trial court's statement that Ms. Forcier "stood liable for accessory after the fact" perhaps went too far in its forcefulness; however, we also note that Ms. Forcier's testimony in front of the jury might have in fact enhanced her credibility as a witness who felt strongly enough still to testify, even in the face of such threat.[1] Accordingly, we find no merit to this assignment of error.

---

[1]Moreover, Ms. Forcier was not the only witness whom the jury saw with her own counsel sitting beside her; the trial judge also instructed the counsel for State witness Rosaida Rivera to sit beside her while she testified and informed the jury that the appointed attorney was there "representing any Fifth Amendment interests that Ms. Rivera may have" and that the attorney "may consult [the witness] at any time concerning any issues that may arise." Similarly, Dr. Kenneth Kastleman, who had provided marital counseling to the Theers, had an attorney present during his testimony to represent his interests. The fact that the jury saw the same treatment of other witnesses lessens the potentially prejudicial impact of the trial court's statements concerning Ms. Forcier.

III.

Defendant next argues that she is entitled to a new trial because the trial court erroneously admitted the State's irrelevant evidence and argument about her bad character, in contravention of Rules of Evidence 401-404 and the Fourteenth Amendment to the U.S. Constitution.[2]

A trial court's rulings under Rule 403 are reviewed for an abuse of discretion, see State v. Lanier, 165 N.C.App. 337, 345, 598 S.E.2d 596, 602, disc. review denied, 359 N.C. 195, 608 S.E.2d 59 (2004), as are those under Rule 404(b). See State v. al-Bayyinah, 359 N.C. 741, 747, 616 S.E.2d 500, 506 (2005) ("Whether to exclude evidence is a decision within the trial court's discretion."), cert. denied, 547 U.S. 1076, 126 S.Ct. 1784, 164 L.Ed.2d 528 (2006). This Court will find an abuse of discretion only where a trial court's ruling "is manifestly unsupported by reason or is so arbitrary that it could not have been the result of a reasoned decision." State v. Campbell, 359 N.C. 644, 673, 617 S.E.2d 1, 19 (2005) (citation and quotation omitted), cert. denied, 547 U.S. 1073, 126 S.Ct. 1773, 164 L.Ed.2d 523 (2006). Although rulings under Rule 401 "are not discretionary and therefore are not reviewed under the abuse of discretion standard," we also note that "such rulings are given great deference on appeal." State v. Wallace, 104 N.C.App. 498, 502, 410 S.E.2d 226, 228 (1991) (internal citations omitted), cert. denied, 506 U.S. 915, 113 S.Ct. 321, 121 L.Ed.2d 241 (1992).

In her appeal, Defendant argued prejudicial, plain, and *ex mero motu* error as to the evidence and testimony challenged in this argument. However, she failed to distinguish as to the specific grounds for objection and appropriate standard of review concerning the testimony of each of the eighteen witnesses she challenges. Nevertheless, even assuming arguendo that the objected-to testimony was error in each instance, thereby giving Defendant the benefit of the most favorable standard of review, we hold that its admission was not prejudicial to Defendant. See N.C. Gen. Stat. § 15A-1443(a) ("A defendant is prejudiced by errors when there is a reasonable possibility that, had the error in question not been committed, a different result would have been reached at the trial out of which the appeal arises. The burden of showing such prejudice is upon the defendant.").

Defendant takes specific issue with witness testimony concerning, among other things, her refusal to have children, her sexual promiscuity and affairs during her marriage and after her husband's death, her "alternative" lifestyle including classified Internet ads seeking sexual partners and "swinging," her belief in the Wiccan religion, and her ability to manipulate others, particularly men.

Regarding the testimony of Charles McLendon, a man with whom Defendant had an extramarital affair from late 1999 to early 2000, the trial court overruled defense counsel's objection "based upon the [North Carolina] rules of evidence," finding that his testimony was "relevant on the issues of motive, pattern of conduct on using the Internet to engage in sexual liaisons, and the status of the apparent disengagement from [Defendant's] husband, Frank Martin Theer." The trial judge also instructed the jury that Mr. McLendon's testimony should be received for only those limited purposes, as well as for the mental state of Defendant.

Likewise, after reviewing eight boxes of some 21,000 documents and computer records, the trial court found that

The marital relationship between the defendant and Frank Martin Theer, the length and depth of the disengagement between the defendant and Frank Martin Theer in their marriage, thus the

---

[2]*Although Defendant refers to a violation of the Fourteenth Amendment in her brief, she offers no argument or citations in support of this contention. Accordingly, she did not preserve her constitutional claims regarding this evidence. See N.C. R.App. P. 28(b)(6).*

motive and marital state of the defendant leading up to December 17, 2000, are relevant for the jury's consideration. It is also relevant on the issue of the process which the defendant utilized during the disengagement from Frank Martin Theer and in corroboration of the testimony of Charles McLendon.

The relationship of the defendant to John Diamond and the defendant's relationship to her husband, Frank Martin Theer, have now become a substantial and material matter and, thus, the mental state of the defendant at the time of the death of Frank Martin Theer as well as the motive on the part of the defendant. The matters dealing with an alternative lifestyle may reflect not only the degree of engagement with John Diamond but also the degree of disengagement from her husband, Frank Martin Theer, at the time of his death.

The Court has considered this matter under Rule 403. The defendant's motion is denied. The Court will give a limiting instruction accordingly.

A limiting instruction was later given to the jury, bidding them to receive evidence as to Defendant's Internet posting and alternative lifestyle for the "limited purpose of [their] evaluation of the marital status of the defendant and Frank Martin Theer, any motive in this particular case, corroboration of the prior testimony of Charles McLendon and, thus, [their] evaluation of the mental state of the defendant."

Defendant argues that this testimony about the computer documents and e-mails should have been excluded as bad character evidence, as it made her out to be a "moral degenerate" and went beyond simply chronicling her extramarital affairs. See State v. Small, 301 N.C. 407, 432-33, 272 S.E.2d 128, 143-44 (1980), superseded by statute on other grounds as stated in State v. Woods, 307 N.C. 213, 217-18, 297 S.E.2d 574, 577 (1982). However, as our Supreme Court similarly concluded in Small, "[w]e are satisfied that given the admissibility of the fact that defendant had sexual relations with other[s], the outcome of the trial would not have been different had this bit of embellishment not been admitted." Id. at 433, 272 S.E.2d at 144.

Moreover, as the trial court found and instructed the jury, the evidence in question was properly admitted for another, permissible purpose, such as "proof of motive, opportunity, intent, preparation, plan, knowledge, identity, or absence of mistake." N.C. Gen.Stat. § 8C-1, Rule 404(b). Likewise, in light of the trial court's extensive findings on the record concerning his reasons for admitting this evidence, we conclude his rulings were neither unsupported by reason nor arbitrary and thus were not an abuse of discretion. See Campbell, 359 N.C. at 673, 617 S.E.2d at 19. As such, we uphold the trial court's finding that the probative value of this evidence was not "substantially outweighed" by its prejudicial effect. N.C. Gen.Stat. § 8C-1, Rule 403.

Turning now to the evidence of Defendant's affairs while living in Florida after her husband's death, as well as her alleged practice of the Wiccan religion and her behavior while in jail, we acknowledge that this evidence had a tenuous, at best, relevance to the question of Defendant's guilt. However, even assuming arguendo that it was error to admit this evidence, we hold that it was not prejudicial in light of the overwhelming amount of evidence presented by the State as to Defendant's alleged motive and involvement in the murder. After reviewing all of the testimony and transcript in this case, we are unpersuaded that, but for this evidence, Defendant would have been acquitted of the crimes charged. See N.C. Gen.Stat. § 15A-1443(a).

Additionally, although Defendant seems to argue that the cumulative effect of these evidentiary rulings should entitle her to a new trial, we believe that, even when taken as a whole, the evidentiary rulings in question did not deprive Defendant of a fair trial. This evidence went to Defendant's motive and state of mind with respect to her husband's death; it did not include any suggestion that she had committed similar crimes in the past. See State v. Anthony, 354 N.C. 372, 423, 555 S.E.2d 557, 589 ("In light of the great weight of evidence against defendant presented at trial, we hold that the combined effect of any erroneous evidentiary rulings was not prejudicial to defendant.") (2001), cert. denied, 536 U.S. 930, 122 S.Ct. 2605, 153 L.Ed.2d 791 (2002); State v. Beane, 146 N.C.App. 220, 234, 552 S.E.2d 193, 202 (2001) ("[W]e find no merit in defendant's final argument that he was prejudiced by the cumulative effect of the trial court's alleged errors."), appeal dismissed, 355 N.C. 350, 563 S.E.2d 562 (2002); but see State v. White, 331 N.C. 604, 616, 419 S.E.2d 557, 564 (1992) (finding the cumulative effect of evidence as to the defendant's commission of two similar crimes in the past to have deprived him of his fundamental right to a fair trial).

For the foregoing reasons, we find no merit in this assignment of error.

IV.

Next, Defendant argues she is entitled to a new trial because the trial court improperly denied her motion for a mistrial following inadmissible bad character evidence offered by witness Rosaida Rivera, including the suggestion of an improper relationship between Defendant and her trial counsel. Defendant contends that admission of the testimony was plain error, and that denial of the motion for mistrial was an abuse of discretion. She specifically objects to the following statements made by Ms. Rivera on direct examination:

A: I told her about her lawyer, about her and her lawyer used to get these-these special contact visits. How they were real close. She used to-before she'd go see her lawyer, she always used to take these little-a whole bunch of paper, which-about her case and stuff like that that she would take to her lawyer. She would brag on her lawyer was so good and how sweet her lawyer is. And people suspected, you know, that her and her lawyer were a little too close than most lawyers would be with a client but how she'd get little special things that no other inmate can get unless her lawyer would bring it in. That would be like erasers and pads, what else?

These statements were made in response to an unrelated question by the prosecution, and in fact came in the midst of what might be characterized as a rambling non-answer by Ms. Rivera. Defendant asserts that the suggestion of an improper relationship with her trial counsel impaired the latter's ability to effectively represent her and caused her substantial and irreparable prejudice.

The plain error rule "is always to be applied cautiously and only in the exceptional case where, after reviewing the entire record," the error is found to have been "so basic, so prejudicial, so lacking in its elements that justice cannot have been done" or that it had "a probable impact on the jury's finding that the defendant was guilty." State v. Odom, 307 N.C. 655, 660, 300 S.E.2d 375, 378 (1983) (internal citation and quotation omitted).

Here, because defense counsel did not object at trial to the substance of Ms. Rivera's testimony, and thus did not preserve the issue on appeal, we may only review the evidence under the plain error standard. To that end, we note that defense counsel did cross-examine Ms. Rivera concerning her claims of an improper relationship, drawing the jury's attention to the strict conditions of Defendant's imprisonment and monitored meetings with her attorneys.[3] He further impeached Ms. Rivera's credibility by reviewing her extensive criminal record. Moreover, at the close of all evidence, the trial court specifically instructed the jury that

---

[3]We also point out that, after Ms. Rivera made the statement recounted above, the prosecution did not pursue the suggestion of an improper relationship any further. In the course of cross-examination, however, defense counsel elicited the first and only mention of possible sexual contact between Defendant and himself.

There is evidence which tends to show that the witness Rosaida Rivera solicited help from the State of North Carolina in exchange for her testimony. If you find that she testified in whole or in part for this reason, you should examine her testimony with great care and caution in deciding whether or not to believe it. If, after doing so, you believe her testimony in whole or in part, you should treat what you believe the same as any other believable evidence.

In light of the curative effect of the cross-examination of Ms. Rivera and the trial court's instructions to the jury concerning her testimony, we decline to find plain error in the admission of Ms. Rivera's testimony.

The trial court is required to declare a mistrial upon a defendant's motion "if there occurs during the trial an error or legal defect in the proceedings, resulting in substantial and irreparable prejudice to the defendant's case." N.C. Gen.Stat. § 15A-1061 (2005); State v. Tirado, 358 N.C. 551, 585, 599 S.E.2d 515, 538 (2004), cert. denied, Queen v. North Carolina, 544 U.S. 909, 125 S.Ct. 1600, 161 L.Ed.2d 285 (2005). The decision whether to grant a mistrial is within the trial court's discretion and will be given "great deference since he is in a far better position than an appellate court to determine whether the degree of influence on the jury was irreparable." State v. Williamson, 333 N.C. 128, 138, 423 S.E.2d 766, 772 (1992). This Court will find an abuse of discretion only where a trial court's ruling "is manifestly unsupported by reason or is so arbitrary that it could not have been the result of a reasoned decision." Campbell, 359 N.C. at 673, 617 S.E.2d at 19.

Here, after reviewing the arguments for the State and Defendant as to Defendant's motion for mistrial, the trial court entered findings as to Ms. Rivera's testimony that included the following:

Paragraph three, there is a substantial body of evidence before the jury that could cause a finder of fact to view Rosaida Rivera's testimony with great care and caution

Paragraph four, it is also worthy of note that no objection nor any motion to strike was raised by the defendant-defendant's counsel cross-examined Rivera about the security when contact visits were permitted including windows through which jail personnel could observe the contact visit.

Paragraph six, it is the Court's judgment borne of 22 years of experience as a trial judge as well as input from fellow trial judges that testimony such as Rosaida Rivera's is generally viewed with skepticism by jurors. Additionally, Rosaida Rivera's testimony represented only a very small piece of a very extensive and substantiated circumstantial case against the defendant.

The trial judge based the denial of the motion for mistrial on these findings, which we conclude to be well supported by reason and the trial judge's superior position to observe the jury. We therefore decline to disturb the trial court's ruling on appeal.

V.

Defendant next contends that she is entitled to a new trial because the trial court erroneously admitted inadmissible and privileged opinion and hearsay testimony from Dr. Kenneth Kastleman, a clinical psychologist who provided marital counseling to Defendant and Captain Theer. We disagree.

At the outset, we note that Defendant's objections at trial to Dr. Kastleman's testimony were based on psychologist-patient and marital privilege, as well as constitutional grounds.[4] Because she did not offer evidentiary arguments at trial regarding the testimony, we review those contentions here

---

[4] In her assignments of error to this Court, Defendant alleges that the admission of this testimony violated her state and federal constitutional rights. However, her brief argues only that the testimony violated various Rules of Evidence. Accordingly, Defendant did not preserve her constitutional claims as to this evidence. See N.C. R.App. P. 28(b)(6).

under a plain error standard, as articulated above. See N.C. R.App. P. 10(c)(4). We review the trial court's decision to compel disclosure of what would otherwise be privileged information under an abuse of discretion standard. See State v. Smith, 347 N.C. 453, 461, 496 S.E.2d 357, 362 ("The decision that disclosure is necessary to a proper administration of justice is one made in the discretion of the trial judge, and the defendant must show an abuse of discretion in order to successfully challenge the ruling.") (internal citation and quotation omitted), cert. denied, 525 U.S. 845, 119 S.Ct. 113, 142 L.Ed.2d 91 (1998).

Defendant specifically objects to Dr. Kastleman's testimony that during their sessions in the summer of 2000, Defendant was "not looking for common ground" in the marriage, that she was "establishing boundaries" toward her husband and getting "separation" from him, and that she was "attempting to distance herself from" the marriage and not "motivated to undertake therapy." He further testified that Captain Theer "did indeed want to make [the marriage] work," was "attempting to accommodate to [Defendant's] wishes," and that he felt "he and [Defendant] could work out their problems together." Dr. Kastleman also stated that Captain Theer said that he was "the one putting all the energy in trying to get things back together" and that he guessed Defendant did not love him anymore and he did not "understand why she doesn't want to be together."

Defendant argues that these statements and opinions constituted impermissible expert testimony on character, in violation of North Carolina Rule of Evidence 405(a). See N.C. Gen.Stat. § 8C-1, Rule 405(a) (2005) ("Expert testimony on character or a trait of character is not admissible as circumstantial evidence of behavior."). After a careful review of all of Dr. Kastleman's testimony, we find that his opinions related to the state of the Theer marriage and Defendant's attitude toward her husband and her marriage, neither of which meet the definition of character evidence. See State v. Baldwin, 125 N.C.App. 530, 536, 482 S.E.2d 1, 5 ("Character is a generalized description of a person's disposition, or of the disposition in respect to a general trait") (internal citation and quotation omitted), disc. review improvidently allowed, 347 N.C. 348, 492 S.E.2d 354 (1997). Additionally, he made no impermissible statements nor suggestions as to Defendant's guilt. See State v. Mixion, 110 N.C.App. 138, 145, 429 S.E.2d 363, 367 ("In North Carolina an expert may not express an opinion regarding the guilt or innocence of a defendant."), disc. review denied, 334 N.C. 437, 433 S.E.2d 183 (1993). We thus conclude that admission of the testimony did not violate Rule 405(a).

Defendant also contends that the testimony violated Rules of Evidence 401-403 as to relevance and prejudicial effect, Rules 701-702 as to opinion and expert testimony, and Rules 801-803 as to hearsay. See N.C. Gen.Stat. § 8C-1, Rules of Evidence (2005). We find these arguments to be without merit, particularly under a plain error standard. See State v. Cummings, 352 N.C. 600, 636-37, 536 S.E.2d 36, 61 (2000) (holding that the "bare assertion" of plain error in an assignment of error, without accompanying explanation, analysis, or specific contentions in a defendant's brief, is insufficient to show plain error), cert. denied, 532 U.S. 997, 121 S.Ct. 1660, 149 L.Ed.2d 641 (2001). In light of the State's theory of the case, that Defendant conspired with and aided and abetted Sergeant Diamond in the murder of her husband, the testimony of their marriage counselor was surely relevant. Furthermore, Defendant has failed to make any argument or showing in her brief that the testimony as to Captain Theer's statements had "a probable impact on the jury's finding that the defendant was guilty." See Odom, 307 N.C. at 660, 300 S.E.2d at 378.

Defendant also argues that the trial court erred by compelling disclosure of Dr. Kastleman's records of his counseling sessions with the Theers. The trial court ordered the disclosure of the counseling session records "in the interest of the administration of justice and pursuant to North Carolina General Statute 8-53.3."

Indeed, our legislature has seen fit to give trial judges such discretion to compel the disclosure of what would otherwise be privileged communications between psychologist and patient. See N.C. Gen.Stat. § 8-53.3 (2005) ("Any resident or presiding judge in the district in which the action is pending may compel disclosure, if in his or her opinion disclosure is necessary to a proper administration of justice."). Given that the state of the Theer marriage was a central issue in the trial as to Defendant's alleged motive for the crime, and that the trial judge himself reviewed the records prior to their disclosure, we find no abuse of discretion by the trial judge regarding this issue.

VI.

Defendant next argues that she is entitled to a new trial because the trial court improperly excluded relevant defense evidence about Captain Theer's alternative lifestyle. We disagree.

We review the admissibility of expert testimony under an abuse of discretion standard. See State v. Anderson, 322 N.C. 22, 28, 366 S.E.2d 459, 463 ("In applying [Rule 702], the trial court is afforded wide discretion and will be reversed only for an abuse of that discretion."), cert. denied, 488 U.S. 975, 109 S.Ct. 513, 102 L.Ed.2d 548 (1988).[5]

Defendant specifically objects to the exclusion of portions of testimony offered by two clinical psychologists, Dr. Deborah Layton-Tholl and Dr. Donald Stewart. Dr. Layton-Tholl was qualified as an expert in the fields of psychology and extramarital affairs; she interviewed Defendant and reviewed documents and e-mails related to the case. Dr. Stewart is a clinical psychologist in Florida who provided marital counseling to Defendant and her husband in 1997.

After hearing from the defense as to what information Dr. Layton-Tholl and Dr. Stewart planned to offer, the trial court excluded any testimony that was based on statements made by Defendant to either psychologist.[6] In doing so, the trial court referred on the record to our Supreme Court's holding in State v. Prevatte, noting that

It is well settled that an expert must be allowed to testify to the basis of her opinion. State v. Ward, 338 N.C. 64, 105-06, 449 S.E.2d 709, 732 (1994), cert. denied, 514 U.S. 1134, 115 S.Ct. 2014, 131 L. Ed.2d 1013 (1995). Nonetheless, admission of the basis of an expert's opinion is not automatic. State v. Workman, 344 N.C. 482, 495, 476 S.E.2d 301, 308 (1996). The trial court, in its discretion, must determine whether the statements in issue are reliable, especially if the statements are self-serving and the defendant is not available for cross-examination. Id. Moreover, if the

[5]Although Defendant again asserts constitutional error in the section of her brief devoted to this issue, she fails to present any argument or citations to that effect. Accordingly, her constitutional arguments are deemed abandoned, see N.C. R.App. P. 28(b)(6), and we consider only her objections on the grounds of the North Carolina Rules of Evidence.

[6]With respect to Dr. Stewart's testimony, the trial court also excluded any information that was gained from statements made by Captain Theer, on the basis that he had not waived the psychotherapist-patient privilege provided by Florida law, even if Defendant had. The Florida statute allows the privilege to be penetratedFor communications relevant to an issue of the mental or emotional condition of the patient in any proceeding in which the patient relies upon the condition as an element of his or her claim or defense or, after the patient's death, in any proceeding in which any party relies upon the condition as an element of the party's claim or defense. Fla. Stat. Ann. § 90.503(4)(c) (2006). Without providing any supporting case law or argument, Defendant asserts that "the State was using Marty's mental condition as an element of a legal claim," such that the privilege should be penetrated, and that "the Trial Court incorrectly applied Florida rather than North Carolina law." Given that the marital counseling in question was conducted in Florida, and that the State put at issue only Defendant's state of mind and the status of the marriage as a whole, not Captain Theer's state of mind, we find these arguments without merit.

statements appear unnecessary to the expert's opinion, exclusion of the basis may be proper. State v. Baldwin, 330 N.C. 446, 457, 412 S.E.2d 31, 38 (1992).

356 N.C. 178, 233, 570 S.E.2d 440, 470 (2002) (emphasis added), cert. denied, 538 U.S. 986, 123 S.Ct. 1800, 155 L.Ed.2d 681 (2003). The trial court here noted that statements made to the two psychologists by Defendant would have been self-serving and that they would be allowed only if Defendant elected to testify. Both witnesses were, however, permitted to testify as to other facts at issue. Dr. Layton-Tholl offered extensive testimony concerning her research into extramarital affairs and specifically her opinions on the relationship between Defendant and Sergeant Diamond, including why Defendant might have vacillated between her husband and Sergeant Diamond and why she might have continued her relationship with Sergeant Diamond after Captain Theer's death. Dr. Stewart testified that he had provided marital counseling to Defendant and her husband and had recommended to Captain Theer's commanding officer that his scheduled transfer be postponed in order for the couple to receive additional counseling.

Defendant contends that, under the trial court's previous evidentiary rulings and Rules of Evidence 401-403 as to relevance, Dr. Layton-Tholl and Dr. Stewart should have been allowed to testify in full as to Captain Theer's extramarital affairs and "alternative lifestyle" in order to show a direct correlation between his behavior and Defendant's state of mind. The trial court found the evidence to be related to Captain Theer's state of mind, not Defendant's; he therefore excluded the expert witness testimony that might have involved their opinions of Captain Theer's state of mind, saying that "The victim's state of mind is not relevant in this trial. Her state of mind is, not what his attitude was towards her."

The trial court's position on this question is reflected in the following exchange from the transcript, conducted outside the presence of the jury:

DEFENSE COUNSEL: But the state and the Court has made Marty's state of mind relevant in this matter. You've admitted, you know, Dr. Kastleman's records. The state has, you know, hammered home how Marty said this and said that and so forth and, you know, that became-that became an issue in this case by them raising Marty's state of mind.

THE COURT: Frank Martin Theer was assassinated on December 17th of 2000. If the facts in this case show that this arose out of spousal abuse and that they had a shoot-out at the O.K. Corral and you wanted to develop the history between these two individuals, then it may be relevant. But the fact pattern in this case is very simple. Some individual, the state contends it being John Diamond, hid behind some bushes and at some point in time, apparently Frank Martin Theer went up the rear steps of 2500 Raeford Road and some person, the state contends being John Diamond, shot Frank Martin Theer four times and apparently the state contends that once he was on the ground, some person came up and put a bullet through his brain. The mental state of Frank Martin Theer in this case is not relevant.

DEFENSE COUNSEL: When they have paraded in front of this jury, you know, the extramarital affairs of Michelle Theer-

THE COURT: They are held relevant as to her state of mind and her reasons or the attribution being made by the state as to why she would want to have Frank Martin Theer killed.

In reviewing this exchange between the trial court and defense counsel, it is clear to us that the trial court did not make a ruling that "is manifestly unsupported by reason or is so arbitrary that it could not have been the result of a reasoned decision." Campbell, 359 N.C. at 673, 617 S.E.2d at 19.

Furthermore, we note that Defendant was able to introduce evidence of Captain Theer's alleged extramarital affairs and Internet activities through other witnesses. Thus, even assuming arguendo that it was error to exclude the evidence, Defendant has failed to show "a reasonable possibility that, had the error in question not been committed, a different result would have been reached at the trial out of which the appeal arises." N.C. Gen.Stat. § 15A-1443(a). We conclude that this assignment of error is without merit.

VII.

Defendant also contends that she is entitled to a new trial because the trial court committed plain and *ex mero motu* error by allowing State evidence and argument about her exercise of her constitutional rights to silence and counsel. We disagree.

Defendant points to a number of instances in which the State made reference at trial to her "pre-trial exercise of her constitutional rights to silence and counsel." It is telling that she refers to this "pre-trial exercise," as the references are all to instances in which a witness testified to Defendant's invocation of her rights to counsel and to remain silent prior to being arrested herself. Witnesses such as police and Army investigators and Defendant's boss testified as to her lack of cooperation with the police during the investigation of her husband's murder; the prosecutor's closing argument likewise referred to her reaction to invoke her right to counsel when Sergeant Diamond was arrested. None of these situations was custodial such that her Fifth and Sixth Amendment rights to counsel and to remain silent would have attached. See Miranda v. Arizona, 384 U.S. 436, 444, 86 S.Ct. 1602, 1612, 16 L.Ed.2d 694, 706 (1966); Kirby v. Illinois, 406 U.S. 682, 688, 92 S.Ct. 1877, 1881-82, 32 L.Ed.2d 411, 417 (1972) (plurality); State v. Phipps, 331 N.C. 427, 441, 418 S.E.2d 178, 185 (1992).

None of the four cases cited by Defendant nor those found by this Court in its review of this argument have awarded a defendant a new trial on the basis of references at trial to the defendant's right to remain silent and right to counsel prior to being arrested or to being in custodial interrogation. See also Jenkins v. Anderson, 447 U.S. 231, 238, 100 S.Ct. 2124, 2129, 65 L.Ed.2d 86, 94-95 (1980) ("We conclude that the Fifth Amendment is not violated by the use of prearrest silence to impeach a criminal defendant's credibility."); State v. Lane, 301 N.C. 382, 384-85, 271 S.E.2d 273, 275 (1980) (distinguishing between impermissible references to the decision to remain silent after arrest and allowable references to silence prior to arrest). We decline to do so now. We hold that this assignment of error is without merit.

VIII.

Defendant next contends she is entitled to a new trial because the trial court made nine improper negative comments before the jury that belittled her trial counsel, and also improperly denied her motion for a mistrial based on this conduct. We disagree.

"In evaluating whether a judge's comments cross into the realm of impermissible opinion, a totality of the circumstances test is utilized." State v. Larrimore, 340 N.C. 119, 155, 456 S.E.2d 789, 808 (1995); see also State v. Blackstock, 314 N.C. 232, 236, 333 S.E.2d 245, 248 (1985); State v. Allen, 283 N.C. 354, 358-59, 196 S.E.2d 256, 259 (1973). Furthermore, "[e]ven if it cannot be said that a remark or comment is prejudicial in itself, an examination of the record may indicate a general tone or trend of hostility or ridicule which has a cumulative effect of prejudice." State v. Staley, 292 N.C. 160, 165, 232 S.E.2d 680, 684 (1977). A judge must remain impartial towards defense counsel and should "refrain from remarks which tend to belittle or humiliate counsel since a jury hearing such remarks may tend to disbelieve evidence adduced in defendant's behalf." State v. Wright, 172 N.C.App. 464, 469, 616 S.E.2d 366, 369 (quoting State v. Coleman, 65 N.C.App. 23, 29,

308 S.E.2d 742, 746 (1983), cert. denied, 311 N.C. 404, 319 S.E.2d 275 (1984)), aff'd per curiam, 360 N.C. 80, 621 S.E.2d 874 (2005).

Nevertheless, "unless it is apparent that such infraction of the rules might reasonably have had a prejudicial effect on the result of the trial, the error will be considered harmless." State v. Perry, 231 N.C. 467, 471, 57 S.E.2d 774, 777 (1950). This burden to show prejudice "rests upon the defendant to show that the remarks of the trial judge deprived him of a fair trial." State v. Waters, 87 N.C.App. 502, 504, 361 S.E.2d 416, 417 (1987).

In the instant case, after carefully reviewing in context the nine comments complained of by Defendant,[7] we find that none rise to the level seen in any of the cases cited by Defendant in which a new trial was ordered. See, e.g., Staley, 292 N.C. at 165, 232 S.E.2d at 684 (finding prejudice and ordering a new trial where the trial judge had made comments to the jury including, "'Ladies and gentlemen if these witnesses are not telling the truth, then the court, I think it is obvious what the facts are. Now, I have made your speech again for you.'); (emphasis in original); Wright, 172 N.C.App. at 464-65, 616 S.E.2d at 367 (finding prejudice and ordering a new trial where trial judge mocked defense counsel in front of jury on several occasions and made comments such as, "'I have done everything I can possibly do, except end your cross examination. Whatever you need to do, as I have now told you three times, whatever you need to do to help yourself not do that, do it.").

Rather, as in Larrimore and State v. Agnew, the trial court's statements in this case "reflected efforts on the part of the trial judge to maintain progress and proper decorum in what was evidently a prolonged and tedious trial." Larrimore, 340 N.C. at 155, 456 S.E.2d at 808 (quoting State v. Agnew, 294 N.C. 382, 395, 241 S.E.2d 684, 692, cert. denied, 439 U.S. 830, 99 S.Ct. 107, 58 L. Ed.2d 124 (1978)). In a ten-week trial with over 6,300 pages of transcript, we find that the nine comments by which the trial court admonished Defendant's counsel when he asked inappropriate or improper questions did not prejudice Defendant nor deprive her of a fair trial. Accordingly, we find no merit to this assignment of error.

IX.

Defendant also contends that she is entitled to a new trial because the prosecutor's closing argument was *ex mero motu* error, such that the trial court should have intervened. We disagree.

---

[7]*The nine comments objected to by Defendant, with some parenthetical relevant context, were as follows: (1) "[L]et's move on to something reasonable, please." (Defense counsel questioned a forensic technician for the Fayetteville Police Department as to whether her watch was coordinated with the watch at the department and, if not, how far off it might be.) (2) "Well, that makes it an unfair question then." (Defense counsel questioned the forensic technician about blood testing that she did not conduct.) (3) "That's an unfair question." (Defense counsel questioned a Fayetteville Police detective as to whether a signature was that of Defendant.) (4) "[Y]ou know that's not appropriate." (Defense counsel continued asking the same question after an objection by the State had twice been sustained by the trial court.) (5) "You know that's inappropriate, please, sir." (Defense counsel made a statement in front of the jury in response to a sustained objection, then continued and finished the statement over an additional sustained objection.) (6) "Let's not make any gratuitous remarks." (Defense counsel made a statement about not knowing a witness before the trial, during the State's redirect examination of that witness.) (7) "That's not a proper question for the jury. Specifically prohibited by the rules of evidence." (Defense counsel asked an agent with the U.S. Army Criminal Investigations Division whether she had noticed anything about interviewees being untruthful when they made statements to her.) (8) "Don't do that again." (The State objected, after defense counsel used a third redirect examination to ask a witness the same questions and make the same points that had been made on the previous redirects.) (9) "So that's a mischaracter-misstatement. Do you acknowledge that?" (Defense counsel asked a defense witness if she had been threatened with prosecution in the case, suggesting that it was the trial court who had done so.)*

In cases where a defendant does not object at trial to the prosecutor's closing arguments, "the impropriety of the argument must be gross indeed in order for [an appellate court] to hold that a trial judge abused his discretion in not recognizing and correcting *ex mero motu* an argument which defense counsel apparently did not believe was prejudicial when he heard it." State v. Hoffman, 349 N.C. 167, 185, 505 S.E.2d 80, 91 (1998) (internal quotations and citations omitted), cert. denied, 526 U.S. 1053, 119 S.Ct. 1362, 143 L.Ed.2d 522 (1999). Additionally, our Supreme Court has repeatedly held that "counsel must be allowed wide latitude in the argument of hotly contested cases." State v. Berry, 356 N.C. 490, 518, 573 S.E.2d 132, 150 (2002) (citation and quotations omitted).

Here, after carefully reviewing the entirety of the prosecutor's closing argument to the jury, we find that none of the comments challenged by Defendant were so grossly improper as to require the *ex mero motu* intervention by the trial court. Defendant specifically objects to the prosecutor's statements (1) that Defendant had "a burden there once they put on evidence and you can reject it or you can accept it"; (2) concerning Captain Theer's character and his mother; (3) assuring the jury that "[e]verything I argued to you is supported by the facts in this case"; and, (4)referring to occasions on which Defendant had lied.

We note that the prosecutor also explicitly said in his closing argument, "The defendant doesn't have to prove anything. The state has the burden of proof. We have the burden of proof. We put on evidence." In a criminal case, "the defendant's failure to produce exculpatory evidence or to contradict evidence presented by the State may properly be brought to the jury's attention by the State in its closing argument.' State v. Taylor, 337 N.C. 597, 613, 447 S.E.2d 360, 370 (1994). The prosecutor's reference here to Defendant's "burden" was not grossly improper when it followed a clear statement of the State's burden of proof in the case, and was instead designed to suggest to the jury that Defendant had failed to contradict the State's evidence.

Furthermore, the prosecutor's passing references to Captain Theer's character and to his mother "did not improperly emphasize sympathy or pity for the victim's family." State v. Alford, 339 N.C. 562, 572, 453 S.E.2d 512, 517 (1995). Moreover, when "[v]iewed in the context of his entire argument, these comments did not attempt to make sympathy for the victim or his family the focus of the jury's deliberation." Id. As such, they were not improper. A prosecutor is similarly permitted to give reasons why the jury should believe the State's evidence or not believe a witness, and the prosecutor's comments here did not rise to the level of gross impropriety that would have warranted *ex mero motu* intervention by the trial court. See State v. Bunning, 338 N.C. 483, 489, 450 S.E.2d 462, 464-65 (1994), sentence vacated, 346 N.C. 253, 485 S.E.2d 290 (1997); State v. McKenna, 289 N.C. 668, 687, 224 S.E.2d 537, 550, sentence vacated, 429 U.S. 912, 97 S.Ct. 301, 50 L.Ed.2d 278 (1976).

This assignment of error is therefore without merit.

X.

Next, Defendant argues she is entitled to a new trial because the trial court erroneously admitted the State's evidence about computer documents related to body bags, specifically, concerning alleged searches on the website eBay for "body bag disaster pouches" stored in the memory of Defendant's home computer. Defendant asserts that the evidence was irrelevant and inadmissible under Rules of Evidence 401-403 and 901, as well as the Fourteenth Amendment to the Constitution.[8]

[8]*Although Defendant's brief refers to the Fourteenth Amendment as grounds for finding this evidence to have been inadmissible, she offers no argument to support the constitutional grounds. We therefore consider only her evidentiary claims, under an abuse of discretion standard. See N.C. R.App. P. 28(b)(6).*

In its ruling on Defendant's motion to exclude the evidence, the trial court noted that it had "reviewed eight boxes of computer records which have now been represented to be an approximately 21,000 documents." He further stated,

It was a rare occurrence that a document could be interpreted as having been produced by a third party. The computers were found in a locale at least in the constructive possession of the defendant. The State always has the burden of showing relevancy and attributions to the defendant which the Court will have to judge as to its admissibility as offered.

At trial, after overruling the defense objection to the evidence in question, the trial court instructed the jury that

this evidence concerning with this issue dealing with the body bag is offered and received concerning the defendant's then existing state of mind or emotion such as intent, plan, motive or design. It's offered and received for that limited purpose and your consideration thereof.

Even assuming arguendo that the admission of this testimony was error and an abuse of the trial court's discretion, we find that it was not prejudicial to Defendant. See N.C. Gen.Stat. § 15A-1443(a) (prejudice results where, "had the error in question not been committed, a different result would have been reached at the trial out of which the appeal arises."). The evidence referring to the body bags comprised just three documents out of the 21,000 reviewed by the trial court, and out of over five hundred exhibits submitted by the State. The trial court made findings that the computer was in the constructive possession of Defendant, and defense counsel cross-examined the State's computer expert as to whether Captain Theer could perhaps have conducted the searches rather than Defendant.

In light of the other overwhelming evidence presented to the jury as to Defendant's guilt, we conclude that this evidence, even if irrelevant, was not so prejudicial as to have affected the outcome of the trial. This assignment of error is without merit.

XI.

Lastly, Defendant argues that her conviction for first-degree murder should be vacated because the short-form indictment was insufficient. As recognized by Defendant in her brief, however, our courts have previously rejected the argument she makes, and this issue was raised and decided against Defendant at trial. See State v. Hunt, 357 N.C. 257, 278, 582 S.E.2d 593, 607, cert. denied, 539 U.S. 985, 124 S.Ct. 44, 156 L.Ed.2d 702 (2003). This assignment of error is accordingly dismissed.

CONCLUSION

For the foregoing reasons, we conclude that Defendant's trial was free of prejudicial error. We therefore uphold her convictions for first-degree murder and conspiracy to commit first-degree murder.

No prejudicial error.

WYNN, Judge.

Judges BRYANT and STEPHENS concur.

See more at: http://caselaw.findlaw.com/nc-court-of-appeals/1201672.html#sthash.fUmldC86.dpuf

Retrieved from:

http://caselaw.findlaw.com/nc-court-of-appeals/1201672.html

SUMMARY

Data is everywhere. We leave digital footprints or impressions everywhere we go and by doing anything online or on a computer system, we leave our mark. Most, if not all, of this activity is traceable and can be tracked, and it is also available for data theft. We can attempt to protect ourselves or operate in a stealth manner; however, it is possible that your actions will be logged, tracked, and proven based on many factors. Digital forensic teams are called in to review systems that have been tampered with and/or when data theft has taken place and there are many tools that can be used to prove certain activity has taken place. Lest we forget, there may also be cameras showing you were in the vicinity of a target system proving you were involved. You can remotely access these systems and it can be proven that by a source IP address, you may be involved. Even if it's spoofed, there are other ways to track this activity.

As we see, data tracking and doing forensic work in the digital domain can prove to be helpful; however, it is not always a guarantee that data can be kept secure. As many security analysts learned in the past decade, all of the security measures in the world did not stop a perpetrator from removing classified information about US nuclear weaponry with a thumb drive.

In this chapter, we discussed data at rest and data in motion and discussed how it can be stolen and what is at risk. We also covered the methods of data exploitation and theft as well as how digital forensics can be used to reconstruct a crime scene and provide evidence. Other topics covered include how to mitigate this thread specifically with encryption and how we can safeguard our data and identities.

CHAPTER 8

Protection Methods

PROTECT YOURSELF!

As we end this book on how to defend yourself against surveillance and recon-naissance attacks, the best advice up front would be to protect yourself, your data, and your assets. Protect your identity. Today, the world operates on a digital landscape. Wearable technology is the latest buzz word and everyone seems to be connected via their phones, pads, and laptops. Virtually, everyone everywhere is becoming more and more interconnected and sharing data and socializing. Using this medium has become the norm. While the world contin-ues to grow digitally, so does the risk of exposure. As the landscape grows expo-nentially, so does the threat of those who would, and will, abuse this medium for their own gain. Because this threat is so real, it's imperative to consider your exposure to it, limit it, and protect against it.

Reconnaissance and surveillance have been practiced for centuries, primarily as a way for militaries to conduct observation of enemy activities and moni-tor targets to gain strategic advantage. Reconnaissance and surveillance teams would go out to gather information about enemy activities in hopes to find out location information, size, and strength of their targets and/or to place targeting information for incoming strikes. Today, the battlefield is in your digital world, where everything you do can be revealed. Things you do that you believe are secret are saved on files, logs, and storage maintained by service providers. What is at stake? Currently, much is at stake. Your privacy is at stake. Your safety could be at stake. Your identity can be stolen. You can be impacted financially. As the digital landscape grows, so does the threat.

The Internet fueled by search engines, social media, and the ability to retain all that it collects is a digital spy's goldmine when doing reconnaissance work. Considerably, one of the biggest threats today on the Internet is in the form of search engines and social media. You can virtually learn a person's history, what they like, their location, and who their friends and family are all with the click of a mouse or a stroke of a keypad.

Be Concerned, not Paranoid!

Another topic to discuss is the need to practice due diligence at every turn and try not to be paranoid. As we close on our studies of what can be done digitally and how you could easily be victimized, the goal was to teach you so that you can prepare, not to make you a paranoid wreck! That being said, the trick is to be aware of the risks.

The threat of digital spying is growing at a rapid rate, generationally, more and more are creating an online footprint. As more people get mobile devices and attach to the public Internet, there are more opportunities for attackers to conduct surveillance on selected targets. Your identity can be stolen. You finances can be impacted. Your safety can be threatened. All of this should concern you and enough so that you practice operating safely on the Internet, in social media sites, and as you use your mobile device.

When we discussed how easily your credit card data could be stolen, this did not mean carry around a stack of cash everywhere you go. That too creates a risk. What exposing you to the risks should do is, train you to minimize them.

Information privacy should be practiced as much as possible. If you want something to remain safe, it's best not to talk about it, record it, or write it down. If you do so, then you should consider that it could be at risk. This is incredibly difficult to do. There are things that we must simply record and write. As you navigate from place to place, consider that your actions are being recorded as seen in Figure 8.1. You're on video camera; your actions are logged so how do you keep your information private? To keep your information private, you need to secure it the best way possible.

To secure your actions, your identity, and your privacy, you need to learn general security practices that we will cover in this chapter. Some of them may seem outlandish; however, you be the judge. You can choose to practice

FIGURE 8.1 Your actions are being viewed.

some of them, or just use them as suggestions. However, one thing is true; if you become the victim of spying, identity theft or an invasion of privacy, and you're also impacted financially, you may find yourself reviewing this chapter or perhaps the entire book to learn or re-learn ways to safeguard against such attacks.

General Security and Mitigation Techniques

In general, you need to practice due diligence. In sum, this means that you need to assess and analyze your actions before you take them. This can be as simple as limiting your digital footprint. Do you really need to post pictures of yourself on vacation in the Bahamas to your friends and family on Facebook? Is it really necessary to tweet about everything you do every single day? Assess why you do this and what you are attempting to get out of releasing this information to the public. You can also limit your digital footprint by asking those you spend time with to do the same – limit what they put about you and of you on the Internet. This can be as simple as asking your great Aunt not to post pictures of you to a public forum and explaining why. Explain what is at risk. If you do post data about yourself or others do of you, you can also limit who views this data with specific privacy and security settings available on most social media sites to limit exposure.

Be aware of your surroundings and practice looking at things you normally would not look at; for example, take a look at the amount of camera's in your local area that are mounted on traffic lights. Assess your path to and from work and look for all of the digital tools that are recording your actions. Be aware of who is around you and who does not fit in, or belong. Is anyone following you? Although this seems to spark a debate about being "paranoid," can you really afford not to?

In general, open your eyes to the bigger picture and be aware that your actions are recorded at every turn. Things posted online may be taken down but they are stored in an archive and can be retrieved and used at a later date. Be aware of your actions and the actions of others as well as what could be recording and tracking you at every turn. Do you really need to carry your phone with you everywhere you go? If the answer is yes, then be aware that everything you do on it and everywhere you go with it is traceable.

Identity Theft

As we have mentioned, identity theft may be funny in the movies, but not funny when it happens to you in real life (and it can). Identity theft, fraud, and other methods of acquiring and using your personal information against you consist of many legal issues today. When banks lose money and insurance rates rise, it costs individuals money and criminals make a lot of money. Social security accounts are stolen and used, bank fraud takes place, and social media

FIGURE 8.2 Physical theft of information.

sites can be duplicated to where an attacker can pose and post as you. Your personal identity can be used to impersonate you to gather more information.

You can limit exposure by considering what you post online. You can limit exposure by paying in cash instead of by credit card and use specific credit cards with fraud protection in places that you do not frequently or often visit in order to track fraud if it takes place. Check your statements often, and review for any possible misuse. There are many ways you can change your habits so that you can better protect your most valuable asset: you.

As seen in Figure 8.2, your information can be taken from you without your knowledge – physically and digitally. Ensure that you are aware of your surroundings, keep your valuables secure. Your personal information can be stolen and used against you physically as well as in the digital realm.

Obviously, due diligence is a general term whereas, more specifically, there are actions you can take to secure yourself from the threat of identity theft:

- Take inventory of your belongings. When was the last time you photocopied what was in your wallet? Are you organized? Do you know what accounts you need to lock down and close if anything was stolen?
- Consider what you store and what can be stolen. If you carry a wallet, do you have ATM receipts and other financial information within it that if stolen could cause an issue? Always remove these items from your wallet or possession and only carry what is absolutely needed.
- Practice general security mitigation by keeping a security mindset. Again, this does not mean "be paranoid," but develop good habits to ensure that you are safe such as checking to make sure you have all of your belongings when going from place to place.

All of these techniques may not eradicate the threat; however, it minimizes the landscape. Be safe, consider that there are threats in the world, and attempt to safeguard yourself, others you care for, and your personal and private belongings.

Harden Systems

Most technology devices you use can be hardened. This means, locked down, secured, and/or applying a greater depth of security. To cover the basics, remember, in general, you do not want to lose these devices to physical theft. There are things you can do to safeguard the data; however, if it is not backed up, it may be lost forever.

There are general guidelines to "hardening" any systems, software, hardware, or application you use. Most come with details on how to do this; however, some do not. In these cases, most restrictive is always recommended and then open up or loosen these restrictions as needed.

Basic system hardening guidelines are as follows:

- Personal computers (PCs) – In general, you want to secure access. Never leave the computer powered on and open for use. Use strong password protection. This will cover access control. Back up critical data. Use a firewall and an antivirus software. Use anti-spyware protection software. Make sure that the operating system and any applications installed are kept up to date with critical system and security patches. Turn on automatic update to keep the system updated. Do not access websites that seem questionable. Use anti-phishing software, generally installed within the browser itself. Set up an e-mail spam filter and make sure you do not open e-mails from those you do not know. Never give out your personal information by request to those you do not know. Turn on auditing and check your logs often. Turn off your webcam when you are not using it.
- Laptops – All of the same hardening rules apply that were covered in PC hardening; however, you need to make sure you do not lose your laptop and prevent against it being stolen. Never use your laptop in public where someone can shoulder surf your activities.
- Mobile devices – Most if not all of the PC and laptop general hardening rules apply; however, some differences are, if you root or jailbreak a device, make sure you install reputable apps with security certificates to ensure it is not malware. Make sure you do not physically lose your device.
- Webcams – Webcams can be hardened by turning off broadcast on any wireless components so that outsiders cannot attach to your cameras. Make sure that you follow all of the hardening steps provided with the application that comes with the system.
- Wireless systems – Make sure you do not broadcast your Service Set Identifier (SSID). Use strong encryption. Change any default passwords that come with your systems.
- Network hardware – Any network devices you use, you should follow the recommended hardening procedures that come with each system.

- Game consoles – Make sure that you secure your devices following recommended best practices that come with the systems. If you have an external camera such as a Kinect, make sure that you secure it and monitor its use.

In theory, you should use encryption whenever possible. You should encrypt data so that if stolen, it cannot be used. Using strong encryption is recommended since weaker versions can be easily cracked. Encryption can in fact be broken, so always consider that this is not 100% secure whenever you use it.

Passwords should always be used and it's recommended that you use strong passwords. This means that you should not use dictionary words, things that can be associated with you (kids and pet's names as an example), or any other easily identifiable information that can be used to guess your credentials. Generally, a password should contain a mixture of letters and numbers, upper and lower case letters, and special characters if possible.

General Reconnaissance and Surveillance

Unfortunately, people are followed. We live in a world where there are good people and there are bad. As we covered in detail over the past series of chapters, the use of technology is designed to provide safety and security; however, it can be manipulated and used in harmful ways. Although difficult to determine, if you are in fact being spied on, it's ok to call law enforcement if you need to. If someone is physically stalking you or you feel endangered, make sure you take the steps necessary to protect yourself.

General reconnaissance and surveillance protection comes in the form of due diligence also. You should always make sure that you are aware of your surroundings and look for things that look out of place. A great example would be if you see that while driving, a car or van behind you is taking the same path as you but attempting to stay out of view. This can be seen by the vehicle not following directly behind you, but a few cars away. A great way to validate this is to make a turn off your normal path and see if the vehicle still remains behind you. A way to protect yourself may be to drive to a police station nearby and park out front.

This may seem scary but believe it or not, it happens. You may have an ex-spouse or mate tracking you and what you are doing. This is also possible if you are in a current court case with someone and they are attempting to gather information on you and what you are doing. For example, if you go to "happy hour" on a Friday evening and attempt to leave the bar and drive. They (or a private investigator) may be videotaping you for evidence.

Although uncommon, there are those out there who may wish to cause you harm randomly, so the same rules apply. Be aware of your surroundings and look for things that are out of place.

General digital surveillance mitigation is similar, whereas with someone physically following you, what is following you are the cameras. In this case, the best form of mitigation is to attempt to be aware of where the cameras are and avoid them. One may ask, why you would want to avoid cameras and that may be answered by two simple answers: either you want what you do to remain private for good reasons or for bad. It may also be because you are attempting to thwart detection and do not want your actions recorded. Either way, there is little you can do to avoid detection without physically or electronically disrupting the cameras, and avoidance is your best method.

Information Gathering

As we discussed, social engineering is a way to gain unauthorized access to trusted resources. This intrusive behavior is done to penetrate defenses to gain information, data, or line of sight into a target. It's done to commit fraud or espionage. Another common goal is to gain access to commit identity theft. Other malicious behavior could be to cause harm or disruption. That being said, it is important that you learn to protect yourself and your interests carefully. Before we learn how to mitigate this threat, we should discuss how attackers use social engineering to gather data. Earlier in this book, we used a brief example of how an attacker may use a simple phone call to trick someone into providing trusted information. Other ways attackers violate the sanctity of trust through social engineering and trickery is by doing the following:

- Dumpster diving – Ensure that you do not throw away anything that can be retrieved and used against you. Ensure that all papers are burned, shredded (shredded correctly and cannot be reassembled), or destroyed beyond repair. Ensure that hard disks are erased correctly, systems thrown away have disks removed, phones have subscriber identity module (SIM) chips removed and are erased correctly, and so on. Simply put, do not throw anything away that someone can retrieve and reuse.
- Shoulder surfing – Protect yourself by being aware of your surroundings and covering up your actions so that those nearby cannot glean any information from your actions. Cover your hands while typing in pins, and make sure nobody is behind you when entering sensitive information at a terminal or on a keyboard. Block the wandering eyes that are around you from viewing what you do.
- Phishing – Make sure that when you open e-mails and/or get links to sites that they are legitimate. There are phishing filters that come with most if not all standard web browsers. Validate the site you go to so that you do not give your personal information away.
- Keystroke logger – Although difficult to determine, if you have a logger on your system or phone, there are ways to check the running process

on your system to see if anything is running in memory that maps to a keystroke logger. Use anti-malware software to ensure that there is nothing running on your system that can steal your information from you. Physical devices can be installed on your system without your knowledge and out of view, so a physical check of your system periodically make sense, any key fobs or odd looking devices should be questioned.

- Bugging – You can physically check for bugging devices. There are tools available online to help you find bugging devices; however, digitally, running specific anti-malware software should find and remove spying tools fairly quickly.
- Recording – This is difficult to mitigate because there are so many ways to record someone's activities. For example, if you are in a meeting with someone, you may be recorded by a device in which you cannot see and/or mitigate against. In this case, it's safe to say that to mitigate, ensure that you do not say anything you want to remain private. Otherwise, you can use the same mitigation techniques as already mentioned for the other attacks listed: due diligence, awareness, software scanning, and anti-malware sweeps should find any recording software present.

To mitigate information gathering in general, attempt to practice restraint when posting, putting information online, or giving information away. The public Internet is a goldmine for those conducting intelligence. When used in non-malicious ways, the Internet can be a source of a lot of information. Researching a homework assignment, locating the best travel path, or getting movie times are all simple examples of what can be done in seconds without having to leave your home or pick up your phone. When used for good reasons, the Internet can prove to be extremely helpful; however, when used for bad reasons, the Internet can be used to gather information to conduct attacks.

Another issue with the Internet is that once you put something on a server such as a blog post, a data file, or other source of data, it could remain there for a long time, possibly forever. Data backups collect data from servers and archive it. Data can also be added without your knowledge. In the world of social media, it's common for people you connect to and with to, and "post" data such as an old picture of you. It can also be done in real time. For example, a favorite bar you visit frequently can quickly be online news if someone posts about it, tags a picture of you within it, or posts that you are in a group at a certain location. Attackers can use this information to ascertain your habits, favorite frequented places, and many other facts about you.

Data can also be doctored. Pictures can be digitally edited, words can be manipulated, and if someone has stolen your identity and posing (and posting) as you on the Internet, could cause serious issues for you. Information is also added willingly, almost too willingly by many. Social media sites today encourage those who are part of them to post data, connect to others for no reason other than to increase their numbers, and like things you normally wouldn't ever comment on outside of the digital world.

Without any effort at all, your information can be added to the publically searchable Internet within seconds, stay within it indefinitely, and even if you think you have had it removed, it could still be archived somewhere for retrieval. To add, this does not include the data that can be obtained from globally interconnected devices that can also provide those who seek information a source to get it. Servers cache data as an example to speed up Internet browsing and if this system was hacked, could reveal the browsing habits of an entire community as an example.

We should be concerned as a society that if those who wish to do us harm, need only to first have an Internet connection and second a "will" to be interested in gathering data on you, that's all it takes is a few clicks of their mouse to obtain it. To mitigate, restraint is the key. Observe others as well, who may put information online about you and attempt to have it removed if you do not want it online.

Physical security is equally important. When at work, take the security policies enforced in your organization seriously. No, do not hold the door open for someone you do not know to let them into your office suite. Yes, it's great manners; however, there have been dozens if not hundreds of penetration attacks conducted by allowing someone into an office suite by simply holding the door for someone to be nice, they do not need to use the biometrics or card reader and you have just been hacked.

Be aware of your actions. Do not allow someone to dig through your trash. Do not allow someone to watch over your shoulder. You can protect yourself by destroying information such as using a shredder as seen in Figure 8.3.

Shred or burn important papers you decide to trash and do not leave anything that can be reused. Do not sit somewhere with your back facing an open crowd, and do not do personal or private work on your laptop or phone, mobile device, or pad if you cannot safeguard it from being overseen.

When you are talking to someone on the phone, be aware of your audience. Could you be on conference? Could the phone be tapped? Can the room you're in be bugged? Don't believe it can happen? Hopefully, by reading this book and others like it, you can start to realize that yes it does happen and it happens often.

When opening e-mails or receiving texts, take the extra time to perform a seconds worth of due diligence. Check the entire e-mail header, review the domain name in which the e-mail was sent, and validate with a phone call to the

FIGURE 8.3 Shred all important documents.

originator based on a trusted source (not from the e-mail itself) that this was in fact sent on purpose and not a scam.

Do not openly trust. Since this is tough to do, it's no question as to why this is one of the biggest attacks performed today and why it's the most difficult to mitigate. As you can see, there are many ways to mitigate this form of attack but it comes down to not trusting everything you see and hear and trusting everyone you do or do not know. It simply comes down to verifying and validating things and ensuring that they are safe if possible.

Social Engineering

Security is built on the foundation of trust. You can secure your identity, computer, or access to your home, but you do give this information and access to those you trust. As an example, you hold the door for someone because you practice chivalry. Your kindness just thwarted the electronic badge system used to ensure that unauthorized users do not enter a facility. Attackers, hackers, and stalkers all hope that you let your guard down for this exact reason so that they can gain access to a trusted location. The main reason social engineering takes place is because it is easier to gain access to a trusted source by simply manipulating someone who can give you access instead of breaking in through technological means. This is the basic foundation of social engineering.

There are many definitions for social engineering. As we just discussed, manipulating human control in order to gain unauthorized access is one of them. Another could be, using a human to provide needed information to gain access to trusted resources. When considering technology specifically, it can sometimes be defined as malware used to trick a user into providing trusted data. In all of these examples, manipulation and trickery are key words used to define the basic underlying principles of social engineering.

In relation to information gathering, social engineering can be used to gain technical data such as passwords, physical and logical access to resources, and many other pieces of information that could be used to conduct a larger attack. Another example, you trick someone through simple conversation to produce answers you need. For example, I place a call to you from a spoofed phone number that appears to you to be from a trusted source. I then tell you things that relate to you, us, or our conversation so that I can gain your trust. By asking specific questions and getting answers, I may be able to ascertain information from you needed to do another task, such as your account information to get into a personal website or bank account. This can then be leveraged into the digital world by exploiting the gathered information.

It is difficult to mitigate social engineering attacks. It strikes at the very root of how human beings treat each other; defending against social engineering means that you need to be aware of your surroundings, who you are dealing with, and no, you cannot trust everyone you meet or know. In fact, social engineers scout for this overly trusting, gullible behavior in people in order to know who to manipulate and how to manipulate them. They are considered easy targets. An act of kindness could be, in fact, the launch of an attack as seen in Figure 8.4.

If you could openly trust everyone and everything, there would be no reason for security. No locks on doors and banks would leave their vaults wide open. The fact is that historically, this is not the case and security grows as an industry

FIGURE 8.4 Bypass security biometrics with chivalry.

exponentially every year. As we have covered, there is a thin line between being overly safe and being paranoid. That does not mean you should not have faith in people and believe that you can trust them; it just means precautions are in order for your benefit and the benefit of your finances, your loved ones, and your safety.

You can remain safe by being aware. Be aware of your surroundings. Who are you talking to, who can be listening?

Are you typing something? Are you being recorded? If you remain aware and vigilant about your own personal security, you will understand how to mitigate social engineering attacks. Do not openly trust those you do not know and think about the actions of those you do.

Mobile Phone Tracking

In previous chapters, we covered how dangerous a phone can be, whether it be an old PSTN-based phone or a new digital mobile phone. Although the chapter focuses on mobile phone attacks, it should be considered that just about every device with network connectivity these days can place you at the scene of the crime. It is also very disturbing that with mobile technology, devices are carried with you and not left in your home, placing you directly at the scene of the crime. That being said, your movements are being tracked and recorded and you should be aware.

When you are tracked with your mobile phone (or device), you are essentially giving your exact geographical position away to your telecommunications carrier. The radio towers that you use to obtain and maintain your signal are also used as reference to your exact position. Global positioning system (GPS) technology also aids in placing your location, which we will discuss further in the chapter. Carriers can also track movement based on technology called location-based services. This technology can be used to help assess specific co-ordinates as you use your mobile device. We will also discuss this technology further within the chapter.

In this chapter, we will also address how the US government is taking advantage of an outdated law on privacy and technology to track Americans. If you use your mobile phone, it will register its position with cell towers every few minutes, whether the phone is being used or not – and mobile carriers are retaining location data on their customers. As the government collects and uses this data, a record of your movements is being kept without your permission or knowledge. Why is spying on mobile devices so important to understand? If you are a victim, let's look at what could be at risk:

- View SMS messages – applications can record all SMS activities from the target phone. All sent and received messages can be recorded in an online account, even if the messages are deleted from the mobile phone.

- View call logs – Each call can also be logged by the application that will also be uploaded to your online account. This provides the caller and the time of call.
- Track GPS location – GPS tracking can provide your location at any time and recorded to an online account.
- View photos and videos – All photos and videos taken can be recorded and sent to an online account.
- View contact list – A contact list of phone numbers can also be viewed and sent to an online account.
- Website uniform resource locator logs – This can show which websites are visited and can be sent to an online account.
- Call recording – Your calls and messages can be recorded and retrieved and sent to an online account.

As you can see, with a simple application, your privacy is no longer secure and everything you say and do as well as where you go can be tracked. Pretty scary don't you think?

Physical Device Tracking

In previous chapters, we covered the fundamentals of tracking and focused on the mobile device that is likely to be your cell phone, although we find ourselves carrying or within devices that can also be tracked such as your car. We carry our cell phone's everywhere we go that basically gives those with access a clear line of sight into your movement, activities, communications, and more. However, beyond the cell phone, there are many other products, services, devices, and applications we are using that also track our behavior. In this chapter, we will look at not only the mobile phone but also other mobile devices that can be tracked. We will also look at other devices that you may not know can be tracked, such as your vehicle.

Another interesting trend emerging in technology today is the "physical tracking" of items with devices. Other devices exist that help those who are forgetful. New devices are coming to the market that allow you to place trackers on items you would normally misplace, for example, a set of keys. More commonly, tools are being sold to "track your pets" with sensors that although only operate with Bluetooth and can only be tracked so far, some offerings can track you within larger radiuses. Another growing trend is with wearable technology where a new market has opened. This technology will allow tracking and the data collected is used with an application so that you can track your health, track your diet, and track your medical condition. There are many devices on the market today that can be placed on a target to "track" them without their knowledge as well such as the locator seen in Figure 8.5.

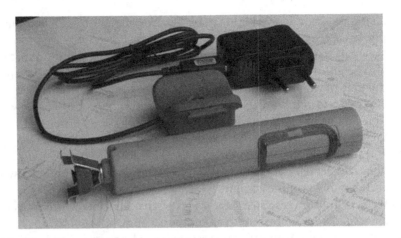

FIGURE 8.5 Physical device tracker.

Other physical tracking such as finding a lost phone has been around for some time now; however, the technology has been evolving. By registering a device online, offerings such as Apple's MobileMe (iCloud) allows for the recovery of a lost or stolen device by tracking it. Our vehicles are now coming equipped from the factory with tracking devices installed in them. LoJack that has been around for years is also another form of an advanced anti-theft device that allows for the tracking and recovery of a stolen car. LoJack can also be used with other devices such as laptops. Surveillance gear to track someone physically is also emerging, such as USB devices that can be placed within a car or on a person (perhaps in a pocketbook) to track movement of an individual without their knowledge.

As you can see, tracking is nothing new and it's growing at an alarming rate. It's growing in availability and ease of use. It's being offered as a service for the forgetful and it is appear as a standard feature in devices everywhere. This goes beyond the tracking being done without your knowledge. Within the chapter we will also make reference to tracking without technology, stalking, etc. however the bulk of this chapter will revolve around the technical tracking devices used to physically bug you with or without your knowledge.

When you are charged with a crime and go through the process of getting fingerprinted, you are put into a database so that you can be tracked. Since fingerprints are unique to an individual, it seems likely that if you are caught after being fingerprinted, you will be found to be a possible target of investigation if your prints show up at another crime scene. Similar to physical human fingerprinting, devices can also leave a unique mark. Device fingerprints can be tracked easily; however, there are ways to secure against them. With technology you need to understand that there are unique characteristics that pinpoint or associate you to a device.

- Username – When you log into a device with a set of credentials (username and password), you are leaving a logical fingerprint logged in a system. You can ensure that you are protected by using strong passwords as well as uncommon usernames. For example, do not use your e-mail address as a username if you do not have to.
- Internet protocol (IP) address – When you use a device that uses transmission control protocol/IP, your IP address leaves a fingerprint that can be tracked. You can spoof an IP address or keep them hidden so that you cannot be tracked. Generally, hackers will launch an attack from an unidentified IP or one that is taken over from another machine so that they cannot be tracked.
- Phone number – Your phone number assigned by your carrier is another logical fingerprint that associates you to your mobile device or location. You can spoof your phone number or dial anonymously so that your information cannot be tracked.
- MAC address – A burned in address that denotes the NIC manufacturer and a unique hex number that leaves a unique fingerprint that maps to a device. You can change your MAC address so that you can avoid detection.
- Serial number – Serial numbers leave a fingerprint that maps something physical or logical to a unique number. You can use a fake serial number in order to bypass detection.
- SIM – Your SIM has a unique fingerprint associated with it. Never give your personal information out to those who may ask for it claiming to be from your carrier. They can have your service turned off and use your information to process calls.
- Barcode – A barcode can be unique and allow tracking of whatever is associated with the barcode. Barcodes can be faked to avoid detection or commit crimes.

As you can see, tracking is done everyday, in many ways so that devices you use, places you go, and things you buy can all be tracked. It is possible that when you leave your home in the morning and go to work, go out to lunch, and then back to work and return home, your entire day and everything you have done can be tracked. The credit cards you used, the calls you made, and the ticket you got on a busy intersection can all be used to track your patterns, your movements, and your ultimate location.

There are also different ways that you can be tracked, some ways are application specific and others are physical device specific. If you access a server to download files, you likely did this via IP-based devices that then connect to another IP-based device. Yes, the addressing can be spoofed; however, this can be easily mitigated if you know what to look for. Also, you need to consider that every movement you make in an application-centric world can be logged that allows system administrators to look through, log, and review activity. If you are at work and visit a questionable website against company policy, it's likely you can and will be found doing so.

You can also be tracked by wearable technology. Ensure that you practice safety when using these devices and the best mitigation techniques is to first limit your exposure, limit your digital footprint, and, if you do use the technology, take every opportunity to harden it as per the systems guidelines.

Web Camera Tracking

The increased use of mobile devices with cameras, PCs with webcams, and camera systems installed at homes, businesses, and out in the general public are growing at an alarming rate and the threats are growing to expose security issues with them that violate your privacy. In this chapter, we will look at the growing use of this technology, what the technology is capable of, what purposes are served for good and evil, and why we should be concerned.

As we discuss these topics and how they relate to reconnaissance and surveillance, it will become evident that you are now always on camera. We carry one with us everywhere we go. There tends to be a camera located everywhere. Let's consider this example: you wake up and get ready for work, while in your home you are on camera as your home has an active internal security surveillance system. You check your e-mail before you leave the house on your laptop configured with a webcam. You pack up to leave and grab your mobile phone and tablet and get into your car. Your drive to work roughly passing 10 traffic lights before pulling in and parking in the parking garage. There is video surveillance feeds in the garage. You enter work and each entrance/exit and floor contains surveillance equipment. You dock your work laptop (with integrated webcam) and get to work briefly checking your mobile devices that are directly sitting next to you. Each time you leave your desk to move within the office, you take your phone with you. You leave for lunch and go to mall to eat in the food court with a few friends. The mall has video surveillance feeds. After work, you drive back home (10 traffic lights) and settle in for the evening. After dinner, you decide to load a game on your Microsoft Xbox and join a few friends online to play games. After, you check your social media sites online and Skype with a friend.

We can go on and on but I think you get the picture. You are on camera 24 hours a day and this does not include the government's ability to pinpoint and track your whereabouts via satellite. This does not include military or law enforcement being able to use satellite tracking. Digital surveillance is here to stay and will probably become more invasive over time so learning how to mitigate threats and be aware of new threats is the key to regaining your privacy.

Make sure that you are aware that webcams can be exploited. Some put a piece of tape over their cameras on their systems if they do not use them. Other's run anti-malware software to ensure Trojans are not running on their system. Regardless, ensure that you protect against this threat or your private and personal information can be exploited.

Data Capture and Exploitation

Data is everywhere. We leave digital footprints or impressions everywhere we go, and by doing anything online or on a computer system, we leave our mark. Most, if not all, of this activity is traceable and can be tracked, and it is also available for data theft. We can attempt to protect ourselves or operate in a stealth manner; however, it is possible that your actions will be logged, tracked, and proven based on many factors. Digital forensic teams are called into review systems that have been tampered with and/or when data theft has taken place, and there are many tools that can be used to prove certain activity has taken place. Lest we forget, there may also be cameras to prove you were in the vicinity of a target system to prove you were involved. You can remotely access these systems and it can be proven that by a source IP address, you may be involved. Even if it's spoofed, there are other ways to track this activity.

As we see, data tracking and doing forensic work in the digital domain can prove to be helpful; however, it is not always a guarantee that data can be kept secure. As many security analysts learned in the past decade, all of the security measures in the world did not stop a perpetrator from removing classified information about the US nuclear weaponry with a thumb drive. While working as a security analyst, you may be asked to investigate data loss or theft. Data loss prevention is the activity where you or your business entity does whatever possible to safeguard from data leakage or theft. With data everywhere, safeguarding it is a considerable challenge. Data leakage, loss, or theft causes one major problem – it is no longer secure or secret.

Data theft is also a problem that is considerably getting worse. As mobile devices are stolen, data is taken on thumb drives or websites are hacked and credentials are leaked; more and more attackers are able to spy on those they target or find targets through the data they acquire. This data can have confidential information such as passwords to financial accounts, pictures of loved ones that can also become targets, and/or medical information you wish to keep secret.

Data theft can happen in many ways. Physically, a pocketbook or wallet can be stolen. Your phone or mobile device can be taken. Your laptop can be stolen. The data could be with a service provider and they could potentially become a target inadvertently making you the next target. So why is this such an issue when it comes to protecting your assets from surveillance, becoming a target and/or victim? Your data if not protected can be used against you. For example, if your mobile device is lost or stolen and the attacker gains access, they can pose as you which is identity theft. They have access to your private information that can be used to launch a series of attacks against you and those you know.

Due diligence should be done in an effort to protect against becoming a target such as using encryption on your data so that if it is accessed, it cannot be used. Password protection allows those who gain access to a device to be challenged that may dissuade them from attempting to steal your data; however, if your password protection is not strong, it can easily be hacked. When considering surveillance, never store data that can be used against you with protecting it. It is up to you to protect against a data breach to ensure that your data is safe and secure.

Make sure that you safeguard your belongings. Ensure that you use credit or debit cards safely. Protect your data at rest with encryption and protect access. Protect your data in motion with encryption.

GENERAL SECURITY TIPS

Final tips for securing yourself and your data - Be Aware of Everything (spam, scams, things out of place). Harden your identity protection, your systems, and your devices. Never misplace things and prepare to misplace them by limiting the data on them and securing them so that they cannot be used against you. Keep your eyes open and be aware.

Look around.

Protect yourself.

Be vigilant.

SUMMARY

To conclude, we have covered a lot in this book – from digital surveillance and reconnaissance to covert operations, malware attacks, webcam breaches, and much more. Without thinking too deeply about it, we may find ourselves at constant risk of being tracked, violated, and victims of identity theft and other malicious attacks.

Legally, we are just touching the tip of the iceberg as case law for cyber law-related crimes surface more and more. In this book, we attempted to discuss some of the more relevant cases; however, there are many out there to review and learn from.

We have discussed the fundamentals of digital surveillance, what reconnaissance is, and what digital spying is. While discussing the history of digital spying, we looked at how government entities, militaries, and others have been practicing for decades to gain tactical advantage and gather intelligence. While discussing these topics, we covered major legislature put in place to provide privacy to those under the fourth amendment as an example.

Unfortunately, we cannot isolate ourselves from living, and doing so carefully and with due diligence will keep us safe; however, the method of attack and the growing landscape expanding the attack vector puts everyone at risk. By practicing safe security practices such as being aware of your surroundings, being careful about leaving or losing devices or other personal information, and checking to see if your systems are free and clear of malware are all good ways to be safe.

Information gathering will take place; however, it's up to us to limit the amount of information that can be gathered. Stalkers gather information on targets, government agencies collect information on the public, their adversaries, and military targets, and corporate gather information on their competition – it is undeniable that this practice will not stop and we as security analysts must remain vigilant in our attempts to secure, safeguard, and stay on top of the latest threats. – Good luck.

Index

Printed in the United States
By Bookmasters